# GROUP PROCESS
# MADE VISIBLE

# GROUP PROCESS MADE VISIBLE

## Group Art Therapy

**Shirley Riley, M.A., A.T.R., M.F.T.**
*Faculty of Phillips Graduate Institute*
*Marital and Family/Art Therapy Program*

Routledge
Taylor & Francis Group
New York   London

**GROUP PROCESS MADE VISIBLE: Group Art Therapy**

4 5 6 7 8 9 0

Cover design by Robert Williams

A CIP catalog record for this book is available from the British Library.
∞ The paper in this publication meets the requirements of the ANSI Standard Z39.48-1984 (Permanence of Paper)

**Library of Congress Cataloging-in-Publication Data**

Riley, Shirley.
   Group process made visible : group art therapy / Shirley Riley.
      p. cm.
   Includes bibliographical references and index.
   ISBN 1-58391-059-X (case : alk. paper)
   1. Art therapy.   2. Group psychotherapy.   I. Title.

   RC489.A7 R554 2001
   616.89'1656—dc21

                                                              00-051883

ISBN 1-58391-059-X (case)

# CONTENTS

# ABOUT THE
# CONTRIBUTORS

**Jean Noble, M.A.,** is a licensed marriage family therapist and a registered art therapist. She has worked with clients in out-patient clinics, school settings, day treatment programs, and group practice where she specialized in working with children with autistic and other developmental disorders. She now resides and practices in Humboldt County, California.

**Laurel M. Thompson, M.P.S., A.D.T.R., A.T.R.-B.C.,** is Chairperson of the Graduate Creative Arts Therapy Department at Pratt Institute in Brooklyn, New York. She has taught group art therapy, dance therapy, and introduction to creative arts therapy. She is also Director of the Body Balance Program and Creative Arts Therapy at Renfrew Center for Eating Disorders in New York. She has maintained a private practice in Brooklyn since 1987.

**Aimee Loth Rozum, A.T.R.,** is Program Coordinator of Free Arts for Abused Children in Los Angeles, California, where she designs and implements art groups serving families at risk, designs curricula to promote positive interaction between family members, and teaches program volunteers basic art therapy.

# FOREWORD

Art therapy has reached a point in its development where we must appraise and articulate the common qualities that unite us all. In keeping with the model of a successful art therapy group experience, we need to establish the shared purpose of expression while affirming the differences that enrich the mix of what we create together. Shirley Riley's *Group Process Made Visible* displays her personal practice while clearly manifesting the universal healing and life-enhancing qualities of art making that constitute the shared heritage and future mission of art therapy.

In my experience, the creative process generates healing energy that will find its way to areas of need if allowed to circulate freely. "Staying with the art," as Riley suggests, is the basis of practice. The flow of creative energy is environmental. Because creative processes do not follow predictable and linear paths, groups offer ideal conditions for treatment. As one of nature's self-regulating systems, a group of people can fill a space with creative forces that act upon those working within it. Creative transformation corresponds to the process of healing in that both change conflicts and afflictions into affirmations of life.

From our experience as art therapists and from the testimony of the people we treat, we know that art heals. Art may not always cure, but its healing function is reliable if the people involved are open to the influences of the creative process. Healing involves acceptance and understanding, the transformation of suffering into affirmations of life, and the ability to perceive individual struggles as part of a larger life purpose shared by all people. Art enables us to give dignity to our difficulties and find a purpose in our troubles, which accounts for the healing power of art.

C. G. Jung described how healing occurs when we realize that the pain we experience is not ours alone. A 16-year-old girl who participated in one of Riley's art therapy groups made a similar statement about the healing function of art:

Group art therapy helped me because I was able to see my peers having similar problems and expressing them in different ways. . . . Art was my vehicle of communication. Even though there were times my message wasn't getting across to my therapist, I was getting it out of me and my head. Once it was down on paper, it became easier to see my troubles weren't so scary and that knowledge allowed me to begin to open up verbally.

In addition to demonstrating *how* the sharing of a problem with others promotes healing, the girl describes other aspects of artistic healing: *Getting it down on paper helps us get it under control.*

As Riley says, the experience "becomes tangible" through artistic action that connects to the present and a particular place and group of people, even if the subject matter refers to the past. *Art helps us see that our troubles do not have to be "so scary."*

The monsters and demons often take on a less threatening role in our lives through the transformations of the creative process. While art making no doubt helps the person gain a sense of control over frightening emotions and memories, the artistic imagination turns difficulties into affirmations of life. As Samuel Beckett discovered at the end of his life, the darkness that he fought was his purpose. When we honor all of the images that we make, as suggested by Riley, our relationships to them shift. What was once threatening becomes a partner and a source of insight and strength. As we discover in the creative process, the things that disturb us the most often have the most to offer in the expansion of our characters. *Art helps us to open up verbally.*

The art therapy group creates a safe environment where participants can experiment with new ways of expression. "When the problem is the problem and not the person," as Riley says, the person realizes a freedom to explore the area of discontent. Riley declares "that most persons have little difficulty talking about their problem and their goal if they are embedded in an image. The members are encouraged to talk about the drawing and not themselves." *Art was my vehicle of communication.*

As the girl said, art helped in "getting it out of me and my head." Expressing bottled-up feelings within a group setting allows the contents of emotions to enter the world where they are witnessed by other people. Even if the therapist did not totally understand the message, what mattered to this girl was the process of making inner states come alive with physical materials. The act of connecting inside and outside worlds is fundamental to art's healing power.

The value of *Group Process Made Visible* as a guide to universal qualities of the art therapy experience is underscored by the variety of groups described by the author: interns and staff in an early childhood program; an adolescent group, a support group for children recovering from burn trauma, autistic children, behavior disordered children, the elderly, psychiatric hospital and day-treatment groups, women in an eating disorders program, a widow's group, and therapists working with severely abused patients. Each group reveals common art therapy elements as well as unique features determined by the needs of the participants. For example, in the group with elderly clients, Riley described how art becomes the primary mode of therapy and communication, whereas her group of autistic children needed help in making social connections to others through safe and playful art activities that created bridges and mediating structures. It was necessary to help the traumatized burn patients to master their fears and pain; the disruptive boys required structured activities that furthered self-discipline and control; and the adolescents need ways to "catch the imagination." Art therapists continually customize what they do so that universal elements of artistic healing will take effect in different clinical situations.

In keeping with the Los Angeles School of Pragmatic Art Therapy initiated by Helen Landgarten, our mutual mentor, Riley shows very little theoretical bias. Although never stated as an explicit goal of the text, *Group Process Made Visible* displays Shirley Riley's leadership. Successful groups depend upon leaders who establish a sense of community, a common purpose, and a respect for different perspectives. The leader both listens and acts decisively and with a spirit of fairness. Safety is established within environments where people are able to risk new ways of expression and where honest communications are supported. The effective leader knows her subject matter, responds honestly and consistently to challenging situations, and engenders trust through these actions.

"Groups are a minor miracle," Riley declares. When this sense of confidence and wonder is conveyed by the leader, others are motivated to perform. The leader activates and affirms the positive energy that exist within every group and builds the resolve that is required to pass through challenging and new situations. Riley likens the group leader to the conductors of orchestras who hear and see the complexities of the members' interactions. She conveys a sense of total presence and nonjudgmental responsiveness to whatever happens to be moving through a group at a particular time, helping people realize that any mark, scribble, or stick figure is acceptable.

The leader is always charged with maintaining the safety of the group and a clear sense of purpose. Even though Riley prefers a relatively transparent style of leadership, and is reluctant to impose art

tasks, she never forgets that she is a guiding force. The leader culti-
vates confidentiality, realizes how affirming rituals emanate naturally
from every group, and appreciates the normal fluctuation between
trust and distrust. Riley models how mature leaders engage conflicts
and doubts as the subject matter of the work, and in this way builds
the group's confidence when facing difficult situations. The skilled
leader shows group members how to deal with problems calmly when
they might otherwise be prone to destructive panic. Experienced group
leaders will concur with Riley's belief that group treatment provides
an opportunity to respond to behavior as it happens."

Riley reveals her group sagacity when she simply states, "I am very
much in favor of the therapist showing humor as much as possible.
Joy in creating a working group should be shared, and creativity of all
members should be the driving force." Relaxation and enjoyment are
fundamental elements of creative expression. Pleasure is too often
overlooked as a basis of art therapy.

"Art therapy," Riley says, "reduces stress by providing tasks and
projects that are pleasurable." She describes the sensory "pleasure" of
working with materials—smell and touch, and looking at colors. The
experience of beauty is also acknowledged. In my experience, I find
that the measure of beauty in art therapy is determined by the au-
thenticity of the expression. Rather than avoid the issue of artistic
standards, we can give fresh definitions to artistic quality through our
work.

People need help in simply seeing the significance of what they do
and I strongly agree with Riley's belief that art therapist will become
more sensitive to the expressions of others by staying involved the
creative process. The perception of beauty in an image depends upon
our ability to open to its expression, ourselves effaced. Respect for the
image opens us to the perception of its aesthetic significance and personal meaning.

I have worked primarily with groups through every phase of my art
therapy career, starting with groups of patients in a mental hospital
setting in 1970. I wrote my Masters thesis on group art therapy and
published my first journal article in 1973 on this subject. I went on to
lead art therapy retreat groups over the past 20 years and I have
recently concentrated on the community of creation in the workplace.
My early exposure to the therapeutic community work of Maxwell
Jones has had a lasting influence on everything I do. The creative
energy and intelligence of groups of people working together has
continuously inspired me to stay focused on the process of collective
creation. I have never lost my sense of awe when witnessing the participation mystique of group creation.

I identify with Shirley Riley's declaration: "I am a pragmatic therapist." I share her fascination with the artistic phenomena and I do my best to objectively perceive what they manifest. I am challenged by the idea of staying with the art and allowing it to enlarge participation. As a "group person" I am inclined toward constantly inviting others to participate and forever widening the circle of artistic healing. There is something in art therapy for everyone. Like Shirley Riley, I have discovered that with groups of people the most elementary concentration on art therapy goals and values will grow into a richer encounter and almost guarantees, if not a cure, a healing experience for the group.

I also share her belief that artistic products can influence healing as much the process of creation. "Many issues," Riley says, "may be concentrated in the image." The process of creation and the images it generates integrate the complete complex of a person's life and emotional condition. This integration in both artworks and dreams is itself a source of healing. The imagination is capable of treating itself and reconstituting its afflictions. Since the creative process brings things together in ways that are beyond the reach of linear thought and narrative discussion, art has always been my first and primary therapeutic language.

When the work is done in groups, the effects are magnified. We gain the benefits of witnessing the creative integrations of others, which act upon ourselves and inspire an ongoing ecology of creation. The pictures themselves are vital members of the community of creation. Groups are enriched and augmented as soon as the images begin to arrive. The artworks convey energy and the gifts of creation. Meditation on the many intriguing illustrations included in this book further enlarge its effects.

I feel a sense of homecoming when reading and reflecting upon *Group Process Made Visible*. The book renews the vision that inspired my first days of art therapy practice. Where our profession has spent so much energy during its early years of formation trying to control what people do, this book demonstrates the many things that art can do for people. *Group Process Made Visible* defines our common ground in advancing the healing and life enhancing qualities of art.

*Shaun McNiff*
*Gloucester, Massachusetts*

# PREFACE

Every book has a personality and belief system that underlies all the words and information. I had a particular approach in mind when setting out on this literary journey. I definitely did not want to imitate the many excellent texts on group dynamics that have become a classic in the field of mental health. The hope I held was to make the discussion about leading groups for various populations and in varied settings, a shared experience between myself and the reader. Although the consumer of a text on group therapy probably did not pick it up with the hopes of being engaged in a novel, still, it seems to me, there is no reason to make a "professional" book a reading hurdle. For that reason, I have reduced citation of names and dates to a minimum, and relied on the reader to check out the suggested readings list for the many fine books that informed me as I thought about conducting the groups I have led.

This is a book that is based on real-life experiences. The groups are either ongoing or others like them are alive. Art was a tremendous help in sustaining the groups, and a stimulus for the leaders. Hopefully, the reader will imagine him or herself offering media and enjoying a respite from having to rely on words alone, which when they do come forth, often are misunderstood. I have attempted to clarify how helpful it is when the group members and the therapist look at a visual product. Together they can focus on an image; together they can explore the meaning. The therapist is the student of the client as he or she teaches the therapist the significance of the expressive rendition.

My basic philosophy is postmodern in attitude, although I go where the client takes me in the choice of theory. Theories are suppositions about how people live in this world, some fit one situation, and some another. I choose a postmodern label for several reasons: I avoid pathologizing, I believe what the client tells me, I think humor is as valuable as agony and a lot more tolerable, and I have faith that the client will work with me to find a solution to their problems. I provide the vehicle, they do the driving. I watch out for bends in the road and unusual bumps on the highway. Some groups are in high gear almost all the time, others seem to prefer low gear. They all stop and start as they choose, but most of the time we reach our destination.

I believe the successful group leader should have a "here-and-now-ear." Researching the past does not stimulate interactive process or lead to the growth of the group. As an example: If a group member reports that they are "submerged in difficulties" I would inquire, not about the difficulties, but how it is to be "submerged." What bodily sensations accompany this condition and what is the plan to emerge from this state? The group can relate to these feelings and the difficulties can be explored in due time. The trained ear listens for descriptive words that invite metaphor and can be translated to a visual rendition. The created product, which could be made by all members who share this type of feeling, brings the group together in an immediate situation.

## ☐ The Magic of Group Process

Groups are a minor miracle. A group of people come together and, gradually, their very disparate personalities and behaviors come together in some strange way that transforms the group into a personality, an entity in itself. Because of this witchery, there are no groups that are exactly alike and that is part of the fascination. When you add the art expressions to the mix, another mysterious amulet is a part of the process. Now a group has voice, behavior, and eyes! To see forms together and share a vision takes therapeutic intimacy to another level.

Group leaders are like orchestra leaders, they hear and see the complexities of the members' interactions. However, sometimes the "orchestra" is mostly winds, or sometimes over-staffed with percussive instruments, but music can be created in spite of the dissonance.

There seems to be a basic quality that is necessary to be a group leader: The therapist should like to be with people. *People* in contrast to *person*. Enjoying the excitement of a group and weaving together the complexities of human behaviors and opinions is a talent. In addition, when adding the art component to the conversation, it is essential that the therapist rely on the intelligent knowing of his or her right (imaging) brain. *Seeing* the whole problem in the space in which it lives, and simultaneously perceiving in graphic form an intervention that would modify or complement that difficulty, is right brain imagery interacting with left brain cognition. Later, the cognitive faculty makes logical sense of it all, but first is the vision.

# ☐ Brief Comments

Looking over the contents of this text, I realized that I have not made a special point of the issue of culture and race, and how this impacts a group, perhaps because I live in Los Angeles where Whites are no longer a majority. Every group I conducted in the clinic was a mix of cultures, in fact they were usually dominantly Hispanic. They were group members, not because of some flaw in the Hispanic families, but because the clinic was based in a Latino neighborhood. It is clear that Whites still hold privilege in L.A., but the policies are changing. What is a dominant culture in a large part of the city, and of many other cities, is that of poverty, and that knows no color. The stress between first- and second-generation immigrants has been the theme of many groups, particularly the adolescent groups. I believe another book could hardly begin to cover all the conflicts that exist in this area.

It seems to me that by now the need for a broad understanding of all the cultures that are a part of our daily lives has been vigorously emphasized. I doubt if there are group leaders still unaware of these issues. The proof will be demonstrated in the life of the group. If there is neglect of this fundamental issue and a lack of awareness, the group will fail.

There is one group situation with which I have had experience which is not included in this text. Multifamily groups are hard to arrange, but are extraordinarily helpful. I have written about a plan for multi-family treatment in my 1994 book, *Integrative Approaches to Family Therapy*. I would like to encourage therapists to experiment and introduce this form of treatment in their practice.

# ☐ Context, Context, and More Context

Throughout the presentations of the groups using art as communication, I hope I have made the point that where, when, and with whom you conduct group is the key. Context is everything. The physical surroundings themselves are a consideration, as well as the demands of the administration. One group will be self-motivated; others will need structure and strong leadership. One group will profit from open studio, and in context, another group would be at a loss in an art environment. In every case, I have attempted to be as clear as possible why a group was structured in a certain manner, and give rationale for asking the group members (or not asking) to pictorialize their dilemmas.

However, the actual group I have described can be generalized to other parallel groups of clients. For example, when reading about the burn injured children, one could substitute other form of physical disabilities, and the construction of the group would still be workable. The principles of group process underlie all of the group structures.

## ☐ The Therapist

In several chapters I tried to bring to the reader's attention, that the position of the therapist is of greatest importance. How we interact with our clients and our philosophical stance is a presence in the room whether we like it or not. There is no faking relationships! My most strongly held conviction is that the therapist is the deciding factor when it comes to client satisfaction and growth. A group therapist is a key to opening new vistas, and the key often unlocks the abilities of the group to be their own "therapist." Fading in and out of leadership is a talent that must be developed.

In our new millennium culture there seems to be a group for every situation that the human race can imagine. There are more groups than one therapist-type person can possibly know about or even conceive. Some of the theme groups with which I am acquainted are presented in a more condensed format. It allowed me to discuss a variety of therapy groups, ones with which I have had experience, and with which I have had personal involvement. Some of the chapters are more detailed than others—that depended entirely on the material and the complexity of the treatment. Length does not correlate with importance. In every case the use of art as communication has been utilized. In some groups art expression takes center stage, in others it is less prominent. However, creativity is always a prime mover.

## ☐ The Reliable Co-Leader

Adding the art to group is like having a co-leader. This "co" can facilitate creative tasks that speed up interactions that lead to group cohesion and the installation of trust. I have suggested many ways in the first chapter that a competent therapist can integrate, introduce, and utilize graphic or three-dimensional communication. For the professional who has not had training in art therapy, it is most helpful to work with an art therapist and read some of the literature. Using art without understanding its potential and limits should be a serious consideration. A cautious approach should be taken until the therapist has become aware of the complexities of visual language. However, if the professional confines the art to an adjunct position in the group dynamics, the visual component can still be a vital and binding force in the group.

As I focused on various populations, the use of the art varied. At times the art was structured, a stimulus that was necessary to help the group move ahead toward their chosen goals. Other times the sheer fascination of the product growing under the hands of the group members gave permission for emotions or recollections to surface in memory. Perhaps the reflections that were stimulated in either of the approaches would not be discussed, or discussed at a later date.

Art products can speak to their creator without verbal interpretation. The significant personal communication that happens between the art product and the observant self of the artist is a rare occurrence. For the therapist to learn to trust that intimate process comes from their experience and the information gathered from clients after they have left the group. Often the ex-member recalls moments that were non-verbal but memorable, memories that were held though a process of visual awareness and sensory reactions. Touch and movement brought the "changing" moment into mindfulness more than the words used at the time. Many times the image was imprinted on the mind, while the words were lost. Imagery often resists exact interpretations and is better understood in its metaphorical state.

## ☐ The Choice of Groups

The discussions about the group experience are offered in context of where they were held and with whom. The social environment and the cultural beliefs of the group members absolutely influenced the process of the group. Without attention to gender and prejudices that define sex roles and status, the group dialogue would be a formality. Feel-good groups do not interest me, therefore all the groups described in the following chapters were formed to contend with serious difficulties, although being serious was not at all the preferred mood. People learn best from one another, so I have offered the reader some examples of how this learning took place.

## ☐ The Contents

Chapter 1 is a broad overview of the process of group formation and how the language of art becomes an intrinsic part of the process. The suggestions and examples are applicable to many groups of clients and is written to stimulate ides about introducing a visual form of creativity.

Chapter 2 explores a group which set its goal on integrating the latest neuro/psychological/developmental theories with art tasks to further the attachment behaviors of caretaker and child. Many cases of poor attachment and subsequent parent-child distress were addressed by using art as a mode of improving intimacy. The group demonstrated that it was possible to employ the mind/brain knowledge in a pragmatic manner. Cutting-edge research can be applied to clinical treatment.

Chapter 3 relates a story of the bravery and adaptability of burn injured children as they faced their trauma and coped with their recovery. Their narratives were worthy of recording and their coping skills inspiring. The group was with burn-injured children, but it could as well have been with medically ill or abused children. The format is flexible.

Chapter 4 demonstrates how creativity in the therapist flows into the treatment of youths who have traditionally been seen as asocial. Jean Noble takes you through the small steps that are needed to help autistic children have a socializing experience in a small group. A great accomplishment.

Chapter 5 is an opportunity for Aimee Loth Rozum to describe a program based on a cognitive-behavioral approach that has proved successful with pre-adolescent boys. The majority of the youngsters carry the label of ADHD. Most therapists are reluctant to combine the freedom of art with a structured behavioral procedure, but she has demonstrated how to make these two modes fuse and create a therapeutic program that works.

Chapter 6 is a brief sampling of adolescent group treatment. The art is all-important, and the attitude of the therapist equally so. The changing world of mental health services for adolescents has made a tremendous impact on the services provided to this important segment of our society. As the need for youth services becomes more critical, the only youth services extended are at the level of last resort.

Chapter 7 is an inspiring journey in an area where inspiration is not expected. Rather than a depressing experience with the elderly members of a "high-functioning" group diagnosed with dementia, we find humor and kindness. This chapter takes the reader though the evolution of a long-term group that has made a difference in the lives of its members. In addition the rationale for art as a psycho/social/neurological stimulus is addressed.

Chapter 8 looks at the challenge the therapist and patients face when hospitalized patients are offered treatment in chaotic environments.

There are suggestions how art as support and communication can relieve some of the stress in a difficult situation. Hospital and daycare treatment programs are doing their best in difficult times. The groups described are often islands of comfort when the circumstances of hospitalization are frightening to the disturbed patient.

Chapter 9 shifts the therapeutic stance to a more psychodynamic view as Laurel Thompson shares her expertise as a dance therapist and an art therapist with a women's eating disorder group. This population is extremely hard to reach, and the reader will be interested in how Thompson creatively combines movement, art, and verbal groups into a synergistic whole.

Chapter 10 takes the reader through the life of 10 meetings with a widow's group. The stages of facing the new status in life and the necessary mourning that are necessary for newly widowed women is the heart of this chapter. Rituals and ceremonies that help to mediate bereavement and grief are discussed, as well as specialized approaches for this type of group.

Chapter 11 explores an overlooked area in the professional lives of therapists. When working with the severely abused client, the art expressions spontaneously created by the client often are very hard to experience. The client's imagery often enters into the memory bank of the therapist and causes stress and anxiety. How this group of therapists dealt with their secondary post-traumatic stress is challenging and gratifying.

Chapter 12 looks back briefly at the many groups and their members and attempts to make some generalizations that summarize the value of group treatment.

## ☐ To The Reader

My final wish is that you will use the information in this book as a incentive to add the language of art to your groups or, based on some of these suggestions, find personal arenas for your own creation. I am a pragmatic therapist, I want clients to make progress and write their own stories in ways that are more satisfactory. However, I find that imagery and metaphor translated into visual statements turn the practical goals into a much richer encounter and almost guarantees, if not a cure, a healing experience for the group. Group is like weaving a beautiful basket—when it is finished, it is impossible to follow a single strand. It is a complex whole that in the end is the work of art.

# ACKNOWLEDGMENTS

I am more than pleased to acknowledge the additional perspective that Shaun McNiff adds to this book by his thoughtful and stimulating foreword. He brings years of experience and a fine literary style to the world of therapeutic texts. I am equally indebted to the three excellent therapists who added their thoughts and clinical knowledge to this book. Laurel Thompson, Jean Noble, and Aimee Loth Rozum, each experts in their field, provide the reader with clinical observations that I could not. I thank them for their time and dedication to my project. I thank Victoria von Brauchitsch for the photographs that she helped me with, as well as the students of Pratt College and Phillips Graduate Institute who allowed me to add some photos of their group work to the book. The Well-Designed Day Program addressed in Chapter 7 is a reflection of the outstanding opportunities offered to the elderly at OPICA in West Los Angeles, California. I am indebted to Lauren Naumoff, ATR, Director, who allowed me to give my interpretation of their activities. I also wish to acknowledge Tamy Polland and Anne Gaibraith who were the co-therapists. I am additionally grateful to the many students and clients who joined me in the group process and added their art to the conversation. This text is a compilation of 20 years of group work, two decades of many adolescents and adults taking the voyage of self-discovery with me.

Always most important to me is the exceptional encouragement I have from my husband, and the support from our children and grandchildren. It was a memorable honor when I was chosen by Laura (my granddaughter) to be the "subject" of her school project.

In particular I thank my friend who started me on this tract of writing: Cathy Malchiodi, a role model of intelligent clinical thinking. This book is a gathering of memories and life experiences made possible with the help of those named and others unnamed—a clinical life experience translated into print. I thank the publishers and the Editors of Brunner-Routledge for their immediate acceptance of the format and contents of the book, a presentation that reflects my desire to offer this text as a narrative and resource useful to professionals of many disciplines.

# The Language of Art in Group Therapy

The concept of group therapy has changed as the services of mental health professionals have changed. The fantasy that often comes to mind for many when the phrase "group therapy" is used is an uninviting room, chairs in a circle, eight to ten persons looking somewhat miserable, and a therapist evoking "painful" material from one member after the other. Another picture is one where the members are the target of a cross-examination by the therapist, interrogated by the other members, and (in the movies) given a hard time. If that fantasy still survives it should be erased. Although the prevailing concept of group therapy is much more benign, few, if any, first-time consumers of mental health services would imagine a group drawing, painting, and constructing art objects—and enjoying the activity while learning from the process and the related discussion.

The therapist of the twenty-first century accepts that group treatment is as flexible as any other therapeutic process and can be reinvented to fit societal and cultural needs. The size of the group is a moot point: For some populations a group of three is helpful. However, because a health insurance plan or state funding demands group treatment for every client, every other day, larger groups may be necessary. To answer such requirements, many candidates are assigned to a group session, sometimes more than the therapist can even focus on. Overcrowding can be managed in ways that are nontraditional; the challenge is to not lose the unique qualities that group therapy

1

has to offer, but instead find creative solutions to the pressures of today's health care system (Cross, 1994).

This first chapter will address many issues and offer an overview both of basic group therapy processes and the advantage of adding the language of art to group treatment. The following chapters will address specific populations and emphasize how the group approach can be modified to the context of the environment and to the needs of the members.

Group therapy is not individual therapy practiced with a group of people; it is not family therapy, although a family is a group of people; it is not an interpersonal forum for couples solving problems. Paradoxically, group therapy is all of the above in some situations and some contexts. There is nothing static about group dynamics, they are the palpable life of the group and no two groups are exactly the same. Group therapy has many facets; some are brilliant and catch the eye, and others are without that power and conceal their light within.

"Group" is an extraordinary opportunity to look in the mirror of another's eyes and see one's own behaviors and prejudices reflected back with a clarity that is hard to receive. Often the reflections are difficult to accept, therefore it is helpful to see these images through a screen that provides protection. Because interactions that take place in group are one of immediacy and are in the here-and-now, they are many times spontaneous and unpredictable. It is important that the therapist and members find a mode of communication that does not distort information but provides enough distance that it may be received without rejection.

Vinogradov and Yalom (1998) offer this brief description of group therapy:

> In group therapy both patient—patient interactions and patient—therapist interactions as they occur in the context of the group setting are used to effect changes in the maladaptive behaviors of the group members. The group itself, as well as the application of specific techniques and interventions, serves as a tool for change. This gives group psychotherapy its unique therapeutic potential. (p. 1)

When art is the tool of communication the "techniques and interventions" can take on a singular form that modifies the above description to an extent.

## ☐ Complexities and Singular Issues

The composition of personalities and group process that constitute a therapy group is formed by countless variations of human traits, discourses, and interactions—a microcosm of the world. The unpredict-ability of group therapy is creative and challenging, it also may be dangerous and hurtful. In other forms of therapy, such as family or conjoint treatment, the therapeutic balance that is needed is just as crucial but is more easily controlled. For example, in group, spontane-ity can be encouraged when it is tempered; impulsivity, on the other hand, may be destructive if it is counter to the growth of the group. If one member is allowed to act out dramatically before the group has become cohesive and can handle disruptions themselves, it can create a problem. There are times that the leader must make decisions that are for the good of the group as a whole, and hope that the individual will continue to be a part of the process.

Relationships are difficult to develop in the manufactured commu-nity of group therapy. If the therapist keeps the group action and dialogue in the here-and-now, the risk of being distracted by unpro-ductive remarks is reduced. The goal is to remain in the present tense and bring the interactions and concerns into the group itself where problem solving can become a part of the group dynamics. If a mem-ber focuses on past events they are moving away from the group and become unavailable for group discussion. Fear and shame may para-lyze a group member and limit the therapeutic possibilities. Such de-fenses are not useful for the client. Countless interrelational situations will arise in every group and with any age population. The group leader needs all the help that can be mustered to pull all these diver-gent factors into a dynamic whole that results in a beneficial experi-ence for all concerned.

## ☐ Introducing Art as an Aid to Communication

Is there a magic panacea to cure problems and establish a cohesive, working group? No, there is not. However, there is a way to bring a mirror into group that is reflective but not confrontive. A creative modality that can keep the members focused on group activity can bring a sense of urgency by using an unfamiliar form of communication. The dictionary meaning of the word "create" is helpful at this point (Funk and Wagnall, 1938): "To cause to come into existence; especially to produce out of nothing; to produce; to be productive" (p. 281).

The goals of therapy also are directed toward having clients bring new interpretations of their difficulties into existence, create new answers, and thus, become more productive in their own lives. The creativity in group rarely comes out of nothing. Group nothing is often an unplanned interaction between members, which activates reactions by stimulating memories, feelings, and connections. When abstract words, such as creativity, are translated into an activity or process, the concept ceases to be abstract and becomes accessible.

When creative thoughts and opportunities for change emerge in the group process, it is essential to anchor them in an observable expression. *Using tangible images, self-created by the group member, as the major mode of group communication can help the leader to enhance the group's overall goals.* Too often the opportunity slips by and the chance to verbally explore a vital issue is lost. Visual expressions punctuate a moment in time. Even if the image conveys a significant message, the art allows the image-maker to control and limit exposure, which reduces anxiety around premature verbal disclosure. The art product can be preserved and re-addressed in the future when further discussion can lead to a more productive awareness. These qualities of safety and timing are inherent in careful use of the art expression and provide a means to solve many of the dilemmas of group interactions.

## Interactive Group Process: The Advantage of the Image

Group interchange can be channeled through the rendering of the art product. Language means different things to different people. This less threatening form of communication provides comfort and reduces confrontation, because the artwork circumvents the quality of the words that may have become toxic, with accrued multiple meanings and meta meanings. The image may also have many meanings, but when it is presented as an artform, it is there for the group, to view and discuss as a concrete feeling; the words are invisible. The group should focus on understanding the explanation and the significance the image has for the art maker. This limits the chance that the members are not simply projecting individual interpretations on a verbalized story. However, there may be exceptions when the artist cannot decode the message in the art because the words that are available to him or her do not seem to "fit" the intended expression. In this case, there may be a delayed revelation or it may remain a mystery.

Ettin (1992) feels strongly that imagery is useful in fostering intimacy and cohesiveness. [I]mages that arise serve to emphasize and reinforce the cohesive ties between the members. Other images may express the difficulties inherent in just this joining process. Some ambivalent images stimulate a consideration of paired opposite reactions, individuation and merger or attraction and repulsion, clearly depicted in within one picture" (p. 188).

The word imagery is often used in art therapy as a condensation of a long explanation of how art expressions are conceived as an image in the brain, scanned and selected to be projected as an art form, and then examined for meaning. Neuro/psychologists use the term image when explaining mind/brain function. Imagery equals an art piece, in many cases.

When art is used, therapy becomes tangible, the action is in the here-and-now, even if the subject matter refers to the past. The members can actually *see* how tying old beliefs to present behaviors can be unprofitable. This process is demonstrated when the client makes images of past solutions that resulted in an unsuccessful attempt to solve present problems. The therapeutic advantage to art expression is that it can be modified and changed immediately, and alternative solutions can be introduced. Discussion that is directed to the artform helps keep the therapeutic dialogue in the here-and-now; it is more difficult to stray from the subject at hand if the artform is present and the focal point of the group's efforts.

Adding imagery to group process benefits individual personalities: it allows the silent group member to be expressive through the art product, while the talkative member is silenced when the image takes preference over words. Members who hold on to shame and guilt seldom may find it difficult to maintain these emotions if they see the entire group is part of the same struggle to make images that have personal meaning and reach beyond representational fine arts. Because persons who hold on to shame often feel their emotions are unique, an open discussion of being ashamed about doing a bad job of making art, will show them that their position is a shared experience. Most persons, when they first begin to make marks on paper, are somewhat self-conscious about their art. This quickly passes when the group leader and the other members put value on the *content* of the representation, not the aesthetic rendering. The "guilty ones" have a chance to see that any mark is valuable if that mark is given respect and attention, that they can contribute without shame.

## ☐ Introducing the Art

The art product provides the group with an activity that has the potential of bringing new awareness to the art maker and to those with whom the drawing is shared. The art can stand by itself as a statement from the "artist" and verbal interpretation can be added when it is appropriate.

The therapist may wish to educate the group about the concept of "visual knowing," or non-verbal observations stored in memory that inform the person. The mind has many intelligences, people think cognitively, emotionally, kinesthetically, and visually (Goleman, 1995). From birth an infant learns about the world by observing, and the early visual concepts of the world remain part of an individual's reactive patterns. Later at about three years of age, the cognitive and visual capacities of the brain are joined, and gradually visual knowing is not considered a primary way of thinking. However, it never loses its power to inform. Consider the many clichés that are based on sight: "Love at first sight;" "He looks like a criminal;" "Don't look at me that way;" "I can see it in your eyes;" and many more. A short quotation from Pinker's (1997) explanation of imagery and the brain touches on the complicated process of how vision is organized: "The brain is ready for the demands of an imagery system, information flows down from memory as well as up from the eyes. The fiber pathways to the visual areas of the brain are two-way. They carry as much information down from the higher, conceptual levels as up from the lower, sensory levels" (p. 287). Gaining a biological understanding about vision, and conceptualizing how information works through sight and imagination, reinforces how important the image is in every phase of living and relating. Having a little knowledge, or at least curiosity, about the "pictures in our mind" stimulates the fascination of incorporating visual expressions into the verbal exchange in therapy.

## Introducing Art into Group Process

Introducing the use of media as communication into a group does not have to be done with long explanations and rationales about the benefit of art expression. In fact, that can put off the client and they may wonder why they have to be burdened with another anxiety when they are troubled enough. The easiest way to start is for the therapist to place a variety of media, such as pastels, pens, and paper, on a table or provide drawing boards, and encourage the participants to express their opinions with a drawing. Clients should know that they can just experiment with the different forms of drawing tools. If they are discomforted by having to start on their own, the facilitator can give a suggestion, for example, "If this paper represents you, how much of it would be filled up with the concern that brought you to therapy? Draw a shape and fill it in with color, if you wish." This is an open ended, non-specific, but still informative introduction; *showing* the therapist and the group the problem. Expect the client to be shy about their talent. Too often a teacher or parent who was critical of the representational qualities of youthful art expressions has inhibited many in childhood. Such early, caustic remarks are felt like attacks on a natural way of expressing a personal view of the world. The inhibition can last a lifetime.

Therefore, in group, the leader must emphasize that any mark, scribble, or stick figure is acceptable. Words may or may not be added to the drawing, and abstract shapes should be encouraged. After the creator observes their product they then have the option of showing it to the group, or an individual in the group, to discuss its meaning. The leader should restrain the group from making interpretations of the images. The artmaker's definition of the content is the one that must be accepted. Reflections on how the images stir up feelings in another member are quite different than projecting one person's meaning on another person's visual statement. Groups then can move quickly past the ordinary mode of communication into the unfamiliar mode of metaphor, imagery, and simple descriptive, concrete visualizations. It is much easier to talk about a drawing that illustrates a difficulty, than talk directly to the other person about a problem. The mirror of feared critical reflections is reflected in a manner that allows the discussion to separate the problem from the person. The problem is on the paper; the person is a member of the group.

## ☐ The Therapist

It is of first importance to consider the philosophy of the creative therapist. Unless the group leader is thinking visually as well as verbally, and understands how to encourage the use of imagery in group, there is no need to introduce media and art expressions into the process. Visual thinking is available to everyone, although to some it is more dominant. It takes interest and a little time to become accustomed to being attentive to one's internal images. It is particularly useful when the therapist is able to recognize these visual messages as the group is in progress. For example, when Joe talks about his loneliness, he creates a drawing of a transparent man with a tiny toddler inside asking to be held. This is not a truth, it is only an informative image. The drawing indicates an "empty" adult, with a neglected child core. Joe is confronted with an image he created of himself and is maybe the first time he was able to conceptualize his needs. He has revealed an internal state in concrete form which provides both himself and the therapist material for explanation. If later, Joe references this drawing and wishes to discuss that he does see himself as without substance, he will be ready to deal with this issue.

In every group the personality and belief systems of the leader will influence the way the group proceeds. Even with the most devoted attention to neutrality, the group leader is a guiding force. It may be favorable for the facilitator to be somewhat transparent, and to show enthusiasm and humor as much as possible. Joy in creating a working group should be shared and the creativity of all members should be the driving force. Some of the basic traits that are essential for the therapist using art in group are:

1. Believing in the process of synthesizing visual communication with verbal discourse in a group setting;
2. Not only knowing all the stages of group development, but being comfortable with channeling these stages into art expressions;
3. Understanding that therapeutic art is not necessarily an aesthetic (fine arts) statement, it is a visible product that reflects the group members' thoughts, emotions, internal processes, and considerations;
4. Recognizing that the process of moving internal concepts into externalized, metaphorical products facilitates and enriches the therapeutic dialogue;
5. Appreciating and honoring how safely a drawing (or any artform) is able to represent traumatic material in a disguised manner;
6. Believing in a therapeutic mode that allows clients to observe their own concerns and remain in control of when they choose to share it;
7. Not being invested in interpreting imagery, and having the patience to allow the material to emerge at its own pace;
8. Being convinced of one's own capacity for creative thinking.

## Training

Many interested therapists question how they can achieve the skills that will help them use art in group practice. The most obvious route is to become a trained art therapist. There are excellent graduate programs across the country that offer a Masters in Art Therapy. There are also certificate programs that follow the guidelines for art therapy education from the American Art Therapy Association. In addition there are workshops and individual teaching and supervision opportunities offered by professionals who have worked with art therapy for a considerable period of time.

It is important to know more about the clinical use of art as therapy: It is not just introducing concrete images as a form of expression, it is an epistemological shift in thinking. If using art is attractive to the group leader, they should seek further training in it and enjoy the full appreciation of this mode of conducting therapy. In the process of becoming trained, the therapist will be aware that clients often are dismayed or retraumatized by the emergent image, and this situation must be carefully handled. At the minimum, supervision by a certified art therapist is recommended.

Even though art can be used in group in many ways, there should not be a feeling that creative therapists cannot join with art therapists and give positive service to clients. Art as therapy should be inclusive, not exclusive, welcoming the well-trained professional into the many arenas where creativity will enliven and inform both client and therapist to a mutual advantage.

## Personal Involvement with Art Making

The ability to use art most effectively in therapy rests on taking the risk to "do" art personally. Art is a therapeutic experience if the art maker lets go of expectations that are married to the word "art." The art that the therapist asks the group member to create is a mental, physical, visual, emotional, experience. Art making is experiential. It makes sense to enter into this adventure before you ask others to do so. However, using art expressions to their fullest therapeutic advantage takes training and a personal commitment on the part of the therapist exploring a client's artwork, moving beyond the obvious into the subtle constructions and deconstructions of creative ideas and physical marks, finding an opening through which an alternative can be viewed, is worth taking the time to learn.

Familiarity with a variety of media, knowledge of the tension at the moment of the first mark on the empty page, realization that creating the art piece takes feelings, thoughts, and concentration to produce, cannot be learned from books. Working with media, and exploring the emotive qualities of line, form, and space, will sensitize a person in a manner that cannot be learned in any other way. Respect for the process will help the therapist have a more empathic understanding of the group while observing them at work. The therapist needs also to appreciate how images can surface that trigger old conflicts and make the artform an unexpectedly emotional encounter. Caution when asking for an art expression from others will naturally result from a personal engagement with the depth of emotions that a visual product can stimulate. Most important, the art "experimenter" will see that the simplest forms can have complicated meanings, that making one's own art sensitizes the self to one's own likes and dislikes about art forms. This brings to consciousness the critical eye one can have for some art. The therapist should be careful not to project these biases on the client's art. The power of the image to communicate will become personal knowledge. There will be heightened appreciation when the art work of a client indicates a situation of potential danger to themselves or others. The therapist who understands that art is communication will take an art expression that indicates risk to an expert in the field of art therapy for additional assessment. Doing art for experimentation and becoming familiar with media is helpful for the therapist and makes introducing the visual mode into the group less difficult.

## Using Art as a Therapeutic Tool

Introduction of art into the group process is not the most difficult problem; the challenge is using the artform to the advantage of the individual artmaker and the entire group. The introduction should be pragmatic (i.e., making marks on paper, shaping clay, using media, taps into others ways of understanding that will hasten and enhance the therapeutic experience). Use art-like expressions to reflect the issues that are important to the group. The art is not the diagnostic tool, it is communication.

The process of exploring imagery can be looked at in two ways. One way is to recognize the vertical, linear thought process when a group member talks about his or her art rendition. The second process is horizontal: The therapist and the other members of the group help the artmaker to explore further meaning in the drawing, they employ the technique of moving *into* the drawing and finding interesting and innovative aspects that have been overlooked.

For example, a group member produces an image that has jagged black lines piercing an amoebic red form, the background consists of swirls of green and blue. This abstract, she says, represents the emotional attack she experienced when her husband wrongly accused her of cheating on him. She relates the story and identifies her feelings through the imagery. That is a vertical explanation, and should be listened to with empathy and sensitivity. Very often the less experienced therapist will stop here. However, after the narrative, the therapist should guide the dialogue by moving into the drawing (the horizontal approach). Ask, "How do the greens and blues affect the red and black image? Are they able to contain or contribute to handling the red and black form? Can you find yourself in the drawing? How can you seek resolution of the forms in conflict and what modification would be helpful? Would introduction of new colors have an influence on the shapes that you have identified?" Although the questions focus on shapes and colors, the client knows they are about how she can better take control of her situation. By modifying the image, the emotional impact of her husband's accusation can also be modified. Taking a once-removed stance, the client is able to begin to solve the problem on paper, which stimulates a parallel thought process to solve the "real" problem.

The example about change within a drawing stimulates thoughts on a metaphorical base that makes change in life an active possibility. As a drawing moves beyond its first meaning, broader concepts emerge in the entire piece, allowing the therapeutic component to be further illuminated. Domestic problems cannot be solved with one drawing; however, new modes of coping can be stimulated, and an observing stance can provide space to look for solutions.

## ☐  Staying with the Art

It is just as important to stay with the artform as it is to allow a person to finish a narrative. Too often the art is done, noted as a reflection, and the attention focused elsewhere. Many opportunities are lost in this manner. The flip side of moving on too fast is the forced examination of the art when the artist may be hesitant to continue. This reluctance to share is often labeled resistance, when actually it is poor timing and a need for the therapist and other group members to press for a deeper meaning. This prevents the art product from being seen as just a drawing and not honored as a personal statement; thus losing its usefulness and leaving the artist with an unfinished feeling.

While a respectful, explorative attitude results in profitable possibilities for change, it also presents a dilemma for the group leader. Since most of the group members will have made an art expression in response to the group's interest in a subject, there will be multiple artforms that will need to be attended to. If the vertical–horizontal approach of exploration is taken, the group may run out of enough time for everyone to share their art. If this happens, members may feel rejected, hurt, angry, and experience other feelings of neglect. When time does run out, it is essential that this issue be confronted and made a focus of group discussion. How to solve the time problem should be a group decision. If the group wants parity of time to explore the art, then perhaps the dissatisfied individual, who feels that his or her art expression represented a turning point, can personally seek resolution. Requests for a special time from the group, might be one option, or an individual session with the therapist where the results are brought back to the group. Whatever the plan of action, a resolution that satisfies the client's needs must be found. The therapist should give this issue some thought before it happens, because it will happen.

## Managing Time

Art making always takes some time. The advantage is that when everyone draws at the same time it is as though everyone is talking simultaneously. This function is economical; it is the exploration of the art expressions that take the extra minutes. Tension occurs between hurrying and touching on only the superficial meanings in the art, and the pressure of time. Time can be an imposition over which the therapist has no control. Time management must be a major consideration when planning a session and how to give fair attention to individual clients, their artwork, and the entire group is a major issue.

There is consolation in the belief that the problems of the individual clients are externalized in the art product and by looking at the difficulty at a distance, the client has still been helped. By separating the problem from other related emotions, by demonstrating that if they can master the problem on paper, they can do so in reality. The client, then, is in charge of his or her own selection of solutions. Even if the verbal exploration must be delayed, the client as an internal observer and evaluator can continue the search for meaning. The image is retained in the artmaker's mind, and the process does not stop with the rendition of the art piece.

## ☐ Synthesizing Group Processes and Art Expressions

There is a general consensus among group therapists that for a group to become cohesive certain therapeutic factors must be addressed (Ettin, 1992; Ormont,1992; Corey,1990; Vinogradov & Yalom, 1998). Yalom, (1995) names 11 of these factors:

1. Installation of hope,
2. Universality,
3. Imparting information,
4. Altruism,
5. The corrective recapitualization of the primary family group,
6. Development of socializing techniques,

7. Imitative behavior,
8. Interpersonal learning,
9. Group cohesiveness,
10. Catharsis, and
11. Existential factors (p. 1).

While some of these goals are essential, some do not seem to be readily achieved in the groups functioning in today's mental health community.

All of these factors grow together to establish the group. They recur in changing relations as the group continues to form, as do all principles that contribute to group cohesion. Groups are formed to support and inform certain selected clients. In today's society there are groups for every type of person at any age. From children's groups to those for the elderly, from highly-structured groups that focus on one set of difficulties to open-ended groups that are created for growth, all of the countless variations will at some time impart information and recognize the universal human traits that they have in common. Some groups are formed around a specific theme, for example a widow's group, but embedded in every group are differences from the theme that arise from the personalities of the group members. Variety and deviations are the factors that enrich group process, the material that makes every group unique.

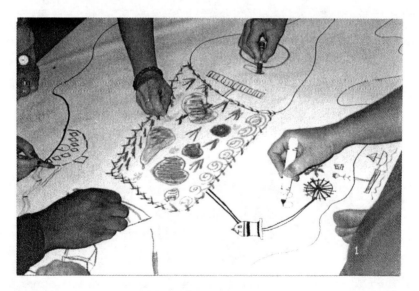

**FIGURE 1.1.** An adult group drawing together, working toward group cohesion.

Group cohesion will gradually grow through socialization, interpersonal learning, and the recognition of extenuating circumstances in all of the members' lives (see Figure 1.1).

## Examining the Synthesis of Art Making with Group Process

As a group gathers together for the first time, the therapist will see six (more or less) people who are strangers to each other and to her. She also sees in her mind's eye not just six people, but six families embedded in each individual's belief system; she sees gender, socioeconomic position in society, race and culture that influence the client, the impact of stress and the question of acceptance, the issue of sexual orientation. She sees that she has a microcosm of the world in one place, in one context. How can all these issues be managed in the allotted time span for a group?

These are some of the many contradictions and complexities that

**FIGURE 1.2.** An enmeshed family. Group member, longs for the past closeness in her family.

people live with daily. However, simply because we find a method to balance all of these realities, it does not mean that the experience is comfortable. In group, there are a self-selected number of people who are not satisfied with the juggling that they have to do so that some of the pressures in life can be reconciled. Most groups are formed around a theme (e.g., divorce, drugs or alcohol abuse, developmental issues, etc.), but the complications mentioned above are still the background that influences the specific problems of the group. Working background and foreground in therapy is inevitable. The more the presenting problem is examined, the more the client and the therapist realize the depth of the impact of family and social issues of creating an alternative resolution (see Figure 1.2).

A remarkable advantage that the therapeutic art product has to offer is that many issues may be concentrated in the image. Ask someone to draw a representation of their life, and they can do it!—Think of the time it would take to hear the story. The image condenses the wide range of thoughts into a gestalt of the whole. Then the events and their emotional connections can be appreciated and become a useful tool for the therapist and client alike. Therefore, the addition of imagery to group process seems to follow as a natural ingredient.

Many groups are time limited, irrespective of the seriousness of the issues to be discussed. Effective methods to accelerate the process without losing the quality of productive change are necessary. This is the challenge that therapists must face in today's health field.

## ☐ The Tools of the Trade: Media

If members are asked to draw or make other artforms, as part of their communication and interactions in the group, then media needs to be easily available.

Felt pens, broad-tip and narrow are easy to use; oil pastels (Craypays) have intense color and an agreeable texture; dry pastels are similar to chalk; collage pictures, cut from magazines with the words removed, are a short cut to imagery that is hard to represent; blunt-tipped scissors, glue sticks, masking tape to use with collages and post pictures on the wall; Plasticine (a form of non-drying clay) or real clay, give an opportunity to do three-dimensional work; paint in blocks that will not spill, along with the necessary brushes are just some of the tools to get started.

The easiest way to have paper of all sizes is to have a roll of white butcher paper mounted on a cutter. In this manner small or large paper can be torn to fit the task at hand (see Figure 1.3).

**FIGURE 1.3.** Mixed media collage with magazine pictures and plasticine.

Special media will need to be offered for children, adolescents, and adults. There will be some crossover, but special projects for a given age group may require media not mentioned above. (See Malchiodi, 1998 for a more comprehensive list pp. 87–100.)

This author's choice of media is solely practical: Easy to handle, easy to move media are selected for several reasons. The first, is because these tools are familiar to the client. The second, because often the space where an art group is conducted is not designed for this purpose. If the therapist is lucky enough to have a permanent space with a table, cupboards for storage, and a sink for water and wash-up, the possibilities can be greatly expanded. The following chapters will introduce the reader to situations where the media was tailored within the context of the therapeutic goals and the capabilities of the population served.

The agency or the facilitator can supply the media, but if the individual client has his or her own tools they begin to have an attachment to them and a respect for preserving them. The tools can also be used outside the group after the client becomes enchanted with the pleasure that making art can provide. The range of supplies should be modified for some age groups or in some agencies, but since the media has a life of its own and impacts the execution of the client's plan, no tools should be overlooked.

Soft media moves the expressive response in a different manner than resistant drawing tools. Paint imposes a need for control that felt pens do not. Clay moves, forms to the hand, and can be easily changed and reformed. All of these possibilities can be used to the advantage of the client, coupled with suggestions from the group leader. Proper use of media can advance the progress of therapy by adding the tactile-emotive sense to the process of discovery. The addition of a spectrum of external stimuli, kinesthetic, sensory, and olfactory, activates areas of the brain that are not stimulated by words and images alone. This leads to improved comprehension of patterned behaviors and blocks to making change.

## Implications Inherent in Art Media

In some situations the introduction of various media is the first step in group formation. Moving the colors around on paper, exploring line qualities, becoming aware of texture and form, are ways of starting a conversation on a metaphorical basis. Members can relate to which colors evoke certain emotions, and which art tasks remind them of other confrontations with new situations. Much information can be shared through metamessages that are implied in this nonthreatening activity. An unstructured chance to become acquainted with art materials may be sufficient to start relationships at this early stage.

Some groups stay with the art experience alone. They are called open studio groups, and serve a population that needs the freedom to create and have a dialogue with their own art (McNiff, 1998; Allen, 1995). For many groups, the therapist can sense when it is appropriate for the members to have a session where they stay with the art, or if the art should be used to convey a message and aid in problem solving. As in all good therapy, flexibility in the service of the client is primary. The therapist must always think about the context in which the therapy is offered. An unstructured environment might be anti-therapeutic in a psychiatric day treatment program, but successful in the inpatient setting. However, this example could be exactly the opposite depending on the degree of illness, the medication, the hospital itself. Media can be dangerous if it is a weapon that can be thrown or used to hurt another. Therefore, it is important to know the clients, know their ability to stay controlled, and keep the environment safe for interactions and dialogue.

Most group rooms are set up with a circle of chairs, without a surface on which to do artwork. For children, the group can make art on the floor, for adults drawing boards can be supplied, but a table is best, and for more than convenience. A table is a symbol in many ways: It is conventionally seen as a place around which people meet to eat, talk, do homework, read the paper, and other activities. It

**FIGURE 1.4.** Two examples of an adult group working in triads: constructing an environment from construction paper in three dimensions.

provides separation from the others at the table, while providing a connection as well. It makes doing artwork easier and more spontaneous because the tools can be readily available, and a stack of paper can be left in one corner. The client can reach for the necessary material to make a point, a visible point. Pastels can be placed in a shallow basket, the pens in another basket, and the collage materials also in another basket or flat box. A conscious effort should be made to separate the media from their image as "precious" and used only for "works of art." In the group situation, if members do not bring in their own supplies, several smaller baskets filled with the media will be needed so that the tools are easily available to each individual.

## Sharing the Pleasure of Art Materials

Make it a point, particularly with children and adolescents, to open a new box of pastels in their presence. Share the pleasure of looking at the pristine colors, the new smell, and the pleasant smooth feeling of the pastel stick. The new pastels, paints, or pens are for the individual or the group to use as they see fit. Perhaps many of the youths have never had the experience of a box of new crayons, of the implied potential of a fresh set of materials, and the possibilities that color invites (Riley, 1999). This encounter with potential beauty is not confined to the younger person. Adults too can respond to an engagement with media, they may either feel excited or become sad thinking of deprivations in their childhood. Many people tell of times when they were a child and were punished because they broke the crayon or messed up the paint box. The therapist can offer a curative experience through a simple transaction such as opening a new box of crayons. The gift of the media is not conditional and the creative opportunities will not be withdrawn. This often runs counter to the client's life experience.

## Issues of Safety

Do not assume that innocent media cannot turn into a weapon in a moment. Do not have sharp scissors available; make sure that the client will not throw the clay or mark up the walls. Such difficulties are rare in group unless the setting is one where either the clients are mentally unstable or they are young, severely damaged youths. Simple precautions will keep active anger out of use of media.

One example is between a therapist and a new hospital patient in a psychiatric unit. The session started with a basket of pastels on the table while the initial discussion took place. Everything seemed to be progressing well until the patient realized the therapist had not understood his drawing, and was attempting to gain more information about it. He became rageful and took the basket of pastels and threw them at the therapist. Fortunately the pastels were light and did not reach across the table. While this situation was lucky, a therapist must stay aware of the surroundings and not underestimate either clients or the objects they are given.

# ☐  Visual Knowing

Everything done with artforms and tools are evocative on a surprisingly powerful level. Imagery stimulates visual knowing and memories that are complex and interrelate with many associations. Emotional stimulation through form, color, texture, composition, and line have moved mankind since history began. Neurologists are beginning to understand the pathways that produce the emotional reaction; therapists appreciate and channel the evocative powers even without fully comprehending the physiology. Although therapists may be naïve about neurology, when group members use media to create a creative product they are engaged in a process that requires their "whole" attention. Cognitive, emotional, instinctive, or patterned reactions, inner verbal dialogue, selective choices, kinesthetic movement, auditory stimulus, even smell plays a part of image making. Are there other therapeutic means easily available, where a person can corral multiple reactions and decisions in a moment? Being able to condense all of the mind and body functions to create a visible statement is the unique quality of art used in therapy.

There is also a hazard inherent in the process of using visual expressions in a session. In addition to the pervasive issue of countertransference that is constantly informing each person with messages, there is the countertransference to the image. Personal preferences in art may cloud the message that the artmaker has constructed in the drawing. Therapists must be very attentive to their own reactions to another person's imagery, and be aware when that same reaction is present in other group members. This bias may be very subtle and hard to uncover, however it is a serious matter that should be a subject of group discussion when the opportunity arises.

# ☐  Development of the Group

## Basic Structure and Development

Corey (1990) lists some of the themes that he has observed typically emerge during the life of a group. The list is helpful as a starting place of using art in group and facilitates dealing with these themes.

1. Clarifying personal goals
2. Creating and maintaining trust
3. Dealing with fears and resistances
4. Coping with loneliness and isolation

5. Resolving dependence/independence conflicts
6. Overcoming the fear of intimacy
7. Dealing with depression
8. Searching for meaning in life
9. Challenging and clarifying values
10. Dealing with the termination of the group (p. 486)

These themes are appropriate for adults and older adolescents, however when dealing with children's groups, the list must be modified to meet their developmental needs. However, if the parents share the group with their youngsters these themes would apply.

## Beginnings

Bearing these principles in mind aids the therapist in structuring goals and monitoring the group's progress. After the group has been selected and the members interviewed, they arrive for the first session. Hopefully the framework and general goals of the group, as well as the length of each session and the number of meetings, were established in the original interview. Now, as the members look shyly at each other and entertain their first impressions, there is a moment of uncomfortable silence and glances at the facilitator, hoping that the tension will be broken. The leader might say something like, "I can imagine that this may be a little awkward for most of you to be here for the first time. Strangers to each other, and to me as well. I suggest that we put therapy aside for these first meetings and do something that is a little different. Take a piece of paper that you see on the table, and make a scribble with any color marker you choose. The scribble will represent why you are here." After a few minutes have passed and everyone has made his or her scribble, the leader may ask. "Now please take another color and trim, expand, color in this drawing, or do anything else that occurs to you to make the reason you are here have a positive outcome. In other words, change it from a problem shape to a solution shape. Remember, you are only changing the shape, not solving a real problem. We can discuss your experience after the scribble has been changed. Please remember that you are not obliged to share verbally, just to hold up your drawing. If you wish to discuss the process the group will appreciate your sharing and reply if the story fits their own life exposure. The art is not fine art, it is communication.

This is only one of many ways to start a group, a personal choice on the part of this author for several reasons. The first reason is that the request in unexpected. This may seem odd, but most people bring a very dour view of therapy to group; they are tense and have preplanned how they will start, what they will allow themselves to say, and how much pain they are prepared to tolerate. Doing a scribble is far from what they likely expected. When asked to change the scribble they begin to get the idea that this isn't all nonsense and could lead to something. However, when everyone holds up their scribble the "eyes" have it—there are likely to be some similarities in the drawings and these indicate (silently) that there is some commonality in their stressors. Most people have little difficulty talking about their problems and goals if they are embedded in an image. The members are encouraged to talk about the drawing not themselves. Group members can look and point at their scribble, and not have to face the strangers in this new group. The entire activity is received on a playful, yet respectful, level. Communication starts even if there is limited verbalizations; the drawings have an energy of their own.

## Style and Meta-Messages

The therapist can set the tone for these first sessions. For example when looking at the scribble drawings they can be talked about in a playful manner. "This seems to be a loopy, purple group. Everyone has looped all over the page, and really poked the space out of the loops with their second color. Maybe we should name this session the Loops?" It is nonsense, but it is purposeful. By projecting commonalties that probably will soon surface, by noting that the first problem issue was modified by the second solution gesture, the group has the strength to solve problems, work as a team, and enjoy being together. Talking in metaphor allows the message to be heard on a metalevel. It is the opposite of confrontation.

This style may not suit anyone else in the world, so each therapist should create an opening task that does not avoid the fact that people come to therapy for a reason. Acknowledge that fact, then find a task that takes the focus away from pure cognition into the broader field of reactions, behaviors and nonconfrontive interactions. Create an activity that reflects the goals of group process in an oblique manner.

The leader can direct the group's interactions to be appropriate for the first phase of group formation; they can be confrontive or nonconfrontive, depending on the style of the therapist. Encourage activities that both reveal and screen simultaneously, allowing traumatic material to surface at a moderate pace. Creating an opportunity for group members to externalize their problems by making it into an object, activates the notion of mastery. If one can bring the problem "into being," there becomes the opportunity to look at it from a new per-spective and take action. The other group members can also "see" the problem and view it apart from the creator. When the focus is on the problem not the person, there is freedom to confront the problem as a team. Each person in group can draw their difficulty and place it away from themselves, literally in the center of the table or floor. As a group of drawings (problems) they make a different impact and stimulate solutions. These mild beginnings offer hope to the participants and punctuate commonalties. This is the first step toward group cohesion (see Figure 1.4).

## Useful Techniques

From the beginning each group should start with the question, "Is there any unfinished business left from last week that needs to be addressed?" The discussion that follows may be solely verbal, but often the ques-tions that are asked have something to do with a dialogue that stemmed from the previous session's artwork. The art can be brought back into the group, since all art products should be preserved and kept at hand. The concrete expressions help to refocus the memories and perplexi-ties that lingered around their presentation. If the group relied on recall alone, there would be many more ambiguous statements. The solidity of therapeutic art is one of the great advantages of this form of therapy.

**FIGURE 1.5.** A group shares their family sculptures.

Introducing image making from the first group meeting adds to clarification and goal setting, as well as demonstrates the processes of group formation in a tangible manner. Seeing the art product of fellow group members gives each person a unique view of the others' personalities and conflicts. The shared experience of pain and joy emerges, and a sense of commonality accelerates the process of group cohesion. The memory of another person's art piece impacts an area of the brain that is not in the same location that stores verbal memory, so that art and words work together to produce a more complete recollection and evaluation of the problem. The image very often lingers beyond the recall of a person's name or verbal description of a situation. Solutions are confronted more quickly as a broad range of skills are activated to solve the problem. It is equally helpful to the therapist, who can use the visual memory as a tool to recall interactions in the past group sessions

## ☐ The Stylistic Signature

Often the signature of the artmaker's artistic style evokes group transactions more than words. For example, John is known for his overlapping triangles and ovals done in heavy warm colors, while Mary has trouble using any other media than light colored pencils to make partially finished flower-like forms. John's drawings refer to his questions about identity; Mary's drawings represent her guilty wish to eliminate her parents and escape their domination. Who would know that by just looking at the art? The lines and colors require the clients' narrative to bring clarity to the art. Images impact visual memory and are stored with the narratives which are available for future explanation. It is the combination of created image and verbal explanation that gives the whole picture (see Figure 1.5).

### Structured and Nonstructured Directives

Do not give preconceived directives to a group or an individual in therapy. Listen carefully to the discussion and interchange among the members of the group as they settle down to start group. Often the therapist can pick up a theme or a viewpoint that seems to be a segue into material that the group is ready to examine. Openly say that, for example, this week several members seem to have had a difficult time with their families. Would that be a subject that the group would like to focus on at this time? If the suggestion doesn't fit, the idea will be rejected, but usually another thought will be offered from the group in its place. This method insures that all the art tasks are reflective of the therapeutic process and not an imposition. It also relieves the therapist from the omnipotent position of knowing what the group wishes to discuss. This follows the principle of coconstruction of the transactions in therapy (Anderson & Goolishian, 1988). In this approach the client and therapist are equally vested in finding solutions to the problems that engage the group members (Riley, 1999).

However, there are times when it is helpful to provide an art task to accelerate or solidify group process. Some of the more common opening activities could be:

1. An individual drawing can be shared with one other group member;
2. A dual drawing (subject of choice) is nonverbally created, followed by the same directive done with talking allowed, to contrast the two experiences;
3. The "pass-around-drawing," where each person places an abstract symbol in the center of the page and on cue the drawing is passed to the right and the next person adds to it. This continues until the original artist receives their work again.

There are many more preconstructed exercises, which, can be useful only if they are offered in context and responsive to the needs of the group.

If there is a reason to stimulate discourse between members, then yes, structuring a shared, dual drawing may break the ice. However, to run a group by managing the art activities without regard for the unique personality of the group itself, is staying on the surface and not encouraging the creativity and individuality of the members. The clients grow dependent on the leader for ideas and the dynamic force of group is attenuated. Sometimes, even the most inventive therapist needs a boost from an experienced art therapist. A book that has many creative suggestions is *Art Therapy for Groups: A Handbook of Themes, Games, and Exercises* by Marian Liebmann (1998), another is *Therapeutic Art Directives and Resources* by Susan Makin (2000).

## ☐ Rituals and the Formation of Group Identity

Every group will at some point in their evolution, create a sense of uniqueness, an identity of their own. However, it is helpful to establish some rituals that will hasten and reinforce this process. When a group has created a ritual for starting each session, a group personality emerges. Some visible means of recognizing the individuality of the group can be enhanced by appropriate expressive tasks.

## A Ritual of Confidentiality

Offer the group an opportunity to make their pledge to confidentiality concrete. A piece of sturdy paper, about 12 × 12 can be given to the person on the right (or left) of the therapist. She is asked to trace around her hand with a colored felt pen. The paper and basket of pens are passed to the next person, and so on. With their color of choice, each person traces their hand superimposed on the first tracing. It travels around the circle, ending with a complexity of hand tracings, one on top of the other that exemplifies the group. Each hand is still recognizable, but the method of overdrawing creates a composite image. The symbolism is instantly recognized. To add to this ritual, ask each person to verbally pledge confidentiality as they complete their hand tracing. When this "hands" paper is placed in the center of the room it assumes a mystic of its own. It is also impactful to bring this testimony to every group. Place it in an obvious place each time and it will be a group-created commitment to trust. This is similar to children's ritual of becoming "blood brothers" (see Figure 1.6)

**FIGURE 1.6.** Beginning group ritual. As the hands were traced, the group members verbally committed to confidentiality.

## Rituals of Placement and Sharing

Where people sit, and how they stay or rotate their choice of seats in relation to the therapist and other emergent leaders, is a kind of ritual dance. When working with groups larger than four, work with a co-leader; the movement around the two therapists is interesting to watch. Parallel to this form of behavioral dynamics, is the mode of exploring the artwork. For example, the people who "go" first, the ones that linger to the last; the member that makes remarks about the similarities or differences in the stylist renderings of the art; the member who places his art piece forward to be easily seen, to the extreme opposite action of turning the art face downward on the floor behind the chair. Some members favor one media above the rest, and resist experimenting with new techniques. As these characteristics emerge some group members will notice them and the opportunity may present itself to reframe the observation into a discussion of behaviors and personalities. Whether it is discussed or not, these behaviors inform the therapist and add to their ability to manage group transactions.

## Ritual of "Naming"

A group can be asked to give themselves a name. For example, the "Passionate Purple group," based on the recognition that purple seems to be a dominant color used in the artwork. The name becomes a metaphor and is based on the art products rather than the behaviors of the members. A group drawing or painting, created in any manner that the group decides, can become their banner placed on the wall. Preferably the banner should be made up of abstract forms, contributed by all members of the group. The name can change at any time and the group drawing can be replaced by a new one. The new drawing should be placed on top of the first, signifying the growth of the group and respect for the past therapeutic work that has lead to the current developmental stage.

These are just suggestions. Each group leader and each group composition has to develop their own visual expression of continuity and uniqueness. The above rituals may seem to lack in originality, however, do not discount the power of the group to make a visible projection of themselves in the context of the group to which they are committed. The artform assumes a place of distinction, and the group often becomes very protective of the art product.

This realization can come about very gradually, and the therapist may be rather surprised at the intensity of the power that the group

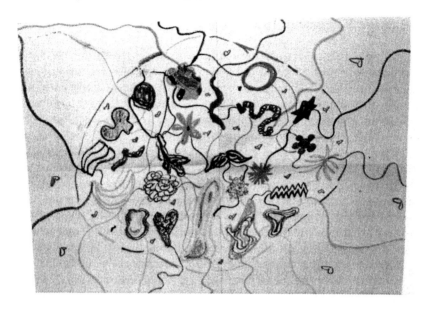

**FIGURE 1.7.** Group mural. Personal symbols with lines of "connection," establishing commonality of purpose while protecting individuality.

endowed on their product. Over time, how the ceremonial expressions and the rituals of creating are reflective of the group personality becomes more and more impressive. This may come about by recognizing that every group creates an overriding persona, a composite of the whole which transcends the individual traits of each group member. The therapist may also be amused at how titles precreated before the sessions did or did not coincide with the group's perceptions of themselves (see Figure 1.7).

## ☐ After the "Beginning"

The creative move for self-structure is the kernel of the next phase of group growth, the "middle phase" of group development. However, "middle" often may be the entire duration of the group until it is time to terminate, because the group moves forward and backward in a rhythm peculiar to itself. It can be metaphorically compared to the tide coming up to the shore and then retreating back into the surf. As every wave washes up, it leaves behind some residue that a beachcomber might wish to recover and hold. The "beachcomber" is the group facilitator who makes the collection, arranges it, and then displays it to the other people in the group.

What ever floats to shore is added to the treasure chest and is equally valuable. Thus, the group addresses one issue, which leads to a related one, or makes decisions about the value of one piece of detritus over the other. In collaborative therapy terms, the growth of the group lies in their continuous attention to the issues that surface and how they add to their collective appreciation of the complexities of problem solving. Group members will choose issues that they believe are notable, as well as those that are not worthy of their attention. How they arrive at this consensus is the power of group therapy contrasted to individual treatment. A situation that was ignored one week, becomes a topic of passionate dialogue the next; the member who was ignored takes the spotlight when the circumstances shift. This is the ebb and flow of group process.

The leader can evaluate this flow by paying attention to the art. If, for example, the art products are all stereotyped drawings that are without content, then it is time to pull out a collection of art pieces, images of unresolved issues that have been lying dormant. This does not mean it is the group leader's responsibility to come up with new material, it does, however, mean that he or she can speculate on "Did we ever solve the problem of —————?" Invite the group to create a drawing that recalls " the solution to the ————— problem of Mary's divorce."

Recalling a neglected topic must be based on reality, it can not be a false concern injected into the group. Chances are that there will be multiple ways that a solution is pictured in the art. That, in itself, will stimulate interchange and discussion. Alternative solutions may arise that were not previously offered, or there may be awareness that this issue was never addressed, and these group members may still be feeling isolated. Group leaders can use modified techniques from deShazer's (1985) solution-focused model to stimulate renewed vitality.

When the group does not have to be guided by structured directives or suggestions about media, there is no need for the group leader to impose ideas or control the expressions. After the members have established trust and become acquainted with their shared concerns and individual stories, they will probably, without prompting, go to the paper, drawing material, and three-dimensional media that is available in the room. They will be self-directed in their choices and find media which reflects the image they have conjured in their mind. The visual schema that reflects on the issue they choose to address will become a spontaneous expression; their timing and pacing of the sharing process will also be self-motivated.

# ☐ Group Differentiation

Following the establishment of a secure working environment through speech and art, there is no single path that can provide satisfactory progress for all groups. For most groups, introducing simple tasks that make the bridge from discomfort to trust can follow similar lines, modified for the developmental and psychological capacities of the members. However, after the first steps have been established there is a dramatic

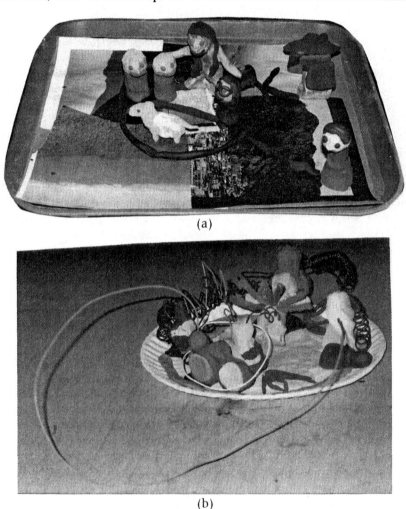

(a)

(b)

**FIGURE 1.8.** Two examples of visualizing family relations. (a) Issues of emotional connection, closeness, distance, and power rendered in plasticine; (b) collage used to indicate the "heat" or "cold" of the family environment.

difference in the manner the group will proceed if they are serving youngsters, adolescents, or adults.

Age-appropriate creative tasks will be addressed in the following chapters. The philosophy of the therapist may remain constant with every group experience, but she must constantly question the validity of her theoretical constructs and offer modifications of activities that are reflective of the individual group. It is essential to accommodate to each group. It is necessary to re-invent and re-evaluate the process and progress of the group on an ongoing basis.

For every specialized group there must be specialized treatment, and that does not exclude how the art will serve the expressive needs of the group. Commonalities can be learned; specialization must be carefully developed. As the following chapters discuss the age of clients, cultural and psychological belief systems, the context in which the therapy is offered, the care devoted to tailoring the verbal and non-verbal tasks will become apparent (see Figure 1.8).

## ☐ Summary

Earlier in this chapter 10 themes were quoted from Corey (1990). These 10 themes can serve as the underlying foundation of the art directives. Each emergent theme can translate into a tangible product and provide a record for the growth of the group. Forming opportunities that facilitate the building of trust, facing fears and resistance, loneliness and isolation, dependencies and intimacy, depression and the meaning of life projects the path of growth that groups often travel. If the group leader were able to ask the members to make art renditions of each of these major milestones toward group cohesion, and by making the art, the forward movement was accomplished, group therapy would be predictable. However, this evolutionary progression is not likely to take place so smoothly. The group will trust, make a leap forward, demonstrate willingness to be intimate, then fall back to distrust. This normal fluctuation should be expected. In spite of this knowledge therapists have an obligation to be as helpful and creative as possible. Therapists should be dedicated to stimulating skills in their clients and mastery over their problems.

By using the power of the art to record, challenge, and bring forth abilities to find alternative solutions, the group is able to regroup when in crisis and rejoice when in success. The art product testifies to progress and change as both visual and verbal process develop simultaneously. The art, as a second language, speaks for the flow of the group and indicates the best direction toward change.

Art as an integral part of the communication in group is invaluable. It is a support and provocation to change. As this chapter has reviewed, the inclusion of graphic expressions in group allows more of a client's sensorial reinforcements to be involved, and that involvement stimulates brain patterns that lead to fresh conclusions and alternative choices. The therapist and group members both benefit from better understanding of problem issues when the difficulties are seen.

Group facilitators should experiment and enjoy incorporating art tasks to their group's activities. Creativity is not confined to great artists; therapy itself can be a creative art of the highest degree.

# ☐ References

Allen. P. (1995). *Art is a way of knowing.* Boston: Shambala.

Anderson, H., & Goolishian, H. (1988). Human systems as linguistic systems: Preliminary and evolving ideas about the implications for clinical theory. *Family Process,* 27, 371–394.

Author, I. (1938). Funk & Wagnalls: Practical Standard dictionary, ed. Frank H. Vizetelly. New York: Funk & Wagnalls.

Carter, R. (1998). *Mapping the mind.* Berkeley, CA: University of California Press.

deShazer, S. (1985). *Keys to solutions in brief therapy.* New York: W. W. Norton.

Ettin, M. F. (1992). *Group psychotherapy.* Boston: Allyn & Bacon.

Goleman, D. (1995). *Emotional intelligence.* New York: Bantam Books.

Leibmann, M. (1986). *Art therapy for groups.* Cambridge, MA: Bookline Books.

Liebmann, M. (1998). *Art therapy for groups: A handbook of themes, games, and exercises.* Cambridge, MA: Brookline Books.

Makin, S. (2000). *Therapeutic art directives and resources.* London: Jessica Kingsley.

Malchiodi, C. (1998). *The art therapy source book.* Lincolynwood, IL: Lowell House Kingsley.

McNiff, S. (1988). *Fundamentals of art therapy.* Springfield, IL: Charles C. Thomas.

Ormont, L. R. (1992). *Group therapy experience: From theory to practice.* New York: St. Martin's Press.

Pinker, S. (1997). *How the mind works.* New York: W.W. Norton.

Riley, S. (1999). *Contemporary art therapy with adolescents.* London: Jessica Kingsley.

Vinogradov, S., & Yalom, I. D. (1998). *A concise guide to group psychotherapy.* Washington, DC: American Psychiatric Press.

Yalom, I. D. (1995). *The theory and practice of group psychotherapy.* New York: Basic Books.

# ☐ Suggested Readings

Betensky, M. (1973). *Self-discovery through self-expression: Use of art in psychotherapy with children and adolescents.* Springfield, IL: Charles C. Thomas.

Cane, F. (1983). *The artist in each of us.* Craftsbury Common, VT: Art Therapy Publications. (Originally work published by Pantheon, New York, 1951).

Case, C., & Dalley, T. (1992). *The handbook of art therapy.* New York: Tavistock Routledge.

Corey, G. (1981). *Theory and practice of group counseling* (3rd ed.). Pacific Grove, CA: Brooks/Cole.

Cross, D. C. (1994). Organizing group psychiatric programming in managed care settings. In K. R. MacKenzie (Ed.), *Effective use of group therapy in managed care* (pp. 27–42). Washington. DC: American Psychiatric Press.

DiLeo, J. H. (1983). *Interpreting children's drawings.* New York: Brunner/Mazel.

Dissanayake, E. (1992). *Homo aestheticus: Where art comes from and why.* Seattle, WA: University of Washington Press.

Freeman, J., Epston, D., & Lobovits, D. (1997). *Playful approaches to serious problems: Narrative therapy with children and their families.* New York: Norton.

Furth, G. M. (1988). *The secret world of drawings: Healing through art.* Boston, MA: Sigo Press.

Hogan, S. (Ed.). (1997). *Feminist approaches to art therapy.* London: Routledge.

Jennings, S., & Minde, A. (1993). *Art therapy and drama therapy: Masks of the soul.* Bristol, PA: Taylor & Francis.

Killick, K., & Schaverien, J. (Eds.). (1997). *Art, psychotherapy and psychosis.* New York: Routledge.

Kramer, E. (1971). *Art as therapy with children.* New York: Schocken Books.

Landgarten, H., & Lubbers, D. (Eds.). (1991). *Adult art psychotherapy: Issues and applications.* New York: Brunner/Mazel.

Malchiodi, C. (Ed.). (1999). *Medical art therapy with adults.* London: Jessica Kingsley.

Malchiodi, C. (Ed.). (1999). *Medical art therapy with children.* London: Jessica Kingsley.

McNiff, S. (1995). Keeping the studio. *Art Therapy, 12*(3), 179–183.

Oster, G. D., & Gould, P. (1987). *Using drawings in assessment and therapy: A guide for mental health professionals.* New York: Brunner/Mazel.

Skaife, S., & Huet, V. (Eds.). (1998). *Art psychotherapy groups: Between pictures and words.* London: Routledge.

Virshup, E. (Ed.). (1993). *California art therapy trends.* Chicago: Magnolia Street.

Wadeson, H. (1980). *Art psychotherapy.* New York: John Wiley.

Wadeson, H. (1987). *The dynamics of art psychotherapy.* New York: Wiley.

Waller, D. (1998). *Treatment of addiction: Current issues for art therapies.* London: Routledge.

Waller. D. (1993). *Group interactive art therapy.* London: Routledge.

Weisberg, N., & Wilder, R. (Eds.). (1985). *Creative arts with older adults: A sourcebook.* New York: Human Sciences.

Weiser, J. (1993). *Phototherapy techniques: Exploring the secrets of personal snapshots and family albums.* San Francisco: Jossey Bass.

Winegar, N. (1992). *The clinician's guide to managed mental health care.* New York: Haworth Press.

Wohl, A., & Kaufman, B. (1985). *Silent screams and hidden cries: An interpretation of art work by children from violent homes.* New York: Brunner/Mazel.

**2**

CHAPTER

# Introducing the Language of Art to Interns and Staff in an Early Childhood Attachment Theory Program

The early childhood program at Thalians, the mental health component of Cedars Sinai Hospital in Los Angeles, has created a program that is concerned with evaluating and reconstructing early childhood attachment experiences of the clients they see in treatment. The therapeutic approach is based on material discussed in the works of Schore (1994), Siegel (1999), Lillas (1999), Greenspan and Benderly (1997), and others. Bowlby (1969) has been resurrected and given even greater credence through psycho/neuro/biological research. CAT scans, PET scans, and observation has added to the practical knowledge of "good enough" parenting that Winnicott (1965) has written about. As I became involved in the program, both as a supervisor and in dialogue with other clinicians, I had the notion that the addition of art tasks and psychoeducational narration would be a useful component to the already excellent service provided. The department agreed to add this training opportunity for those persons on staff who were interested.

## ☐ Group Composition

Eight post-Masters interns and staff members, all with excellent training and experience, agreed to explore this project with me. We met as a group for eight weeks for an hour and half, and co-constructed the format together. Each meeting I shared with them some of the simple art tasks often employed by art therapists to evaluate relationships, communication, and issues of cooperation, boundaries and power. The members of the group made art expressions themselves and also role-played doing the exercise with another member. By the addition of the art form to parenting and attachment techniques, we hoped the integration would enhance or reprogram some of the weak attachment behaviors between parent and child. A discussion of how we transformed these expressive tasks in ways specific to the needs of the clients follows. We chose the term parent or mother to designate the primary caretaker of the child, the one to which we felt would provide the ongoing care and desire to bond with the child.

## ☐ Attachment

Siegel (1999) puts great emphasis on the importance of the attachment process. He explains the system in this manner:

> "Attachment" is an inborn system in the brain that evolves in ways that influence and organizes motivational, emotional, and memory processes with respect to significant caregiving figures. . . . At the level of the mind, attachment establishes an interpersonal relationship that helps the immature brain use the mature functions of the parent's brain to organize its own processes. . . . Attachment relationships thus serve a vital function in providing the infant with protection from dangers of many kinds. These relationships are crucial in organizing not only ongoing experiences, but the neuronal growth of the developing brain (p. 67).

He feels that this early relationship provides the foundation from which the mind develops, and furnishes the basics of memory, emotions, representations, and states of mind.

Learning about the interrelationship between neuronal growth and parent child activities stimulated me to speculate if there were art activities that could reapproach these bonding experiences in a manner that aroused interest between the parental/child dyad. Pleasant and creative tasks that were structured to bypass the verbal-informational format and would counteract past negative interpretations that may have left the parent feeling blamed. A chance to reprogram old patterns of behavior was the goal.

In addition I read that, "the right hemisphere (of the brain) has a nonverbal 'language' of its own, focusing on the gist, context, or social meaning of experiences. Just as the left hemisphere requires exposure to linguistically based language in order to grow properly, one can propose that the right hemisphere may require emotional stimulation from the environment to develop properly. Attachment research clearly demonstrates that communication between caregiver and infant shapes the way the child's developing mind learns to process information" (Siegel, 1999, p.189).

It also seemed to me that these clinicians had not appreciated how important their dedication to their clients influenced the efficacy of their therapy. Vanderheide (2000) condensed the essence of the emotional-cognitive impact of therapy in an excellent article where he brought forth the important point "that the exchange of emotions in therapy is a bidirectional process. There are emotions generated in both the client and the therapist and these emotions are being communicated both consciously and non consciously as well as verbally and non verbally. The emotional exchange develops into a dyadic affective system that may either enhance regulation or lead to deregulation for the client and the therapist" (p. 59).

My goal was to explore how the relationships between therapists and their clients could be vindicated as reparative if the understanding of emotional intelligence was made more conscious.

## Neuro/psycho/biology and Art Interactions

The more I thought about brain functions the more I understood that the integration of right brain activities (creating visible imagery) and the voluntary exploration of that image through the left brain, activated language and cognition. These basic activities could be correlated with the processes of the art therapy modality. It also seemed possible to revisit the attachment "window of opportunity" if we provided the appropriate environment to encourage reprogramming of this vital function. Granted this seemed ambitious, but the group and I were encouraged by the thought that if we could create circumstances to improve interpersonal communication between parent and child, better self-regulation skills may develop and the ability to mind-speak might be strengthened. We researched texts that supported the notion that poor early attachment could be improved even after the optimum period in development had passed.

## ☐  Introduction to the Art Material

The members of the learning group brought to the first meeting a variety of media. As mentioned earlier, there are intrinsic psychological possibilities built in to the media. We spent some time in trying out pencils, pens, pastels, collage, plasticine, and discussing our reactions to the marks the tools made, the physical reaction to the touch, smell, and the memories elicited by the various media. The discussion broadened to experiences with children who used drawing or painting as spontaneous expressions, and how or if they had explored these products with the children. The conversation also turned to disasters. For example, paint being smeared around the room or liquid glue squeezed recklessly over toys and walls.

The purpose was to allow the group members to "feel" their way into media, and not associate these tools with "art" as aesthetics.

## The Process

At the beginning of each group meeting the clinicians discussed a clinical difficulty or family constellation of clients they were serving. In general, the child presented was six years or younger. Often the parent was an adolescent single mother with multiple stressors in her life. Historically, the child, a baby, was reported to have been restless, a poor sleeper, and cried a great deal; the mother often felt she had failed to bond, that something was amiss with the ability of the child to self-regulate. Sometimes the mother felt the baby had a "character" that pushed her away, other times she openly admitted to feeling distance and a lack of attraction to the child. The cases all seemed to have present-day relationship difficulties that stemmed from a lack of reciprocal attachment at birth. Both the mother and child had trouble making friends, or in the child's case, playing with peers. Complaints from the pre-school were a common occurrence.

The child while in treatment displayed behaviors described as "avoidant, an inability to self regulate, and fearful and lacking in trust." It was speculated that this was because the primary relationship was insecure and ambivalent, and was an accumulation of distressful happenings and frustration that brought the child to treatment. At this juncture, the mother felt guilty and that she was blamed by family, acquaintances, and school personnel, and was less than eager to hear the same diagnosis repeated from a therapist. I hasten to say that these clinicians in our group were not the instigators of this failure–blame cycle. Society expects a great deal from mothers and many of the mothers that were in treatment were children themselves. Adolescents as parents are immature developmentally as well as chronologically.

## First Example

Members of our group were taught that one of the most common directives that art therapists use for observing interactions and dynamics between a dyad is the "two-way scribble drawing" (refer to chapter 1). This activity is also called the "two-way conversation." The mother and child are asked to make a drawing together. They are encouraged to just make scribbles and find images in the forms, or if the child is older, make a story drawing. Taking turns and engaging the other by asking for help and being respectful of the other person's marks were the rules of this game. The scribble was introduced as a vehicle to promote a shared experience for reasons that differ from the explanations given in other texts in other contexts: The scribble is the natural form that most young children, two to six or even younger, make (Lowenfeld, 1987). We chose the scribble because it is probably a mark that will emerge no matter what we ask of a child at this developmental stage. The mother can be coached to expect this form of drawing and not to have unrealistic expectations of form and realism.

With an early childhood population, the first time a drawing is attempted, the child often scribbles all over the mother's drawing or avoids making any marks, the mother vainly attempting to join with her child's marks on the page. Trying again, this time the mother is coached to prepare the child for the exercise. First, she is encouraged to ask the child to look her in the eyes, this may be difficult, but gentle support from the clinician can help. The parent does not have to keep eye contact for more than a brief time. During the time of eye contact the mother suggests that they are going to have a "play game." She is also coached to make physical contact with the child, perhaps no more then a light caress on the upper back. They are asked to place their chairs close together. Both parent and therapist admire the colored drawing tools that are available, and then let the child have freedom to choose any color he or she wishes. There should be no remarks about "what the color means."

This time the mother is taught to shadow the child's scribble marks and ask her son or daughter to do the same for her. In other words, the child's lines will be mirrored by the mother at a close, respectful distance. The child may not be able to control his or her mirroring, and may mark over the mother's line. The therapist must be alert so that the mother does not interpret this move as aggressive or negative. The young child has no concept of territory or boundaries, and has limited fine motor control. The dialogue should be positive. For example, the mother might say, "It makes me happy when our lines are touching. They are happy lines when they touch." Even better, these remarks could be interspersed with humming and melodic murmuring sounds without words. The mother should be prepared for slow change and be ready to relinquish the need of immediate gratification.

It is absolutely unimportant how the finished drawing appears. It is the process that is significant, that of primitive communication through movement, touch, and gesture. This is instigated by using simple lines and color to engage the child in an easy, nonthreatening activity. Both participants are focused on the movement on the page, and thus the usual, aversive behavior can be modified, if only briefly. The mother and child can put their customary interactions aside and let the interest in an evolving image focus their attention away from friction and on to a cooperative task. The mother can let go of her anxiety, at least momentarily, since she has been assured beforehand that there is no wrong way to make a scribble.

With this nonchallenging image making we are trying to stimulate a process that uses right brain "knowing" and avoid the judgmental, evaluative process of the left brain being in charge. We introduce physical touching, both deliberate and accidental, such as the hands brushing together during the art activity. We also have a visible product that can be held and shared. This product gives memory an opportunity to store a positive experience. Using the felt pens that smell like fruit or flowers add another sensory level to the memory; kinesthetic movements also add to the experience, and perhaps music in the background would be useful. Hopefully, both mother and child have an enjoyable moment together. The time period should be ended as soon as it becomes unpleasant for both mother and child (see Figure 2.1).

## ☐ Right Brain Process

Referring again to the material offered by Siegel (1999), which gives some understanding of the way the right brain processes, he writes:

> In contrast to the left, the right hemisphere appears to be able to make sense of the essential meaning of the input it is able to perceive: Contextual information is perceived and processed, and the gist of a situation is sized up and understood. The right brain does not use syllogistic logic to deduce conclusions about cause-effect relationships, but rather represents information about the environment. Such information includes the relationship of various components of experience, including elements of mental processes and spatial relationships. Since the right brain is nonverbal, the output of its processing must be expressed in non-word-based ways, such as drawing a picture or pointing to a pictorial set of options to make its output known to the external world (p. 326).

**FIGURE 2.1.** An adolescent single mother's drawing of her relationship with her child (*left*). How she wishes it to be (*center*). How it is, each facing away (*right*). Therapist encourages her to hold the child and make eye contact.

The above explanation of the way we recall the tone of a memory, as well as the image, encouraged a further exploration of the premise of art and attachment working together.

## Discussion

The art activity itself was not unique. It was chosen to introduce a simple interactive task that resulted in an image. The image gave the mother and child a relational activity that had no critical evaluation connected to it. The learning came from the "doing." We moved from left brain associative, logical activity to the right brain pictorial, emotional arena. The image making was not enough; the mother needed to be coached in a new method of interacting with her child. She was given a nonthreatening education about the manner that attachment forms, and a rationale for doing the art task in a way that enriched the experience for both her child and herself. For example, one of the therapists in the group reported that when teenaged mothers who were finally able to engage the eyes of their toddlers, they had a deeply moving experience, since they had never experienced this connection. These tasks are reparative for both adult and child.

In our learning group, other clinicians discussed that they had possibly developed a new tool to lessen the guilt syndrome. This occurred when they moved into uncomplicated psychobiological education about the possibility of reestablishing pathways and reprogramming attachment patterns, even though the beginning relationship had been successful. There was little, if any, reluctance from the parent/child dyad to perform the art task. The adults needed a reason to scribble, otherwise they entered the task with hesitation and a feeling of being infantilized. In other words, it was not so much what we did with the clients, as it was *how* we did it.

## Expanding the Concepts

With every art expression introduced to the group, the focus was first on how they responded to the art project (their own reactions to doing the art), then, what physical, nonverbal activities that blend with the artwork (e.g., planning the integration of making an image or art-form with physical touching, eye contact, soft-voiced verbal noises, and spontaneous caresses). We questioned if there were windows of opportunity in developmental growth that could be reprogrammed with information, activity, and parenting techniques. The group members were very attentive and observant of the reactions of their clients, which on the whole, were favorable. The feedback of clients' responses were the resources upon which the group experience grew.

## Other Experiments

The opportunity to make plasticine forms is not appropriate for any child who still is exploring the universe orally. Although plasticine is non–toxic, it is not recommended as a snack. Using a malleable media can be a powerful experience for the mother and child. The movement of the clay illicits a different set of responses compared to drawing. Plasticine is slightly oily, nondrying, and gets softer with more handling. Any sculpting requires fine motor coordination, so it does not lend itself to accurate representations when used with the younger children. However, the less differentiated shapes can be representations just as well as realistic renderings.

There should be no attempt to make a realistic artistic product. The plasticity, malleability of shapes, and the opportunity to merge two shapes into one should be emphasized. Thus, a parent can offer a piece of her clay to be added on to the child's molded shape, implying attachment. This limited fusion can be admired, played with, spoken to, and amplified. The child can be invited to add a bit of his or her colored clay to the mother's. The therapist can comment on how much more interesting the combined forms are than the single-colored forms. There can be a guessing game where mother and child can "guess" what feeling the other's clay piece is experiencing. The mother can offer to soothe the "bad feelings" in the clay—but she must resist actually smoothing the shape unless the child requests it. The final move is to encourage the mother and child to put their clay pieces together on a surface and experiment with moving them around, and making the clay pieces "happy" on the tray.

## Metaphors and Improvisations

If the clay pieces can make contact and lean against each other, the therapist might have the parent and child take the same position as the sculptures and then decide on the noise the two clay pieces would make. The drama of the plasticine creations can be extended into stories and reshaped to fit the new narrative. Any number of variations on this improvisation can allow the mother and child to experiment with a fresh form of relating to one another. The shapes can be preserved for the next session, when the dyad and the therapist can either revisit the play or continue to modify the preceding activity with the plasticine.

## Repetition and Repatterning

The permanence of self-created therapeutic objects opens up channels to stimulate the retrieval of memories and the replacement of dysfunctional patterns with preferred models of behavior. Repetition reinforces patterns of thought that are then translated into behaviors. If the mother and child are offered repeated positive interactions that are experienced through sensory stimulus rather than the common verbal ones, there is perhaps, a higher chance of change to occur. For the therapist to be able to reintroduce the previous session by bringing last week's product into this week's encounter, reminds the dyad of their interactions. They are reminded not through words, but through the sight of the created image. Thus, continuity is established from session to session, which seems to deepen the bonding relationship.

With very young children the repetition of simple tasks is comforting and allows trust to build. For the mother the repetition is also comforting since she can appreciate that it is not only that they have created a form together, but they (child and mother) have entered into a state of

**FIGURE 2.2.** An 8-year-old boy's collage of "how my mother sees me," addressing severe problems around rejection and abandonment.

"falling in love" (Lillas, 1999). Other clinicians have named that amazing atunement with another person by many names: therapists also experience harmony when they are able to connect with a client. That mysterious connection is what we hope to create between the child and parent with these simple exercises (see Figure 2.2).

## ☐ Older Children

When working with the mother-child dyad, the principle of reparation remains the same with the child entering into childhood and early latency, when difficulties with attachment are apparent. The parent and child experiment with reattachment through activities that are not reminiscent of the failed interactions of the past.

One of the therapists in the group reported that his five-year-old client would not draw anything but Pokeman. The task became to find ways that his mother and he could make an "environment" for Pokeman to live, to construct a world where Pokeman could find happiness. Pokeman and other characters in this game could be constructed of sturdy paper and a painted world or plasticine environment created for them to live. The same eye contact, nonjudgmental vocabulary, physical exchange can be introduced for a child at the next stage of development. We know that change is possible, we also know that a few basic principles help, but only at the pace of the clients. Self-regulation and attachment can be reprogrammed, but it is best reprogrammed within the parental relationship.

## Reciprocal Patterns of Emotional Exchange

Our group did the "pass around drawing" (see chapter 1), which can be used to serve a variety ends. In this case, the value lay in the method of passing more than the drawing itself. As the drawing was passed the group members paid extra attention to the face of the other person, looked them in the eyes, and were watchful of the expression on the "receivers" face. There was an attempt to mirror the expression before turning to pass the next drawing. Considerable time was spent on exploring how each group member felt about their drawing that had been passed around the room. Parallels between loosing touch of one's own product, being out of control of one's image, feeling pleasure or disappointment with the final returned drawing were dwelt on for some time. We anchored the discussion by placing it in the context of the parent/child dyad.

The subliminal emotions evoked by this art task gave the group an opportunity to imagine how seeing one's artwork modified by another—an action over which there is little control—could easily be seen as a process parallel to a child feeling disengaged from their caretaker by circumstances beyond their control.

The group became cohesive at an emotional level, in spite of the fact that the purpose was to teach a creative approach to helping mothers, fathers, and children regain closeness hindered by neglect. Merging into the roles of parent and child plus the evocative power of artmaking, inevitably brought personal associations into the dialogue. The personal dialogue was not explored in depth since this was a learning-group experience, however, the process of creating visible images affected each individual. It was a safe experience for these group members who were just becoming aware of the capacity of artwork to access explicit and implicit memories and emotions (see Figures 2.3 and 2.4).

## ☐ Reflections on a Case

I am grateful to a member of the group, Catherine Mary Hutto Gordon, who shared this reflection on a case she was treating at the time.

**FIGURE 2.3.** An overwhelmed single parent. Entitled "My Day," about a single mother with three children, doing the daily chores, driving the children to school and picking them up, going to get school clothes, eating at McDonalds, and trying to rest for a moment (the tree). Expresses feelings of working and parenting.

**FIGURE 2.4.** Positive attachment memory: A family picnic where the mother holds the baby close, standing under the tree. The client was encouraged to honor this memory and pass it on to her child.

She said, "the art group gave me new ways to understand my relationship-based work with early childhood clients."

Catherine used art to resolve a difficult relational problem. Her case example follows.

> A seven-year-old- boy, Z, had been placed permanently with his maternal uncle when his mother could no longer care for either him or herself. He was confused, angry, and unsure of his new relationship with his uncle, and extremely distressed as his mother became more and more distant due to her progressive illness.
>
> Z's new guardian had no previous experience with children and was baffled by the boy's angry and ambivalent behavior. He expected the child to appreciate his generosity in taking him into his life. They came into treatment to help the uncle deal with Z's expression of feelings that alternated between biting and clinging. Both the uncle and Z were confused and hurting.
>
> Using colored markers, the child drew his anxiety about the recent, questionable relationship, and fashioned a family with clay figures with which he and his uncle could explore their relationship. Through these activities the boy was able to conceptualize his place in the family and trust his uncle. He accepted that he could rely on his new environment as a permanent place. The artmaking allowed a seven-year-old-boy to work through the dramatically changed circumstances in his life. The uncle could appreciate the dynamics that stressed the boy, and move into the child's worldview. Words alone could not have made this transition possible.

## ☐  Summary

For the group to first experience the art tasks was important, then to share their thoughts and emotions. Following this personalized group interaction the attention turned to imagining how to integrate the techniques of parenting, information about the principles of reworking attachment, exploring cases, and distinguishing where these art tasks might be useful. The clinicians combined their knowledge of child development with appropriate expressive tools of form and media. It became apparent that much of what we did with the art as group projects, they had tried before. However, they had not found it particularly effective until the therapeutic qualities inherent in the art process, synthesized with therapeutic goals and informed by neuropsychology, united to form an encompassing philosophy of treatment.

The fact that the education was conducted in a group format was essential for success. The group was coconstructed in a manner that responded to the clinicians needs, as well as the population that they served. They benefited from each other's expertise and creatively modified the simple art tasks to serve the individual families or children they had in treatment. The consensus was that the nonverbal dimension of creating images or forms answered some of their requirements for an avenue into early relational states before words were dominant.

There are many other areas of treatment with children and their families where the knowledge of the psychoneurological processes can give the therapist greater appreciation of interplay between emotions and cognition. This appreciation provides therapists with an understanding that broadens their field of vision and stimulates greater creative resources to conduct their therapeutic interventions (Damasio, 1999). As we begin to appreciate how emotions and cognition form a whole that leads the client to more competent decisions, it is worthwhile to find languages that allow these processes to integrate. The language of art gives access to feelings, and the use of the product in therapeutic play combined with a narrative, achieves the synthesis that is needed to change relationships. Establishing new patterns between mother (caretaker) and child is the greatest gift that any therapist could desire.

# ☐ References

Bowlby, J. (1969). *Attachment*. New York: Basic Books.

Damasio, A. R. (1999). *The feeling of what happens: Body and emotion in the making of consciousness*. New York: Harcourt Brace.

Greenspan, S. L., & Benderly, B. L. (1997). *The growth of the mind and the endangered origins of intelligence*. Reading, MA: Addison–Wesley.

Lillas, C. (1999). *A paradigm shift in infant mental health and adult treatment: A psychoneurobiological model.* Workshop at the Early Childhood Center of Cedars-Sinai Medical Center, Audiotape. Los Angeles, California.

Lowenfield, V. (1987). *Creative and mental growth* (8th ed.). New York: Macmillan.

Schore, A. (1994). *Affect regulation and the origin of the self: The neurobiology of emotional development*. Hillsdale, NJ: Arlbaum.

Siegel, D. J. (1999). *The developing mind*. New York: Guilford.

Vanderheide, S. (2000). What the therapist feels makes a difference. *The California Therapist: Magazine of the California Association of Marriage and Family Therapists, 12*, 58–60.

Winnicott, D. W. (1965). *The maturational process and the facillitating processes and the facillitating environment*. New York: International Universities Press.

# ☐ Suggested Readings

Damasio, A. R. (1994). *Descartes' error: Emotion, reason, and the human brain*. New York: Avon Books.

Gardner, H. (1980). *Artful scribbles: The significance of children's drawings*. New York: Basic Books.

Gardner, H. (1982). *Art, mind and brain: A cognitive approach to creativity*. New York: Basic Books.

Goleman, D. (1994). *Emotional intelligence*. New York: Bantam Books.

Greenspan, S. L. (1985). *First feelings*. New York: Viking Penguin.

Pert, C. B. (1997). *Molecules of emotion*. New York: Scribner.

Sapolsky, R. (1998). *Why zebras don't get ulcers*. New York: W. H. Freeman.

Schore, A. (1966). The experience-dependent maturation of a regulatory system in the orbital prefrontal cortex and the origin of developmental psychopathology. *Development and Psychopathology, 8*, 59–87.

# 3

# Psychosocial Support Groups for Children Recovering from the Traumatic Experience of Severe Burns

This chapter presents the reader with guidelines and a description of how groups for children who had experienced the trauma of a burn injury were constructed. This format is also useful for children with other forms of physical trauma. The scarring from burns are visible, as are scars from operations, automobile accidents, and other external insults to the body. The psychological scars of trauma are less visible but often more lasting and unattended than the physical injury. In addition, there is often some hesitation on the part of therapists to expose themselves to this type of injured population. It is not a case of lack of empathy, more a situation of fear that the empathy will be stronger than the expertise needed to be therapeutic.

Therapists may be concerned that they may not be able to function well if their emotional involvement dominated their ability to be useful to these children. Let the children lead the way. Therapists may find that the children are able to talk about their particular problem, to tell the story of the burn incident and the subsequent treatment, and are openly seeking peers that will understand their unique experience. Their overt desire to be supported adds vitality to the group and stimulates creativity and pleasure in a situation that one would hesitate to project as gratifying. By careful planning the therapist can succeed in reaching therapeutic goals within the framework of a support group.

# ☐ Introduction

Of the many misfortunes that can happen to a child, the trauma of burns has a particularly lasting and debilitating effect on their bodies and emotions. Unlike most other serious physical illnesses, burns often leave a visible reminder of the traumatic event. Even hair loss and other somatic signs of cancer treatment usually dissipate in due time upon recovery; scarring from burns can only be improved up to a point. The obvious signs of this misfortune are sometimes less scarring than the loss of self-esteem, confidence in the future, rapport with peers, and withdrawal from family. Parents and caretakers are also scarred by the tragedy. The pervasive guilt syndrome, rational or not, weighs on parents and cannot be alleviated easily. In response to these concerns, child life specialist, Linda Garcia, created an in-depth program tailored to the needs of toddlers, latency-age children, and adolescents for the Grossman Burn Center in Sherman Oaks, California.

# ☐ Philosophical Approach

The philosophy of the Grossman Burn Center program rests on addressing the multiple needs of these children and their parents who have undergone the burn trauma. The goal is to bring support and psychosocial education to the child and the family in a manner that is tailored to their requirements. For example, when groups are formed careful attention is paid to the developmental capacities of the group members. Medical trauma often can cause a child to regress to an earlier level of achievement; therefore, the actual chronological age of the child is not always consistent with their performance. This is reflected in the parent-child relationship where, often, the parent is forced (or chooses) to become more protective and involved with the child than is normal. Enforced separations during the early stages of painful hospital treatment leave their toll, and emotional distress on both sides often leaves both parent and child struggling to communicate.

The resiliency of the child is also a major factor to be evaluated, with proper attention paid to reinforce strengths and coping skills. Scarring and possible disfigurement from burns leaves a child open to remarks from their peers that are based on curiosity and are sometimes cruel. The parent cannot protect the child from these social traumas, which in some instances seem to have the same degree of hurt as the physical burn damage. The only real recovery for the burned child is to be accepted by peers and thus, regain a feeling of self-worth. The support group program that uses art enhances mastery in the young victims and provides a pleasurable experience that accomplishes therapeutic goals. (Groups for survivors of burns are not called therapy groups, however, they are therapeutic.)

In response to the special needs of the burned toddler, school-aged child, and adolescent, a program was tailored to strengthen resiliency, restore social confidence, and address psychological damage through action-oriented, experiential groups. The groups were structured around developmentally appropriate creative tasks and lead by skilled therapists who approach the healing process by building on the adaptable capacities of the clients. This chapter will highlight the latency-age expressive arts group.

## ☐  Developmental Concerns

The issue of developmental stages and the performance of the groups in the context of the environment where the groups are offered will be more thoroughly explored later in this chapter; the material discussed below is an overview. The curative approaches in the groups differ widely with the age of the burn victim, and specific creative tasks are tailored to carry out the restorative goals.

**The burn-injured toddler** is fearful, clings to his mother, and is unwilling to experiment or venture forth in an age-appropriate manner. The child may be emotionally unstable and display psychosomatic distress, such as food rejection or head banging. Youngsters show their insecurities by physically acting out their distress.

When toddlers or pre-schoolers have to make frequent doctor visits or hospital stays, their newly developed sense of autonomy is severely threatened. They may regress and require the type of attention and reassurances they needed when they were younger. For example, the child may stop using the toilet, return to the bottle, and want to be held and rocked excessively. The child may stop talking and use other methods to re-establish control, such as, temper tantrums and refusing medication. The child-like imagination operates significantly unlike an adult's comprehension. The child may assume the blame for the injury, and often misunderstand the adult's explanations. As a result of this conflict, they may be seriously inhibited in expressing their confusion and anger.

How to deal with these psychological fears, as well as the real fears that accompany the trauma of being burned, plus the factor of being with other strange children in a group, are some of the challenges that toddler group leaders face.

**Latency-age children** (school age) who have been burned are able to endure the hospitalization with more understanding, particularly if the primary caretakers are consistent and attentive during the period of separation and medical interventions. However, no matter how supportive the caretakers are, the treatment is not less painful. The memory of the medical procedures and the feeling of helplessness become a part of these children's life experience.

After hospitalization another trauma must be faced: Many school-aged children are at an age where teasing and rejection are the tools of their insecurities, and they often project their own self-doubts on a peer who is vulnerable. Scarring has obviously "marked" them for attention. They have to have strong coping skills to handle these as-saults. They may be angry and confused why they were singled out to bear this burden. Often, they irrationally blame the parent, or imagine the burn to be a punishment for something that they have done wrong. If the burns were the result of abuse, the anger is justified, but even more difficult to reconcile with reality. Children that are abused often make the false assumption that they deserved to be cruelly punished. Many times these feelings of unworthiness are not verbally communicated, only acted upon. These psychological scars impede the forma-tion of self-assurance and interfere with trust. Social learning has to be reworked when trauma occurs with young children.

Some of the goals in this age group include encouraging connec-tions, and all activities are tailored to enhance the group's interactions. For example, learning how to retort to peers without inciting combat or ridicule can best be learned from other boys and girls who have experienced these same social rebuffs. Discussing how they can re-establish appropriate individuation from their parents is another issue. Finding a simpatico group of same-age children who have experi-enced a similar trauma allows them the freedom to speak about their pain and find, with relief, that they are not alone with this misfor-tune. Burned children who have been accidentally burned have dif-ferent issues than those who have been victimized by abusive burning and these differences need to be carefully monitored by the group leaders.

**Adolescents** dealing with trauma and scarring from burns have ad-ditional challenges with which to cope. The main task in the process of adolescence development is for the youth to achieve a sense of iden-tity and competence, and the ability to form long-term stable relation-ships with members of the opposite sex. This process is accompanied by heightened self-consciousness, mood swings based on critical self-evaluation, and intensified narcissism. In view of their deep involvement in their self-image, the slightest deviation from what they perceive as the ideal adolescent appearance causes major distress. If a mild acne condition can depress an adolescent, imagine how devastated they feel with burn scars. Added to their own anxiety regarding their self-image, is the concern that they will not be attractive to the opposite sex. This concern may lead to depression and withdrawal from normal activities.

Because teens do not necessarily trust adult advice, they turn to their peer group for support, but this peer group will not be entirely supportive unless they have a special understanding of this unusual situation and have some guidance and education. Such complex issues are best addressed in a group setting with other teenagers that have shared the commonality of the burn trauma experience.

The activities offered to the adolescent are designed to promote group cohesion and are created to appeal to the teen's worldview. The youths take an active part in shaping the group to their unique needs. A successful group experience at this stage can make a life-long change in a teen's ability to progress through adolescence to adulthood.

## ☐ Parents and Caregivers

For every age group discussed above the overriding need for the child burn patient is support, empathy, and acceptance. Much of this support ideally comes from parents and caregivers, but the psychological healing depends a great deal on the acceptance by, and integration with, peers. For this reason, it is essential that these young burn survivors are offered a support group composed of other youths of their own age—peers who can appreciate the pain, rejection, and struggle to regain a proper place on the developmental track; a group that can talk freely about experiences that only a fellow sufferer can truly understand.

This situation and need is paralleled with the parents of the burn victim. Who else can understand the specific and painful aftermath of living with a child who bears the scars, both internally and externally, of a trauma that often has come about through an accident or by abuse? These parents need to have an appropriate forum with other adults who are attempting to deal with the issues that are of ongoing concern. The parent's pain needs to be addressed for multiple reasons: The obvious is to offer some relief from their difficulties, the other is to educate them on ways to protect and, at the same time, allow their child to re-enter the challenging arena of growing up.

# ☐  Objectives and Team Composition

It is because the traumas and unmet needs of this group became of deep concern to the Grossman team that the following program was instituted.

Six experts in the field of child development and therapy, lead by an experienced authority in childcare of burn patients, were assembled to work as a team. The experts chosen to create and execute the program were from a variety of mental health fields. This was done deliberately, since child-life specialists, art therapists, social workers, and drama and music therapists add to the richness of the program. The facilitators also gained by cross-educating each other.

Three support groups were projected for young burn patients who had left the hospital and were in aftercare or had recovered from their injuries. A toddler group, a latency-age group, and an adolescent group would meet for eight weekly sessions, each with eight of their fellow burn victims and two co-leaders. Simultaneously, the parents of the group members would meet at the same time with another team leader. Both groups focused on problem-solving, education, and issues of loss and reintegration with society.

The team members were specialized therapists, trained to conduct age-appropriate groups for trauma victims. They were schooled in the dynamics of group process, and understood the principles of action-oriented therapeutic tasks, medical play, and play therapy, as well as the symptoms of post-traumatic stress syndrome. They were educated to transform activities into opportunities for each age group so that burn stories could be told and that the clients could share how they dealt with the trauma. They facilitated situations that open the door for sharing other related difficulties that are perceived as a part of the task of reintegration into the main stream.

The toddlers focused mainly on play; the latency-aged group was best served with a variety of action-oriented tasks that kept their interest and appealed to their need to be challenged; adolescents responded to more sophisticated tasks that reflected their creative interests, self-image, and interactions with peers (both of the same and opposite sex). The leader's talent that can be least qualified, but is of the greatest importance, is creativity, flexibility, and the ability to be ready to modify plans to meet the group's immediate needs as they arise. Although there may be a master plan for the program, it is a given that each group will have idiosyncratic differences, and these differences must be respected and responded to by the leaders.

The parent group followed a parallel pattern of focusing on the child in the framework of their child's age, the recent or distant occurrence of the burn, the surrounding circumstances, and their own psychological problems connected to the burn trauma, (i.e., guilt). Activities were offered the parent group, if appropriate, and on occasion they were invited into the children's groups, either briefly or for the whole session if there was a need for special problem solving.

## Framework of the Support Groups

Establishing group confidentiality has proven to be very important for many youths. Confidentiality provides the members an opportunity to unburden thoughts that they might hold back for fear of, for example, distressing their parents. Anger toward parents, even if irrational, is better shared and resolved. One major situation that evokes tension is the adolescent drive to separate and individuate, which becomes much more complicated when parents are overprotective due to their own reaction to the burn trauma. This may be a dominant issue for the adolescent. The latency-age group also treasures some autonomy from parental supervision, and thus enjoys having their "private" group. The exception is in the toddler group, where separation from the parent may be premature until trust with the group leader has been established.

The group becomes a forum for many therapeutic gains in addition to dealing with the issues directly connected to the burn injuries. The group provides an opportunity for observation and assessment of group members behaviors that may call for more intense therapeutic interventions in the future. For this reason, group leaders must be aware of referral resources in the community that could be needed after the eight weeks of group have concluded. To aid termination, a final meeting with the individual families can help bring closure to the group experience. Readmittance for children with special difficulties to a second set of eight weeks of the support group could be recommended. The opportunity for trained personnel to observe a child with their peers provides a very different insight into their needs than individual attention from doctors, nurses, and therapist who see the child one on one.

## ☐ Gains and Goals

The pre-schooler, school-aged child, and adolescent youth, should come away from the group experience with improved tools to cope with their peer society, damaged self-image, and anxieties. It is unrealistic to imagine that these issues will be totally solved in such a short time, however, by introducing permission to face their difficulties, act them out in play or in art, the child will still benefit. This positive experience may encourage the families to seek future professional help if needed. Establishing friendships with peers who have been exposed to the same trauma and promoting enhanced communication between child and parents is often the most important gain from the group experience.

The following descriptions of the group process, the expressive tasks, and material necessary to achieve a satisfactory and therapeutic experience are suggestions, *not* a hard and fast protocol. These are the experiences of the groups and their leaders. Each group, as well as each session should be seen in the context of the personalities, needs, and severity of the burn trauma that the youths suffered. There cannot be an exact formula for success; there can be knowledge, skill, and purpose that offer the best possible chances for children to be well served and to gain some mastery over a life-changing event in their lives.

## Caveat

Art and expressive modalities must be handled with the greatest care and be thoughtfully managed by experienced group leaders. Nonverbal expressions can reactivate emotions and feelings (even pain) associated with the immediate experience of being injured. Without caution, the art task and activities described below possibly can retraumatize the child. Therefore, there was a profound need for the therapist to have a complete understanding of the potential, both for healing and for harm, that is embedded in all these seemingly pleasurable tasks. To guard against the possibility of harm, the team members carefully structured the clinical rationale, the psychological and developmental procedures, and the emotive potential of the media and the narrative process that was attended to in each session. The protection and support for the group members was always the first consideration.

## ☐ Formation of a Support Group for Elementary-School-Age Children Recovering from Burn Injuries: Both Physical and Psychological

Latency-age children are more accustomed to operating in a group since much of their activities are group oriented, for example, sports teams, school and after-school interest groups, and some temple or church activities. Some children are better integrated into their peer-group setting than others, and some are still experimenting with their comfort zone. Latency-age children are in a period of development that loosely covers the ages from seven to twelve. It is clear that children in the first three years of this period have very different needs and developmental tasks than those from 10 to 12. Maturation is always a judgment call, some children mature at a faster rate than others, but in forming a group, it is necessary to start with some structure and modify from there.

## Group Selection

It is useful to divide the latency-age boys and girls into two age-defined groups as suggested above. The interests and psychological capacities for group interchanges and attention spans are more easily addressed if age and social skills are considered. In the traditional view of this developmental period, the child is engaged in achieving mastery over physical and intellectual tasks. The children are usually more comfortable with same sex peers, but are able to interface with the opposite sex if the subject matter is relevant to both girls and boys. This age group are activity minded, competitive, and are engaged in exploring the gender assigned roles that society imposes on them.

Toman (1993) provides a brief overview of the latency period:

> Under favorable circumstances enormously expands his/her knowledge of the world outside the family. The linguistic, intellectual, and motor development, at ages 11–12, reaches the level of young adults, even if the exercise of their abilities and the construction of an adult reality—in which objectivity, truth, honesty, or at least loyalty and causal explanation matters—are only beginning. In contrast, emotional development flattens during the latency period. It is not so much feelings as factual connections between people and things that concern and absorb him/her (p. 43).

Being aware of these characteristics were a guide for constructing the group activities and goals.

With these general developmental goals in mind, the formation of a group to attend to specific, externally-imposed trauma (such as the tragic experience of burns, repeated hospitalizations, and subsequent scarring [major or minor] requires a sensitive plan. Because the average burn victim was not a mental health client before the burn incident they should not be pathologized after they are traumatized. We relied on their basic health and looked for every opportunity to encourage their natural resiliency.

## Assessment Interview

The assessment meeting should focus on the child's adaptability and strengths *before* the burn event. How resilient was the child to other difficulties? Was the child of an outgoing nature, more or less aggressive, curious, or competitive? Questions like these establish the basic personality traits of the potential group member and give the therapist a basis for evaluation. Even at this young age, the burn victim can be suffering from post-traumatic stress syndrome, a reaction that often screens the previous "normal" functioning of the person. Unless the past abilities are known, the therapist may make faulty assumptions. For example, if the child was shy before the accident, it would be unfortunate to see withdrawn reactions after the trauma as foreign to a usual mode of coping.

It is helpful to use an art assessment such as Silver (1978) describes or ask the child to draw a picture that has something to do with memories of the burn incident. The exception to this directive would be to ask a deliberately-burned child to remember the trauma, a child may be too psychologically fragile to remember circumstances of the burn. Others suggestions such as, "draw something about yourself that you would like to share," is also a way of learning about the group member. A drawing in the first interview can establish the notion that the group will be creative and use the language of art.

Another important factor to consider is the chronological age of the group member and their grade in school. A seven-year-old has probably just embarked on the journey to individuation, whereas the twelve-year-old is on the verge of adolescence and is testing his/her independence more vigorously. The reason that the stage of the separation process must be attended is that after a life-threatening event this course may be severely interrupted. Parents and child cling together appropriately at the time of the trauma; comfort and support mean everything. However, in some cases, after recovery either the child or parent (more often) is reluctant to reassume the process of separation. This is an issue to be aware of when the child enters the group. The other extreme is the neglected or abused child whose burns are not accidental. These lonely youths who often have been removed from their home, have had to struggle with their fears and pain without a familiar adult's involvement. They will need more encouragement and more protection.

There are structural considerations, as well, that are general to this age group; for example, should all-boy group include only one girl, and visa versa? Should the cultural and ethnic mix be weighed? Should a child be accepted without a parent representative in the parents' group? We have found that these issues are rarely a problem with a group that is formed for a specific reason and to which the clients' have chosen to attend. All of the group members share a life-changing experience, and they find comfort from the commonality of their problem. It is a great relief for these youths to find a neutral arena where they can talk about their hospital experience, their distress of being scarred, and their difficulties when challenged by their peers to explain their burn experience. The children often remark that no one understands unless they too have been burned (Russel, 1995).

The group is structured to meet for six or eight meetings. Each group lasts for one hour. The co-therapists meet thirty minutes before the session to set up the materials and discuss their latest ideas about the art project at hand.

Each group meeting is organized around an age-appropriate activity that is syntonic with the specific direction that the group seems to need. This goal should be flexible and respond to the clinical or developmental needs of the group. The group should be limited to between six and eight members. This number of members can be attended with two co-leaders whereas four members presents a difficulty if there are several children absent. Children this age often have outside obligations that may interfere with their attendance. It is important that a poorly-attended group be handled in a manner that supports those present, and frames the small group as an "opportunity," for them. Latency-age children, as well as adolescents, have a tendency to see poor attendance as a sign that group may connote social stigma or be failing.

## ☐ Planning the Latency-Age Group

Therapists of a latency-age group require specific skills. They should be familiar with both the developmental tasks and abilities of this age group; be comfortable with the members' differences in attention span, maturity, and outlooks on society; and be well-versed with the process of the "normal" stages of recovery from severe physical trauma.

Activities should be planned based on:

1. The principles of group therapy (i.e., how one moves from individual concerns to a shared group cohesion),

2. The synthesis of the art or expressive task with the goals of the session, and
3. The opportunity to master an individual member's burn trauma with the help of the other group members.

Therapists need to move the group dynamics in a manner that both directs and releases the group process to the group members themselves.

It is of the utmost importance that the activities planned take advantage of the expressive qualities of the media offered. For example, the group should have available a colorful media that handles easily. a media that insures a successful product, a project that does not invite associations of a personal nature too early in the group life, an opportunity that invites creativity and is open to the youths story-making. The creative task should be easy to perform, not take a great deal of time to accomplish, and structured so that a minimum of skill is required. These restrictions are important because built into media are tactile stimuli that evoke nonverbal references that are emotionally based in neural pathways. The therapist utilizing a variety of media should educate themselves as to the evocative powers of paint, pastels, pencils, clay, etc. (Malchiodi, 1998).

## The First Meeting

The first meeting is designed to attract the child on multiple levels: It should provide an easy-going environment and pleasurable tasks that result in a product that is attractive. A well-designed art activity eliminates competition or comparison, and distracts children from the fear of having to perform for a group of strangers. It allows them to engage in a nonthreatening activity that invites normal introductions and story telling while simultaneously letting the art task dilute social pressures. Confidentiality must be emphasized, and safety and permission to speak freely is discussed.

Little eye contact is required as everyone is working on an art piece; that provides a comfort zone for the children that are strangers to each other. To further group process, the therapist can find similarities in the art products that will help to set the stage for future connections. For example, the group may feel more like they have something in common if the therapist observes, "Well, this certainly looks like a 'red-and-green' group since you all have used some of those colors. Let's all put the artwork in the center of the table and look at our group together." The metamessage is that there are commonalties and this is *our* group. Therapists who are aware of how to utilize the power of metaphorical language can accelerate group process with young children. These guidelines are valid for every session.

Expressive, creative opportunities tailored to the therapeutic needs of the group members will keep the children interested, anxious to return, and instill helpful interactions and information in a manner that children can best absorb. The focus of the group should be to confront the multiple difficulties that accompany the trauma of burns, but without attention to group process that goal would be difficult to achieve. A reward of a treat, such as a fruit or candy can be very appreciated by this age group. While permission from the parents is needed, if it is permitted the treat can act as a closing ritual that helps the transition from group to the real world.

## Descriptions of Children from Our Groups

A short description of some of the children that made up our groups follows. The circumstances and names have been altered to cover confidentiality, but the burn situations are real.

One of our members was a girl who was wearing a flowing, gauzy costume when she reached across a table where the candles were burning. Her dress caught on fire and the burn was mainly on her upper arm and chest. When we met she was four years past the incident. She had been treated at the Grossman Burn Center immediately after the burn, and had several reparative operations subsequently. Her scarring was minimal, but she still had residual distress over the trauma and made very sure that she avoided any situation where candles were burning. Her supportive family and natural high resiliency worked in her favor.

A boy had been on a field trip with his class and in an electric plant which serviced the city's electrical needs he put his finger into an electric box that electrocuted him. He was thrown across the room and was rushed to an emergency medical center where he was treated for serious physical complications following this severe trauma. His burned hand was treated at the Grossman Burn Center. He reported that he had made a decision to change his life after this near death experience. He decided to give up his anti-social behaviors.

A girl was severely burned on her upper legs and possibly in her genital region when she reached up on the table and spilled her mother's cup of hot coffee on herself. She felt her burns were no longer visible after a series of skin grafts. However, she was extremely avoidant of situations where coffee is being served.

Two boys had barbeque related burn incidents. One had tripped and fallen into the spilled hot coals, the other doused the fire with what he thought was water but was gasoline. They both had burns and scarring on their arms and chest. One boy faced further skin graft treatment and seemed hyper active, but we did not know if this behavior was the result of the burn injury.

A young girl had the most severe problem with scarring. She was caught in a house fire and her upper body and face were badly burned. Her scars were severe but not to the extent that her features were deformed; however, her family worried that she should never marry because of the scarring.

A girl had been fire bombed in her bedroom by some unknown person. The bomb was thrown from the street. She had burns on her neck, torso, leg, and particularly one hand where she attempted to put out the fire on her hair. There was a possibility of further medical treatment. She was also more psychologically distressed because the attack seemed without reason.

A girl had been burned in a cooking accident. She had assumed some responsibility in the kitchen to help her mother with the younger children. Her burns were not visible to other persons and she was too shy to reveal the site or the severity of the burn. Her shyness was exacerbated by the burn.

A girl was burned on her upper leg and torso by knocking a pan off the stove, which contained hot food. Her scarring had been well repaired but her hyperactivity had escalated and was now the primary problem.

These are just a few examples of the bright, intelligent, and emotionally healthy children in our group. Their emotional problems were appropriate for the trauma they had experienced. Their present need was for support and comfort in relationships with peers. They had all been within the "normal" range of emotional and physical maturation before the burn accident; they demonstrated their resiliency in their recovery patterns.

## Examples of Group Activities for the Opening Session

The first group session and all subsequent sessions should share the same opening rituals (unless a special project has been set up in advance). An example session follows.

The children come into the room, greet each other, sit around a table, and talk about whatever is on their minds.

After casual conversation, the leaders present the activity for the group, answer questions, and lower anxieties about the skill needed. The group is then offered the media that the leaders have prepared ahead of time. Throughout the group activity, the leaders can feed information about the purpose of the group and ask the members how they would like to proceed. The children will be treated at all times as co-constructors of the group and listened to when they have opinions and suggestions. Because the group is structured for a one-hour session, the therapist is forced to offer the most comprehensive experience possible within the time limit. Therefore, the art and verbal communication must be carefully created to synchronize process and content.

The need of the group is always paramount, and pacing and timing are unique to each group. The therapists will know their group best, and they should allow their creativity to respond to the unique composition of the group they are conducting.

The following example of an art directive follows a format for a brief, time-limited group. Because of the time limit, group process must be encouraged with the primary goal being group cohesion.

Two art activities for the early-joining period of group:

- *The paint blob butterfly.* (A therapist who is not familiar with this simple task should experiment before presenting it.) Dribble viscous paint on one half of folded paper that has been creased and then laid flat. Use a modest amount of paint for success. Fold the paper over and press across the paper to spread the paint inside the fold. Open. The colorful paints will have printed on both sides of the paper a shape that often resembles a butterfly. Ask the members what they see in the abstract shape, and have them tell a brief, imaginary story. This activity is fail safe if the paint is controlled and a variety of colors are offered. These prints should be hung on the wall and taken home after they dry. More then one can be made. If there is an over-stimulated child in the group, make it clear that only a certain number of paint blobs will be allowed.
- *The abstract scribble.* An alternate art task is to have each child close their eyes and make a scribble with a felt pen on a paper. When they look at the scribble they can find animals, people, faces, plants, and flowers by filling in the portions that have the "hidden" image (somewhat like finding images in the clouds). This can be amplified with a second scribble by asking the group to work in pairs and be detectives together.

## Discussion

The first session's tasks should be easy to do, colorful, and viewed without psychological interpretation. The children's individual art statements do not force relationships; putting the drawings together at the completion of group indicates a future for group cohesion. Doing art together, particularly when it does not call for a great deal of concentration, frees this age group to talk freely. They seem to be less shy and more willing to get directly to the center of the issues. The stories about the burn incidents come up naturally and are presented differently by each member. Some tell a long story; some just a vignette. Some therapists will be surprised at how spontaneously the trauma is described. Perhaps the ease of discussion comes about because they know that everyone is there for the same reason, or perhaps being burned has become a major part of their identity and, therefore, important to establish early on.

## Second Session: Encouraging the Burn-Story

This session should openly introduce the theme of the group (burn trauma). The leaders set the stage by discussing how all group members have an experience in common, but with each person the common becomes uncommon since no trauma affects any person exactly the same. However, each member is special because few people understand their experience the way they understand each other.

Many times a child is shy about showing their burns, or the injury may be on a part of the body that is private, the following exercise simultaneously allows revelation and protection.

### Body Drawing Indicating Sites of the Burns

On an 18 × 14-inch sheet of drawing paper the group leader prepares for each member of the group, a body outline drawing that resembles a gingerbread man (Figure 3.1). The members are invited to choose a "burn" color and indicate on the drawings where they were burned and the extent of the burn. They are then advised to choose different colors to represent the emotions they felt when they were injured (i.e., scared, worried, lonely in hospital, etc.), and place them inside the body. For example, purple in the head may indicate a headache connected to medication, blue in the stomach represents nausea.

The children then take turns explaining their drawings, telling the story of their burn experience and talking about their feelings at the

**FIGURE 3.1.** Three examples of locating the site of the burns and the location of the feelings that accompanied the trauma.

time of the burns and thereafter. No child should be forced to talk about anything they choose not to discuss. By simply holding up their drawing, each member has shared.

The leaders were surprised at the openness the children have displayed about their injuries and fears. However, these revelations, although they were remarkably frank, did not reach the depth of the distress until later in the group's life.

The theme of the group has been established, and the group now has a commonality of experience, furthering group cohesion and protecting against inappropriate intrusiveness.

## Discussion

The drawings of the burn site and neutralizing anxiety about boy–girl interactions around where they were burned is important. If this is not done through a nonsexual drawing (i.e., the gingerbread man shape), there can be embarrassment and distress in the group. A child may have been burned in the genital area as hot liquid falls on their lap and upper legs, and while the second session is too soon to discuss how the region of the burn affects their image of a future sexual relationship, it subtly introduces the notion to be addressed later. For example, at this age, the group members may be greatly concerned about wearing a bathing suit. Most upper- or lower-torso burns are covered with ordinary clothes, swimsuits reveal too much. Using a theme of summer may also introduce the question of re-entering the hospital for further skin grafts or other procedures. Choosing pain and long recuperation is a difficult decision at any age.

## Third Session: Enhancing Group Cohesion

The group should be encouraged to continue the discussion of the burn experience. The dialogue is directed toward the social stigma the children may have had to deal with in peer encounters. Teasing, rude remarks, exclusion, insecure feelings, prolonged separation due to hospitalization which left them out of school activities, and physical restriction in sports activities as a result of scarring, are all subjects to be explored.

### Pass-Around Support Drawing

**Part one:** On 18 × 24-inch paper the children are encouraged to put down areas of color with oil pastels (Craypods) that represent the mean things that have been said to them, or the insecure feelings they may have had when re-entering school.

**Part two:** After making this abstract image they pass it to their right and, in turn, the next person adds some marks in their special color that indicates support (each child has also selected their own support color, which allows them to be identified when the drawing returns to the originator). The passing around continues until the creator receives back the drawing with everyone's addition identifiable because of the individual colors.

**Part three:** Every child has an enhanced drawing, and they spend a few moments looking at the altered page. Discussion is encouraged about how it feels to see the original shape modified by others. Did they feel supported by the additional marks on their paper? The therapists must allow for the group members to have ambivalent feelings as well as positive ones. There are times a child may not have wanted the image changed. Dialogue about intrusion and control can easily follow this activity.

**Part four:** Some members are then asked to dramatize a "mean" situation. Other members are asked to share how they have handled similar situations or imagine better ways of problem solving.

This drama stimulates physical activity in the room and sufficient space should be anticipated. The leaders must be alert to the sensitivity of each child. The severely scarred may find this too difficult to do, and the role-playing section of this session may not be appropriate for them. Help from peers seems to reduce the hurt and reinforce the cohesion among the members. Feedback from peers is more impactful than a suggestion by an adult.

## "Hands": A Demonstration of Group Membership

**Part one:** Members are asked to trace around their hands with a felt pen; any color is acceptable.

**Part two:** After the hand is traced, they are encouraged to decorate the hand as they wish. (Anything they wish to share with the group, or just make it "pretty.")

**Part three:** Have the children add their name in a special place.

**Part four:** Upon completion, encourage the members to talk about what this activity reminded them of, or what they thought about while they were drawing. Many group members had scarring on their hands and this exercise provided an opportunity to talk about their injury.

**Part five:** The "hands" are then cut out, rolled tape is placed on the back, and each "hand" is attached to a larger piece of paper that has been secured on the wall.

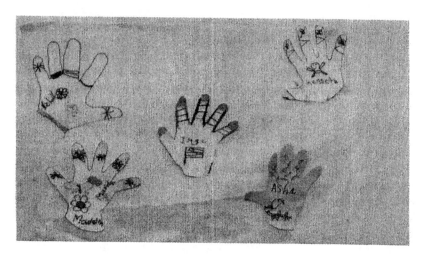

**FIGURE 3.2.** "Hands."

**Part six:** The group then gathers around and talks about how this is *their* group. If anyone wishes to replace their hand, they discuss it with the group. Often, one move will stimulate another move. The grouping of the hands becomes dynamic and symbolic of the dynamics of the group itself (Figure 3.2).

## Discussion

These simple tasks are nonthreatening, impactful ways to bring the ideas of commonality of interests and group cohesion into view. The group now becomes a visible group with an identity. In addition, both of these expressive tasks include some physical activity. School-age children are not noted for their desire to sit for a prolonged period of time, therefore, the movement structured within the art task keeps these children interested. Therapists should be careful, however, when a group includes a child who is hyperactive. This child's problems are often exacerbated by the burn trauma, and therefore, therapists have to limit the physical as well as the art activity to provide appropriate containment and freedom.

## Fourth Session: The Group Tours the Hospital Burn Unit

This is the most powerful session, and the one the group will remember and request to repeat. However, this activity can be done only if the nursing staff and hospital policy allows it.

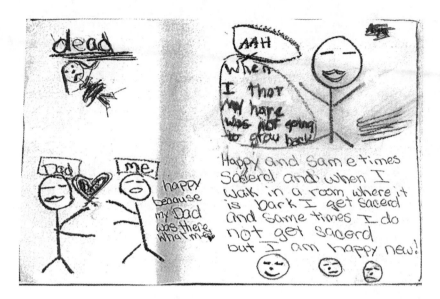

**FIGURE 3.3.** A feeling–memory drawing of a girl badly burned when she was caught in her burning bedroom. "Dead" (when hospitalized), "When I thot my hare (sic) was not going to grow back," "Happy because my Dad was there with me," "Happy and sometimes scared when I walk in a room where it is dark."

The group members and the therapists walk through the treatment center. They remember, and talk about when they were treated in the hyperbaric oxygen tank, the table where the water pressure helped remove the burned skin, the pain and discomfort they felt when they had skin grafts, and many other personal anecdotes that were unique to the individual child. The exchange of experiences, followed by visiting child burn victims who were recently admitted to the ward, is a profound bonding experience of their time together. Group leaders also gain a new insight into their strengths, resiliency, and bravery.

After the first visit, the members may spontaneously ask to make get-well cards, bring small toys to the unit, and discuss their concerns about the children they visited. When the children show their healed scars, that have been greatly improved, the look on the parent's face, as well as the child in the bed, can be heart wrenching.

When the group returned to their session room, the material that they will be anxious to share will be on a much more intimate level, and will likely include what parental or caretaker support they had at the time of hospitalization. The group was eager to visit the burn unit every week.

## *Discussion*

There is no substitute for a visit to the burn unit. In the Grossman program the group benefits because they met in the hospital where many of them were treated. In addition, the nursing staff is cooperative. The group met in the early evening, 6:00 to 7:00 p.m.; therefore, dinner and other medical procedures were completed, and the ward visit did not interrupt the medical routine.

This visit became so vital to the group members that we discussed making it the central focus of an on-going group. Particularly for group members who returned to group for a second time. As therapists who had not been burned, we learned a great deal and were able to respond on a different level to the group members. The subsequent groups all ended with a short visit to the unit before leaving the hospital.

## Fifth Session: Mastery Over the Trauma. A "Feeling and Wish" Box

The entire group shares the activity described here. A shoebox (or another box about that size) is presented to the group. This box is described as a container capable of holding feelings that have been hurtful, wishes for the future, and words they would like say and that they have repressed. The box can hold all the feelings that the group would like to express. The therapist makes it clear that all members of the group can contribute to the material placed inside the box.

The group decides whether the lid should be taped shut or left free to be opened. Usually, they prefer it taped. The outside of the box is covered with the "nice" things that kids are supposed to do and feel. (Collage is recommended, magazine pictures roughly cut from magazines, and then re-cut by the children.) The images are pasted all over the box, and discussion is encouraged as to why they chose a certain picture. The box is handed around as everyone finds a picture that they wish to use.

The leader then cuts a mail box slot on the top (because a sharp knife is necessary, it may be best not to entrust it to a group member).

The next part of this exercise is to have each child write messages on small pieces of paper that express their wishes, fears, anxieties, hurts, hopes, and such that they choose to discuss at this time. They are not asked to share, but sharing is accepted with empathy. The messages are placed in the box through the mail slot.

The idea is to provide a symbolic holding container, similar to the holding that a parent provides for a young child's fears. Providing various colored papers on which to write the messages is useful, so

(a)

(b)

**FIGURE 3.4.** (a) A feeling–memory drawing by a 10-year-old boy, showing the recognition of a new life after a death experience by electrocution. "Changed my head," "I felt like I was hurtid," (then) "I feal very happy" (now). (b) A 12-year-old girl reflecting on how she felt when first hospitalized for her burns and how she feels now: "I was afraid I was going to get a lot of surgery," "Scared," "Hurt." Four years later: "Now I want to be a doctor."

that the colors can be used to identify "bad" feelings, "hot" nasty insults, and so on.

The majority of the time, this age group will be willing to talk about the messages they have placed in the box. No one should be pressured to do so. The therapist can also speculate that some messages may be things that a boy or girl would not feel free to say in front of their parents. This remark introduces the dynamic that often children protect the adult, and to do that they repress their concerns. Countless opportunities arise from this ritual; it is limited only by the creativity of the leaders.

The group may find this exercise to be very helpful. This age group can be well aware of metaphors and second-level communication. Their cooperation with this symbol of containment is a good example of their sophistication.

## Discussion

The box is a variation on the self-box that is regularly used by art therapists to externalize feelings and problems and symbolically control how problems are contained. This opportunity is a reprisal of some of the issues that the group has discussed to date, and a chance to allow more feelings to emerge. It is important to repeat some of the issues that have surfaced, since post-traumatic reactions have been recognized in some members but not addressed. The more ingrained emotions of fear and anger must be processed carefully. The therapists must guard against triggering associations without being prepared to deal with what may be a serious reaction.

The sixth group is designed to build on this introduction to the trauma.

## Sixth Session: Past, Present, and Future

This session involves a three-part drawing designed to explore the past trauma, acknowledge how the children are feeling about themselves at the present time, and project a recovery in the future. A sense of future is important to establish since the installation of hope is a basic part of group dynamics. There is always a high possibility of depression, lingering fears, and other emotions connected to the burn incident. This is the time to bring up these concerns and have a dialogue around preventative resources and future support systems.

Directions should be very simple, "Draw how it felt when you were burned, how it is now, how it will be in the future, and how it has influenced your life." The drawings can be done quickly and cover a large field of memories and decisions. This is a demonstration of how directly material can be presented in a clear and condensed manner through the art project.

Figure 3.4 is all self-explanatory. The reader can understand how group therapeutic discussions can easily arise from the many issues displayed in these visual statements.

Again, therapists will be impressed with the ability of these young children to conceptualize a complicated notion. They talk about the incidents that trigger them, and evoke feelings of fear. For example, a girl who was burned when her gauzy costume was ignited by candles on a Halloween party table, never goes near any candles under any circumstance, described how the sight of flames brings back the trauma, even the pain.

## Discussion

The therapist needs to be mindful that, in working with art in a latency-age group, there is no need to invent tasks that are esoteric or difficult to arrange. When the art reflects the stage of development of both the members and the dynamic life of the group itself, it can be very simple. Each of the sessions described above were intended to build on the other. As the children developed trust in the other members and the adults, the art expressions will reflect this growth. The art can also contain elements that allow new material to rise to consciousness, become visible in the mind, and then visibly tangible on the paper or in three dimensions. All of this process may remain nonverbal. However, the goal is to give words to these images as well. The therapist working with art expressions should understand that if clients can see their problems, they have made them concrete and introduced the ability to handle them.

The past, present, and future project is a good example of a structured/nonstructured directive. The time concept is introduced, but the execution, the decision of how to render the concept of past to future, and the content of the art expression is all left to the individual. In this manner the group member has freedom as well as boundaries. As therapists become more confident of their ability to turn group process and group goals into art tasks that reflect the therapeutic needs of the group, they will be able to use their own pictorial abilities with comfort.

## Seventh Session: Post-Traumatic Stress Triggers

This session is constructed to engage the members in a supportive and interactive group art project. The purpose is to address and master the triggers associated with the burn incident that stirs up fearful feelings. The issue of post-traumatic stress, which was alluded to in previous group meetings is now brought forward.

## Putting the Bad Feelings and Memories in Jail

School-age children can best engage in therapeutic tasks if they are formulated in a manner that fits their mode of coping. This age group has not yet become abstract thinkers, but they are not wholly concrete thinkers either. An art expression that strikes a midpoint between these "ways of knowing" results from an age-appropriate task. The concept of restraining, holding, mastering, and control have all been used in preceding groups. Now, as the group begins to realize that there is only one more session, it is time to work as a group and conquer the "monsters." The monsters are the composite memories of the burn incident. In the following illustration one child was burned by a terrorist, one by a flammable fabric, one by a negligent adult who left gasoline near a barbecue, one by an abuser, one by her own action of reaching for her mother and pulling down the tablecloth. While all are different, they still result in memories, both intrinsic and extrinsic, that interfere with normal daily functions.

**Part one:** The group is directed to place images on the large mural paper that are connected to their burn experience. Everyone should draw simultaneously, exchange ideas, and discussing the process and ideas at will.

The example below from the Grossman project may seem chaotic, and for a short time, a great deal of chaotic activity did occur, but the entire production was charged with emotion and demonstrated how cohesive the group had become.

> The mural was done on the table, each person working simultaneously. The children explained what they were drawing, while they were drawing. They accepted help from one another, "crossing out bad memories," "killing off the bad guy," healing the wounds, and refusing to be hurt by mean words. Each child put their symbol of the accident (i.e., electric switch or burning candles), which still causes them to react with anxiety. Their individual "trigger" was anchored in the drawing.

**Part two:** When the drawings are completed the leaders suggest drawing the "jail," which represents all the work that the group has done together. The children will understand what this metaphor implies and they will demonstrate their understanding by their words. The group shifts attention from one to the other spontaneously, each trauma should be "thrown in jail" with appropriate anger and affect.

**FIGURE 3.5.** Entitled, "Jail of the True Feelings and Friends Group," a composite mural of the burn trauma memories and the present-day triggers (6 × 5). "Spilled coffee that scaulded." "Candles that caused a dress to burn." "The evil man that threw a fire bomb." "The electric socket that electrocuted." An example of externalizing the trauma memories and putting them behind bars (i.e., the group taking charge of their lives and feelings).

**Part three:** Tape the large mural on the wall and review the process and the meaning verbally. By creating distance from the art piece the creators are able to appreciate their work. They need to be given some space to disengage from such an involving experience, and time to evaluate the meaning of the jail in their own way. There will be great pride shown by all after this remarkable expressive piece is taped up on the wall (see Figure 3.5).

## Discussion

Basically, this is the end of the group. The next session, termination, should not be designed to bring up new material, but a time to review and evaluate the group experience. For this reason, the jail art piece is a culmination of the groups attempts to help each other have a better appreciation of their strengths, and to be able to interface with peers with more confidence, and be more capable of expressing thoughts to caretakers.

The choice of drawing tools rather than collage will help the members to make their own mark as a symbolic declaration of their own individuality. The composite artwork will be a dramatic statement of group solidarity and group cohesion.

## Eighth and Final Session: Termination

The group members were advised that their parents (who have been in the parents' group concurrent with the latency-age group) would be invited in the last quarter of the session. They would hear about the final project and share their reactions. The group is reminded that they are to respect the confidentiality of the other members and talk only about their own experience, not speak for others.

**A Termination Mural.** This mural reflects an idea held by the narrative therapist David Epston (1990). He asks his young clients to leave a message at termination for other kids with problems. He suggests that the group members will best know how to give advice and support to the youths who will need help in the future.

The members are presented with this idea, and the mural paper is pre-prepared on the wall. The members are invited to find collage pictures that will send their messages and also help future parents with understanding their children. This is the first group artwork that is designed to be shown to outsiders. Up to now the members have guarded their privacy and taken confidentiality seriously.

The mural (4 × 5 feet) gradually becomes covered with collage pictures and handwritten messages that advise the future group how to cope with trauma, social problems, and other issues that arise after being injured by burns. It also sends messages to the parents—often information that the parents or caretakers are surprised to learn about. The mural is created while the group is actively engaged and talking about what they have learned in the group sessions. They are encouraged to take over the creation of this mural, and through discussion and interaction, the group creates their own statement. They cooperatively decide on a title for the mural, and stand back to admire their

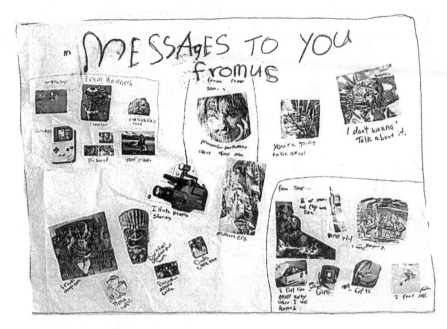

**FIGURE 3.6.** A burn group's collage and message to the next group of kids which was shared with their parents: "You're going to be okay." "I don't wanna talk about it." "I hate people staring." "Don't feel ugly or put down." "Time helps." "Mothers cry.

work. The therapist may wish to take a photograph of this piece and send it to each member. The visual product can be used as a transitional object in many therapeutic situations (see Figure 3.6).

**Sharing with the Parent Group.** After completion of the mural the parents are invited in. The group then shares with them as much of the process as they choose. Generally this age group is anxious to demonstrate how they have used the art, and the parents are encouraged to listen and ask questions. In some cases, the group members may ask their parents to add collage picture to the mural. This addition must always be a group decision.

It is with great satisfaction we observe how appreciative the adults were of the children's creativity, and how immediately they see the underlying therapeutic goals of the weekly tasks. For example, one father was emotional as he commented on the amazing insights that he observed in the termination collage. He felt he had underestimated how deeply his daughter had evaluated her experience and her strength to project into the future. Many parents express their appreciation of the value of the group, and everyone was sad to see it close.

The group leaders freely participate in this meeting. It is a privilege to share with parents and members some of the memorable moments for the therapist in these eight weeks. At the same time, therapists must be aware that they can only share some of the material that did not reveal substance that the members discussed in group. Therapist must be aware before hand what issues the group wishes to keep private. They should, however, feel free to express their admiration of these group members.

## ☐ Summary

The art activities and verbal interchanges that arose from each sessions tasks should be carefully planned to accomplish the following goals:

1. Create a positive, pleasurable, and therapeutic environment for children who have experienced the trauma of being burned.
2. Encourage activities and communication based on achieving group cohesion through group process. Paying attention to the media and art directive that best facilitates this goal.
3. Provide tools to encourage mastery over burn trauma and possible post-traumatic stress symptoms.
4. Learn coping skills from peers.
5. Leave a therapeutic experience with the understanding of the benefit of working with adults and peers to conquer difficult problems.
6. Experience a shift in the members self-concept from negative to positive.

### The Parents' Group: A Brief Overview

The parent's group should meet at the same time as the children's group, in a separate room with their own therapist. The therapist should be part of the team and consulted before and after each group session to alert each leader to possible issues that required attention. There may be a few sessions in the eight weeks where one or two of the parents cannot attend; this will make the group less dynamic. The parents will be grateful for an opportunity to share their distress about their child's burn experience because they feel as their son or daughter does, that no one understands unless they have been there.

The theme of guilt, responsibility, and concern for the future of the child is dominant in every group. However, each parent brings many other issues to the group and shares a great deal of personal material. The parents helped each other with emotional support and with psychoeducational information as well. Often they need referral sources and help with planning additional medical treatment (for example) for scarring and skin graft procedures.

The dominant gain is their appreciation of how focused their children are on their own group, and how much they gain in a short time. They should also be open to consultation if any of the therapists think that some issue with their child required more attention.

In the Grossman program, the parents' group did not use art expressions. In retrospect, the team decided that should have been looked at more carefully, and in the future intend to make a change.

## ☐ Some Random Reflections

There were several art projects that were tried, that were not included in the preceding descriptions. Ideas and projects may be interesting, but if offered at the wrong time present a questionable result. Timing and pacing are vital. Here are two examples.

### Decorated Baseball Hats

Inexpensive white baseball caps were bought and placed, with small tubes of fabric paint, on the table. The paint can be squeezed out to make designs, write names, and other art decorations.

The group members enthusiastically squeezed paint around the cap and onto the brim. They were asked to decorate only the top of the cap. As a project, it was a hit with the group and they wanted to wear them as a "member of the team." All of the above went well; however, the project was offered at the last meeting. The hats were piled with wet paint and a real challenge to take home. The theme of a "group" cap was also lost, since each child went their separate way after this last meeting.

This is an example of poor timing, and an over-ambitious art task. This project should be done again with these changes:

1. Make the caps early on in the process.
2. Limit the paint, so they will dry by the next week.
3. Encourage a little preplanning to ensure that there is more purpose to this task than pure squeezing. (However, if the joy of just mixing colors seemed to be productive, that would be allowed.)

The caps were only a tool toward establishing group cohesion, so how this project is handled should be tailored for the specific group members.

## Eggs and Wishes

Around the Easter and Passover holidays there are many symbols displayed commercially, which can be picked up on. In one group the holidays came about midway through one of the groups, so good-size plastic eggs, about three times the size of a chicken egg were brought in to use as a universal symbol for an art expression. There were no religious connotations to the task.

Each member was asked to write their very private wishes for the future on some small pieces of colored paper, which were provided. The eggs were screwed open, and as many messages that could fit were placed inside, then the egg was closed. Colored tissue paper and white glue, slightly diluted, was distributed and brushes were made available. The egg was brushed with glue and torn pieces of tissue paper applied. The opening was sealed by the layers of tissue, which become semitransparent and had the effect of stained glass. The final product was quite beautiful because the tissue paper bled color, and the layers combined to create other colors.

The group conversation focused on the decision to seal the wishes inside, the symbolism of the egg hatching in the future, and question if the wishes would be fulfilled. The group members took the eggs home with them, and they chose not to share the contents with the family. This exercise held promise, but it did not fit in with the direction of the group process. Perhaps in other circumstances it may be useful. Trial and error are always a condition of art expressions and group process. Sometimes the art does not fit, and sometimes the process takes an unexpected turn. It is best to expect variations and be armed with alternative opportunities.

## ☐ References

Malchiodi, C. A. (1998). *The art therapy source book.* Lincolnwood, IL: Lowell House.

Russel, J. (1995). Art therapy on a hospital burn unit: A step towards healing and recovery. *Art Therapy, 12,* 39–45.

Silver, R. (1978). *Developing cognitive and creative skills through art.* Baltimore: University Park Press.

Toman, W. (1993). *Family constellation: Its effect on personality and social behavior* (4th edition). New York: Springer.

White, M., & Epston, D. (1990). *Narrative means to a therapeutic ends.* New York: W. W. Norton.

# ☐ Suggested Readings

Bush, J. (1997). The development of school art therapy in Dade County public schools: Implications for future change. *Art Therapy, 14,* 9–14.

Drackmik, C. (1995). *Interpreting metaphors in children's drawings.* Burlingame, CA: Abbeygate Press.

Dunn-Snow, P. (1997). The gorilla did it! Integration of art therapy and language arts in the public schools. *Art Therapy, 14,* 50–53.

Essex, M., Frosting, K., & Hertz, J. (1996). In the service of children: Art and expressive therapies in public schools. *Art Therapy, 13,* 181–190.

Kiendl, C., Hooyenga, K., & Trenn, E. (1997). Empowered to scribble. *Art Therapy, 14,* 37–43.

Malchiodi, C. A. (1997). Art therapy in schools. *Art Therapy, 14,* 2–3.

Parashak, S. T. (1997). The richness that surrounds us: Collaboration of classroom and community for art therapy and art education. *Art Therapy, 14,* 241–245.

Prager, A. (1995). Pediatric art therapy: Strategies and applications. *Art Therapy, 12,* 32–38.

Rode, D. C. (1995). Building bridges within the cultural of pediatric medicine: The interface of art therapy and child life programming. *Art Therapy, 12,* 104–110.

Rosal, M. L., McColloch-Vislisel, S., & Neece, S. (1997). Keeping students in school: An art therapy program to benefit ninth-grade students. *Art Therapy, 14,* 30–36.

Silver, R. (1997). Sex and age difference in attitude toward the opposite sex. *Art Therapy, 14,* 268–.

Smitheman-Brown, V., & Church, R. P. (1996). Mandala drawing: Facilitating creative growth in children with ADD or ADHD. *Art Therapy, 13,* 252–260.

CHAPTER

## 4

Jean Noble

# Art as an Instrument for Creating Social Reciprocity: Social Skills Group for Children with Autism

This chapter offers material which will defy a traditional belief, a belief that holds on to the notion that individuals named as autistic are not appropriate for group therapy. The concept suggests that group therapy for this population would be not only unprofitable for learning, but a fearful situation for the group members. The following discussion offers the reader an opportunity to evaluate how a creative plan circumvented these obstacles. The interpretation of the concept of "group" was reinterpreted to fit the autistic population, and the group process was shaped in a variety of unique ways.

The clients who prompted this chapter were primarily referred to me for social skills interventions as part of their overall treatment plan, which was funded by a state regional center, serving clients with developmental delay. Most of these children had been diagnosed with autism and were receiving other services through the center and the school district, including speech and language therapy, behavioral interventions, occupational therapy, and adaptive physical education. About half of the children were fully included, meaning that they were placed in a regular classroom with varying degrees of support to facilitate their functioning. The other half were in special education classes.

To demonstrate the challenges of treatment, consider the example of two seven-year-old boys diagnosed with an autistic spectrum disorder. Both boys were referred for possible inclusion in a "social skills group." They were described as "socially awkward," yet the dynamics of their awkwardness were rooted in different manifestations of autistic traits.

## ☐ Joey's Story

Joey, diagnosed alternately with high-functioning autism and Asperger's[1] syndrome, is an energetic, bright-eyed boy with a strong intelligence and good verbal skills manifested most immediately by his long-winded monologues on trains and Shakespeare. With me, and reportedly with other adults, Joey could display some good competencies with regard to specific social skills (e.g., good manners and cooperative interactions). Referred for social skills, Joey was eager for friends, but was rejected by his peers for social inappropriateness. Joey was painfully aware of this rejection, yet the harder he tried, the more annoying to his peers he became. To address his social difficulties with peers, I brought Joey into a small group of three other latency-age boys. Initially, my prognosis for him in the group was very good in light of his high motivation and his apparent strengths.

However, this child's social functioning within the group fluctuated wildly over the months. Joe demonstrated quick understandings of group dynamics ("Peter is talking too much! It would work better if we took turns!"). On some days he was highly cooperative with other group members, eager to participate, and demonstrated leadership abilities. In spite of these strengths, Joey increasingly showed a strong intolerance for any social failures or misbehaviors of his peers. He would respond, for example, to Chad's monologue on a video game character with anxious, attention-grabbing, and at times flagrantly antisocial behaviors that ranged from refusing to engage in any group activity to name calling, yelling, and running around the room. These behaviors by necessity led to periodic time outs from the group due to my concerns for everyone else's safety.

Pre-group individual coaching was supplemented to provide Joey with additional support, during which Joey's fears of failure with peers

---

[1]Aperger's syndrome and the clinical description of autism are addressed later on in this chapter.

began to manifest more directly when he became comfortable with a supportive adult. Joey showed strong ambivalence toward the group and the group members. For example, he would go into group with great determination toward success and evidence strong attachment to his peers, yet after a mild frustration, ask to be removed. To my distress, we did remove him from the group after several more months. This removal came about as a result of an agreement with Joey's parents that the group had become negatively reinforcing and counterproductive.

Joey, in addition to his social deficits, was struggling with the emotional fallout of his growing awareness of his differentness, the realities of his poor impulse control, and the accumulated impact of delayed intervention following years of problems with peers. The group, in which he so wanted to be successful, became a weekly reminder of his own inadequacies. He saw in his group buddies the social differences that he so feared in himself (compounded by his parent's fears and anxieties in this direction). His anxiety and feelings of shame prompted his impulsive acting out, which only reinforced his feelings of inadequacy.

Despite Joey's clear social deficits rooted in his autistic features—his perseveration, mild language difficulties, sensory sensitivities, difficulties with empathy, and lack of specific social skills—this child's primary social handicap is based, paradoxically, in his relative strengths. Joey's autism lies on the higher end of the autistic spectrum and had a different flavor than the other children in his group. As an illustration, while his groupmates responded with frustration when interrupted in their perseverative monologues, Joey, instead, due to his greater awareness of his differences, experienced hurt and rejection.

## Discussion

Emotional, extremely fragile, and very needy of adult attention and validation, a better referral for Joey would have been individual sessions in tandem with supportive parent education. Joey needed first to be joined by another adult in his world before he could tolerate taking the risk of further rejection by peers. This initial relationship would then be followed by an extremely careful match with a peer with whom he had common interests. In such a setting, and with the support of a trusted adult, Joey would be more available, less anxious, and therefore less impulsive, for concrete interventions to build competencies and self-awareness. Such an experience of social success would have led to a more socially discriminating, more aloof, but happier, Joey. How to evaluate the best possible set of interventions for a "Joey-type" child takes extraordinary sensitivity and the freedom to create a therapeutic plan that can respond exactly to his special needs.

# ☐ Danny's Story

Consider another little boy with moderate language delays, a strong stutter, a severe pattern of perseveration, and social rigidity; one who eagerly engages all strangers with a hello and an inappropriate hug. Danny loves animals, menageries from all continents and seas, and will draw them for anyone who asks, as well as for those who do not. He is as eager to share his pictures as he is to draw them. Danny lacks the component of anxiety and attentional difficulties Joey has, and he has benefited from closely-supervised settings that have buffered him from severe social rejection. He loves to take center stage and has troubles because he always wants to win and be first. Yet, his eagerness to please and "learn how to be a good friend can at times, and with enough reinforcement, override these needs and motivate him toward greater flexibility. Danny was able to enter a small group with two other boys after several individual sessions focused on building Danny's attachment and comfort level with the therapist. He also benefited from coaching on basic "friends rules." He has made slow but steady progress in the group, with the close involvement of his parents, and eagerly looks forward to his weekly group.

# ☐ A Unique Construction

In working with these children whose difficulties largely manifest as problems of relating successfully with others, I have had to reinterpret my concepts of group treatment as well as reconsider my use of "art " as a treatment tool. The needs of these clients stretch assumptions about group process and group size. I have learned to redefine group to respond to the needs of these young people. More importantly, this chapter introduces a notion of group being not only a treatment modality, but a treatment goal. These children punctuate for me a truth for all groups: that the needs of each group member must be considered of primary importance, that respect for the individual and mindfulness of their unique needs must be sustained in tandem with that of the group and its dynamics.

This chapter offers thoughts and insights on using visual nonverbal interventions aimed at developing social behaviors and social competencies with children and adolescents diagnosed with an autistic spectrum disorder. These interventions specifically target, and are primarily aimed to facilitate social process. Rather than the therapeutic attention being focused on the art product, the locus of the power of art is found in exploring how the utilization of creative objects can serve to support and stimulate the dynamics of social reciprocity. Further, the dialogue illustrates process-focused ways to utilize art to support the development of social behaviors. The therapeutic group processes described can also be generalized to other populations with similar needs.

In addition, the use of art in the group setting is explored as a means to allow the client to bring personal meaning and purpose to their interactions with others. Art can be a primary vehicle out of social isolation and towards meaningful connection for clients who struggle with social relatedness.

## ☐  Thoughts on Social Skills Groups

Social skills groups are scattered throughout the therapeutic environment—in special education, community mental health, day treatment settings for both children and adults, and private practice. They target certain populations thought to have greater difficulties with relating socially—the developmentally disabled, people diagnosed with schizophrenia, ADHD, anxiety disorders, and autism. They also target issues present in the general population, such as shyness. Even classes in dating and corporate team building can be considered in essence social skills groups.

Social skills training can be didactic or experiential. This training may involve peers with the same or different levels of social functioning, or include siblings, families, or fellow employees. There are many wonderful and not-so-wonderful models for social skills training for the clinician to choose from. Art making and the art process can be utilized in social skills groups in a myriad of ways to facilitate the learning and development of social competencies.

I have noticed a propensity, especially with treatment providers working with children, to use referrals to social skills groups as a general prescription for a wide range of social difficulties. In my opinion, the greatest flaw of many social skills models is their failure to clearly identify the specific issues, the reasons *why*, a child is needing interventions in this area. It is only after the why has been explored that an appropriate recommendation for group can be made. Before interventions are begun, it is crucial that the clinician accept and fully understand the client for where he or she is operating, developmentally and functionally. There are clients with quite clearly-identified social difficulties for whom, after sensitive weighing, a social skills group is contraindicated.

Making a call against group treatment is often a difficult task for the clinician in the face of the expectations and hopes of parents and providers who are anxious to help a child fit in with peers. In addition, there are systemic pressures that press clinicians to fill up groups, both with the hope to serve more clients and (at the risk of being too blunt) optimizing income. These issues impact the choice of treatment in ways that are not necessarily therapeutic.

## Social Behaviors and Social Skills

A distinction can be made between social behaviors and social skills. There is a greater benefit for focusing on social behaviors rather than social skills with some populations. Social skills training aims to teach and target specific skills and competencies, such as, how do you initiate and keep conversations going (e.g., what are appropriate questions to ask others? What is, and how do you engage in small talk?). Social behaviors are behaviors, not necessarily verbal, that support reciprocal social interactions. Social behaviors must be developed before specific skills can be acquired. For those clients who have not yet mastered basic concepts and skills of social interaction, working to enhance social behaviors means working at a level that is more meaningful for that client. It is best understood within a developmental framework.

I have found Trevarthen and colleagues' (1998) concepts of intersubjectivity to be a particularly useful model. He explains his term in this manner: In the early months of a child's development, children are genetically programmed to interact with their environment, and most especially, with their primary caregiver. The caregiver responds to the child, and with them creates a stimulus loop. Trevarthen has termed this crucial preverbal period of parent–child interaction "primary intersubjectivity." Through the child's sensory experience of the parent and the parent's attention, mirroring, and reinforcing feedback, the dyad engages in a "proto-conversation" of rhythmic turn-taking of expressive acts.

Greater complexities in preverbal social behaviors are observed as a child learns to interact with the world through the experience of joint attention upon an object, secondary intersubjectivity. In the first two years, children develop concepts of self and other and of social causality in general. Children learn that they can do something that affects their environment. From understandings such as, "If I smile at mother, she will smile back at me," the child will begin to initiate acts of meaning upon which meaningful nonverbal and verbal communication is based.

## Assessment for Choice of Treatment

Experience has shown me that for those clients who have adequately mastered basic social behaviors, a referral to a more didactically-oriented social skills group is appropriate. For those younger or less developmentally successful, a referral to individual, conjoint (a group of two), or a small, carefully-matched group, may be necessary to address deficits in social behaviors. For clients who are still developmentally struggling in the stages of primary and secondary intersubjectivity, individual work may be most beneficial. These children, for example, may not yet evidence motivation to interact with peers, may be unable to initiate or sustain social interactions, may not be ready to grasp social causality, and have significant language impairment. Clients whose competencies in social behaviors are compromised by high social anxiety or significant peer rejection may have developed the defense of social avoidance. These clients will best experience progress and a level of success in a placement that acknowledges their particular level of ability. A high-functioning autistic child may seem to be a good candidate for group, but may prove otherwise, and be better supported by other levels of service and means of intervention.

## Social Functioning and the Autistic Spectrum Disorders

A primary indicator of a diagnosis anywhere along the range of the autistic spectrum is sustained abnormal or impaired development in social interaction and communication and a restricted repertoire of activity and interests (American Psychiatric Association, *Diagnostic and Statistical Manual of Mental Disorders*, 1994). A common image of autistic children is of unreachable nonverbal children jumping and flapping their hands while fixated upon a shiny speck on the wall. While this may describe some children, a fuller understanding of this disorder is much more complex and portrays a much more dynamic and hopeful truth. A diagnosis of an autistic disorder defines a child whose social behaviors to one degree or another lack spontaneity and reciprocity and manifests as a disinterest in or an inability to tolerate the anxiety and stimulation of "normal" social interactions. An autistic disorder can be understood as a syndrome resulting in a developmental anomaly evident during the stages of primary and secondary intersubjectivity, and a disorder that is available to varying and, at times, significant degrees of remediation.

I will use the term autism somewhat loosely to refer to diagnoses, including Asperger's syndrome, along the spectrum of the autistic spectrum. Asperger's syndrome, although a diagnosis separate from autism, is considered by many as being on the high end of the autistic spectrum. These individuals lack the clinically-significant delays in language and cognitive development considered a part of classic autism. Yet children with Asperger's frequently have oddities of language, learning disorders and social and cognitive differences that can significantly hinder their ability to successfully utilize their cognitive potential in the real world. I find the concept of an autistic spectrum to be most clinically useful (Attwood, 1997).

The general functioning of individuals diagnosed with autism varies widely along the autistic spectrum. Similarly, so do social functioning and the nature of social impairment as they relate to the individual's other presenting autistic traits. Other associated disorders include sensory differences such as sensitivity to loud noise, attention difficulties, problems with change and transition. Other factors impacting social functions are a child's age and developmental level, their social environment, and their social history.

A minimally-verbal autistic teenager may be unresponsive to direct questions, yet be able to sustain and tolerate some nonverbal social reciprocal interactions. Another child may have mastered some of the skills of language, and be able to parrot appropriate social greetings. However, until the concept of social causality is grasped, simple nonverbal interactions are still unmanageable. It is, therefore, essential that each client's presenting features and strengths be considered when they have been referred for social interventions.

## Categories and Considerations

Individuals with autism broadly can be considered as falling within three social categories: socially avoidant, socially indifferent or passive, and socially awkward. These categories are useful in trying to understand a particular child, but must be overlaid with an understanding of the child's developmental level and a myriad other factors that affect social functioning, such as cognitive level, language skills, and attentional abilities.

It continues to be a common assumption that autistic individuals are deeply and permanently disinterested in relating socially. Yet, it has been my experience that, many children with autism are motivated to make and keep friends despite their social impairments, if they have not yet been overwhelmed by a sense of failure and futility in the social arena. The social deficit may not lie in a lack of desire for social contact. Many awkward, and even supposedly indifferent or avoidant, autistic children are well aware of their differentness and suffer from a sense of isolation. This can be said as well for other populations that have social difficulties, such as individuals who are withdrawn through shyness or even milder manifestations of schizophrenia. I have observed a number of children who, having been indifferent or even avoidant in their preschool years, suddenly develop in their elementary years, a curiosity and interest in their peers. Their newfound emotional investment in peer relating, combined with their social delays, makes them suddenly highly vulnerable to the emotional fallout of social failures. Intervention is highly recommended at this developmental leap to support early successes and avoid a possible spiral toward either a return to social withdrawal or behavioral acting out.

## Evaluation and Referral Considerations

In assessing a child for social skills interventions, it is necessary to consider the child's language skills and cognitive skills. Further questions need also to be asked. Is the problem rooted in the child's inability to attend adequately to social cues, their difficulties in regulating and processing environmental input, or both? Is the child's failure to have friends due to lack of specific skills, or is it also compounded by social anxiety and fears of failure? Does the child grasp social causality and reciprocity? Respond to words as communication? Have sensory sensitivities? Present with any significant behavioral difficulties, such as aggression and frequent tantruming? Is the child even interested in having friends? It would seem obvious that the best interventions would be ones that take the underlying issues fully into account. (Mishna & Muskat, 1998).

A thorough assessment involves observation of the child alone and with parents (and siblings), and within both a semi-structured and unstructured social peer setting (e.g., at school in a circle time and at recess). In addition to the review of any pertinent records, it is important that the assessment process paint an overall picture of the child as well answer questions relating to the "why" of the social difficulties.

A child may be appropriate for a social skills group, however, the specific makeup of an existing social skills group may not be appropriate for him or her. Careful matching of participants is strongly recommended to optimize success for each child. A poor match can prove disastrous and do damage to an autistic child's fragile self-esteem. It can turn a socially indifferent child into one that is socially avoidant, or worse, aggressive.

A broad and developmentally grounded understanding of a child's social functioning is key to identifying successful social interventions. In summary, success of any intervention to address social difficulties is highly determinant on the therapist intervening at the level where the child can be successful and the social interaction meaningful for them (Lewy & Dawson, 1992).

## ☐ Why Art?

I came upon the approach I share in this chapter through my experiential and intuitive process that later became more grounded by the research and theory of others. This is not the most scientific of approaches, but I suspect not an uncommon one. I initially came to the work not as an expert in autism, but rather as an art therapist intrigued by how the tools and concepts of art therapy seemed to particularly resonate with the needs of many individuals with autism and my clinical directive of helping them with socialization.

What I have seen is that art, whether used in individual or group settings, can function as a true grounding, building material—a glue for both verbal or nonverbal social interactions with children diagnosed with an autistic spectrum disorder. Art becomes the potentiator as well as the mediator and facilitator of social reciprocity for these individuals who are easily overwhelmed with direct social interactions. My clinical experience is that the process of creating concrete images or objects can be manipulated to regulate and support a child's social interactions with others. Furthermore, art can be used as a vehicle for reciprocal activities.

### Rationale for the Language of Art and Process

There is something uniquely congruent about the nature of art and art creation and the "world" of autism. Grandin (1995) suggests that many individuals with autism (like herself) are visual thinkers. "Differences between language-based thought and picture-based thought may explain why artists and accountants fail to understand each other. They are like apples and oranges" (p. 160). There is a general consensus that children diagnosed with autism or Asperger's significantly benefit from concrete visual tools in teaching and communication. Visual tools are congruent with the concrete and associational thinking of these children.

Furthermore, these children have, to a greater or lesser degree, retreated from the stress of direct interpersonal interaction to the safety and predictability of object relating, where they have found opportunities for mastery and meaning. Recalling the concepts of primary and secondary intersubjectivity, one can think of the autistic child as being unable or less able to sustain intersubjectivity on either primary or secondary levels. Due to their limited ability to interact with the outside world as mediated by their interactions with others, children with autism have been redirected to the world of objects to serve the function of mediation with the outside world.

## Guidelines

Anyone intending to work with these children would be wise to familiarize themselves with the concepts and tools of social stories and social facilitation, where highly-concrete, specific, directive, repetitively structured stories are constructed to teach individuals with autism specific social and behavioral tasks. Though Gray and Garand (1993) have argued against the use of illustrations, Katz and Yellen (2000) utilize client-specific photographs to illustrate their text. Gray and Garand also outline the use of "comic strip conversations" to offer simple diagrammatic images to help children conceptualize conversational dynamics. They insert color-coding emotions to provide concrete expression of subjective experience. These tools, as tangible objects, can be translated effectively into the group setting, with thought to the specific needs of the group.

An art object, in other words anything made or created by the child client, is different from other objects, such as toys or books. It is, by definition, inculcated with the child's efforts to make his or her world meaningful. The child invests in the process of creating the object, and through that investment, infuses the object with additional meanings. That energy can be tapped to motivate meaningful and spontaneous interactions with others. Through that investment, the children also show something of themselves and their inner process. Certainly, toys and other pre-existing objects can be imbued with meaningfulness by a child and operate as an object of joint attention. But where art objects excel over other materials is that the act of their creation provides rich opportunities for social connection. Object play is a key tool in a child's development of social competency and connection to the world. Art production is a uniquely meaningful means of play.

## Art in the Assessment Process

Often allowing children, at any level of functioning, to draw or utilize any art material that interests them can provide useful information about their social functioning. Do they seek approval or engagement, or remain in their own world? Do they seek to share? Do they ask for materials? Assessment of attentional abilities is often key in understanding a child's social success. Can they attend to objects long enough to gather information and interact successfully? If they are not able to do so, it is probable they will have difficulties interacting with the much more complex social world. In addition, clues to a child's interest are gleaned.

Frequently, autistic disorders manifest as strong fixed interests that are quickly revealed in a nondirective art task. A window to the child's world, and therefore an opportunity for a focus of joint attention and social reciprocity, is accessed and identified early in treatment. Successful use of these persevorative interests are often key to successful social interventions (Baker, Koegel, & Koegel, 1998).

## Art Tasks

There are several art tasks that I have found to be useful as a part of assessment for social skills interventions. A simple turn-taking game consists of the child and the assessor each picking a favorite colored marker and then taking turns making shapes or scribbles on a single piece of paper. If the child is verbal, the turn is prompted by either the assessor or the child saying, "Susie's turn" or "Jean's turn," to concretize the turn-taking dynamic. Observations can be made. Does the child effectively turn-take with or without prompts? Is the child preoccupied with his or her own scribbles or perseverative imagery or are they able to be interested in the contributions of the assessor? Do the child's scribbles mirror the assessor's? How does the child respond to the assessor's mirroring of his or her imagery? How are the child's boundaries as they present on the paper, are they isolative and avoidant (scribbling in a corner), territorial ("this is my side, that's yours"), invasive (scribbling unintentionally or intentionally over the assessor's marks), or seeking contact on the paper (connecting shapes)? Many clues to a client's overall social interactions can be gleaned from this short, enjoyable, and rapport-building task. This task can be translated into three dimensions for children who have fine motor difficulties or are not able to be engaged in drawing. Soft, brightly-colored building blocks can be used to take turns building a tower or making patterns on the floor. This same task can be used to observe dynamics between the child and a parent or sibling.

Simple art directives given to higher-functioning children such as, "Draw yourself on the playground," "Draw yourself with friends," or even "Draw what is hard about making friends," are often remarkably revealing of a child's perspective with regard to relating with peers.

Figures 4.1 through 4.3 show the assessment drawings of a 10-year-old boy with high-functioning autism. Roy was a highly-verbal boy with convoluted sentences, very cheerful and eager to engage, yet highly anxious, with darting eyes and a loud, unmodulated voice. He was able to attend to and respond to concrete questions with some prompting, but frequently interrupted me and his parents. Roy eagerly

**FIGURE 4.1.** In the "Turn-taking" game, Roy's ability to react and reciprocate with the therapist is demonstrated in a joint drawing.

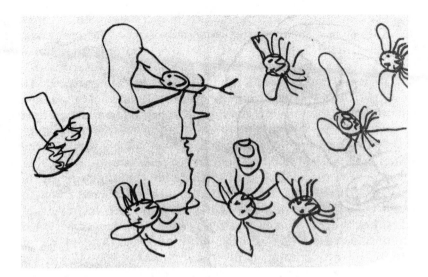

**FIGURE 4.2.** Roy's "spiders" shows his return to his perseverative mode of drawing.

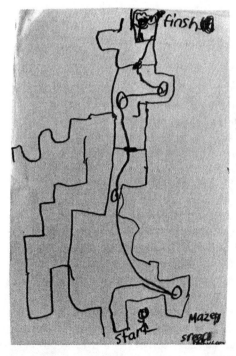

**FIGURE 4.3.** The "maze game" shows Roy's need to control his environment by his staying in command of the art task.

engaged in the turn-taking game, initially successful both in copying and being copied (see how carefully he mirrored my long dark swiggles along the length of the paper with his own). After a short time he became diverted. Roy drew a stick person, I drew a stick person, he then drew a stick person at a computer, drew a "game spider." After this period, he disengaged from the game and launched into a monologue about his favorite computer game. I then offered him an opportunity to do a free drawing. He used this art to continue to elaborate, blow by blow with much enthusiasm, on the spiders from a favorite computer game and how he could successfully battle the bad, flying spiders. I demonstrated interest and attention, and supported his sharing of a favorite topic. Roy responded to my active listening with increased enthusiasm and eye contact. By allowing his diversion, I maintained his engagement and got a sense of his tendency to polarize both his internal and external world into the good and bad, and how this polarization hinders his social interactions.

Later in the assessment session, I raised the topic of friends. Roy talked about the bad other kids who teased him. When asked to draw a picture of something he likes to do with other kids, he drew a game "Roy's Maze" (Figure 4.3). He elaborated in detail as he traced the movement of his man along the game board. When his man reached the finish line of the game, Roy was playing by himself. He enthusiastically yelled, "I won! I won! See I won!"

The drawings provided clues to Roy's social development while confirming observations and parent reports. Roy was able to be successful for brief periods of noncompetitive, structured, and supported, social engagement but has great difficulty sustaining social interactions for long. He was prone to become tangential toward his own preferred topics or activities. He was eager for friends, yet developed negative expectations of, and reactivity toward, peers due to a history of being teased, along with other social hurts and failures. Roy wanted to play games with others, but was so preoccupied with his own part in it, and his desire to control the outcome and be the good winner, that he was unable to successfully survive anything that could be construed as a competitive activity. However, he was eager to have an audience to his world, and in this eagerness for reflective joint attention to his tasks and interests, lies Roy's foundation for successful social interaction.

These assessment observations proved highly useful in Roy's placement—initially in individual work where he could develop a meaningful attachment to an adult. A person who could later motivate him to tolerate the frustration inherent in being in a group with two slightly younger and highly-accepting boys.

# ☐ Treatment: Clinical Needs of Children with an Autistic Spectrum Disorder in Individual and Group Settings

Prokoviev (1998), in her chapter on adapting art therapy for work in children's groups, summarizes key elements about utilizing art in children's groups and working with children in groups in general. Her punctuation of the needs of children to have activities to maintain their interest, to be attentive to developmental levels and needs, and the importance of the therapist in maintaining vigilance toward the group's varying needs for structure, are very applicable to working with children with autism. Also highly relevant for children with an autistic spectrum disorder, is the need for a calm, patient stance by the therapist and great flexibility in the face of an individual's high anxiety or group chaos.

Unique needs for children with autism need to be considered. For example, because autistic children are usually presenting with deeply-rooted difficulties in managing social contact (especially with regard to peers and new situations), they may be unable to sustain any sort of verbal conversation, let alone consistently say hello. They may have strong sensitivities to environmental stimuli. Autistic children are frequently and easily overwhelmed by the all-invasive stimuli that surrounds them. These stimuli can interfere with and prevent successful social interactions. Everything from artificial lighting to walls covered with excessive color and imagery, can impinge on their overly-sensitive senses, overwhelming them and causing either physical or emotional withdrawal. Integrating autistic children with other same-age children with other clinical issues (e.g., ADHD, mood disorders, oppositional defiant disorders) are generally, but not always, contraindicated, and should be done only after much thought. These children are at risk in the face of overwhelming input for yet another round of peer rejection and decompensation. They seem to do best with other autistic children or accepting and supportive peers. Again, attention to the match of social development and functioning, rather than age or degree of clinical severity is essential.

## Multisensory Activities

Because sustained verbal interactions are often a great challenge to children with autism, successful interventions generally require the scaffolding of the shared focus of a concrete and multisensory activity.

A key to success with groups of this population, and arguably, of many other types of groups, is consistent membership. In addition, adequate thought and time spent to anticipate and process any changes, be it changes in the treatment room, in group membership, schedules, or routines. The same goes for individual work. These children often have great difficulties with new situations and transitions in general. Some routines that are highly recommended include: a predictable beginning and end (at least) of each session, such as a ritual check in and check out; an established behavioral plan [I use group "points" which are earned by the group for sustaining a concrete set of "friends rules," and can be earned toward a party (where they can practice their social skills)]; continuity in art activities and materials; and discussion beforehand with the group if there are new activities or upcoming changes. All changes should be anticipated as much as possible.

Many autistic children love to draw, despite a large frequency of these children having fine motor difficulties. I generally limit materials, stay simple, and often use easily manageable washable markers and paper 11 × 14" or larger. Children with severe motor delays often experience frustration in drawing, and for them I provide easily manipulated building materials. Colored dominoes and colorful soft building blocks are often a favorite, stimulating autistic interest in patterns and numbers. I consider the products of these building tools fluid sculptures. Placticine and pastels, despite their colorfulness and maneuverability, are rejected by some children due to their texture and messiness. More adventuresome materials and activities (e.g., popsicle stick structures and puppets) can often be introduced as the group becomes acclimated and masters basic media.

As an aside, I share with many clinicians not having the fortune to have a room designated for my particular needs in running groups, let alone running groups where art tools are used. By necessity I have had to work with the assumption that all media and papers will be put away and cleaned up at the end of the group hour. This has supported the minimalistic approach to the art media that I have also justified clinically above. I imagine that a more bounteous stance to materials and stimulus could be successful and valid, but would probably serve to address a different set of issues than those that I have chosen to focus on in my treatment approach.

Regular involvement of the parents in treatment planning and implementation, and collateral contact with the child's school and other providers to maintain a team effort will help the clinician maintain a holistic view of the child, optimize a clinician's efforts, and help the child (through the support of involved adults) generalize gains in treatment.

# Cultivating Individual Social Skills as Preparation for Group

Bart, a cherubic 6-year-old boy with a diagnosis of high-functioning autism, was referred for social skills training. In the assessment, Bart presented an inability to take turns and showed strong tendencies to verbally perseverate endlessly on favorite topics, usually repeating lines and stories from favorite videos or children's television shows. Despite his evident ability with language, Bart was unable to report on his own experiences and would not answer questions unrelated to his perseverative interest. Bart was prone to dramatic tantrums when unable to get his way. He has strong preferences, which manifest in a severely-limited diet and a preference for the number three and the color yellow. His social rigidity and tantrums, as well as his delays in basic skills of social reciprocity, initially precluded his working with a peer. His social strengths were his affectionate nature with familiar adults, a new interest in making friends, his love of an audience, and his eagerness to learn new things now that he is in kindergarten. He loves to draw and tell stories.

These loves proved to be the jumping-off point for interventions with Bart. As earlier noted, supporting, utilizing and eventually providing respectful containment of an autistic child's perseverative interests can be a powerful way to utilize their own intrinsic motivation and draw them into the world of others. Bart glowed while reciting his favorite animal videos. Initially he was allowed to tell his stories and draw his pictures and was given lots of positive regard and attention from his therapist, his "audience." Which stimulated his interest in coming to therapy. These circumstances presented an opportunity to ask simple questions to help Bart identify the source of his story and begin exploring real versus imaginary stories. His father was frequently brought into the session to help Bart tell real stories about his day. Flexibility was slowly encouraged over the months as Bart was encouraged to draw and tell his own real and imaginary stories and recognize the difference (Figure 4.4).

In addition to the use of Bart's stories, I employed graphic mirroring of his images of his favorite shapes and colors, which prompted Bart's curiosity in me and increased his interest in more reciprocal interactions and activities. This mirroring stimulated Bart's eye contact with me, a powerful dynamic that I have observed with many autistic children, and which has been explored in research (Tiegerman & Primavera, 1984). The process of mirroring captured his attention and stimulated social interaction, and took Bart back to his as-yet-unmastered tasks of the developmental stage of primary intersubjectivity. As Bart

**FIGURE 4.4.** With the "blue elephant," Bart responds to the therapist's suggestion to draw his favorite animal.

became more comfortable with the cooperative rhythm of parallel drawing—as he drew, I mirror—his willingness to engage in reciprocal interactions—where he shared rather than maintained control of the outcome—was increased (Figure 4.5)

The sharing of control through the production of imagery was further encouraged by a very simple turn-taking game. Bart took turns with me, and also with his father, in deciding the content of the parallel drawings. As Bart commanded, "Draw a small blue circle please," and gradually turned concentric blue circles into his favorite animal (an elephant), his adult partners dutifully followed, to his wide-eyed pleasure. His pleasure was less certain when his father asked him to please draw a red circle. (Bart preferred *blue circles* and he was *not* pleased). Gauging Bart's mood and getting a report of Bart's most recent overall functioning helped to determine his frustration tolerance and the direction of the session. The hope was to support Bart's optimal success at his immediate level of social functioning. So, for example, on a day when Bart was more cranky, he, instead of being asked directly to draw a red circle, he was asked to draw several blue circles first and, finally, one little red circle.

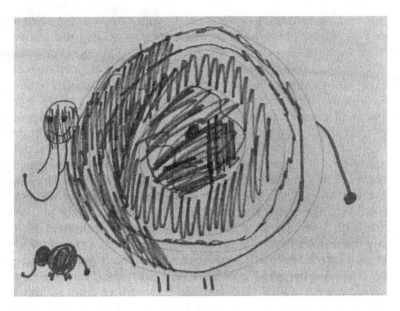

**FIGURE 4.5.** Bart's father copies the blue elephant, demonstrating mirroring as a form of social engagement.

Bart was also helped with this transition toward increased reciprocity with simple reinforcers that also served to support his developing skills of self-regulation. For example, Bart was told that when we were done he can draw whatever he wants or tell his favorite story, which served to motivate him through a challenging round of turn-taking. Along with these reinforcers, were, of course, many words of praise and punctuation of Bart's ability to be a good friend.

The structure of the sessions slowly changed to allow for these new activities, and limits were slowly set, reducing Bart's previous full control of the session's direction. Certainly, this transition to shared control was a big step for Bart and, despite care and caution, resulted in some minor (and occasionally, major), tantrums. However, these tantrums were opportunities to coach Bart's father on basic behavioral techniques of validation and identification of his son's feelings, setting of consistent expectations and limits, and reinforcing and successfully managing Bart's needs for control and predictability in various environments.

Over the months, the turn-taking games grew increasingly complex and challenging as Bart's tolerance for sharing control and enjoyment in the process grew. Bart's pride at his mastery of these new skills became a new source of motivation for him. Turn-taking skills were translated into communications skills, such as asking and answering questions, and talking and listening turn-taking activities. For example, Bart was asked, "What color is in your hand?" and, if I was mysterious enough about my selection process, he was curious enough to want to find out what color was in mine. When he asked, I praised him for asking such a good question. Bart also became able to explore issues of personal and shared space in joint drawings. In addition, social story techniques were practiced as his father increasingly brought in peer issues from school and elsewhere. For example, drawing for Bart a simple, child-friendly sketch of the problematic friend situation at recess: Bart thinks, "No one wants to play with me," as he sits alone in the sandbox. Following the drawing, Bart was concretely coached on simple skills such as saying hello to a specifically-identified child and asking them if they want to dig a hole in the sand or swing with him.

Bart's tantrums subsided, and his interest in having a friend grew to the degree that his social problems were less about self-imposed isolation and more about rejection (by him and to him by others)—rebuffs that occurred when peers did not want to play what he chose. Bart demonstrated his ability to share control with an adult and developed some basic social competencies, such as greeting and saying goodbye, asking questions, and taking turns. He was now ready for greater challenges and graduated to a conjoint setting with another little boy. Bart and his group friend continued therapy with a variety of turn-taking activities and within six months graduated together to a small group of three boys.

## Discussion

Bart's treatment was substantially supported by the close involvement of his father, a nurturing school setting, and a very carefully monitored medication regime. Bart naturally gravitated to art tasks, which were used in nearly every session and were consistently highly motivating and served to pull him into the here-and-now of the session. The art activities provided him with a language and intermediary space with which to share himself as well as contain and manage his social anxiety and interactions with others. The art helped to ground his verbal expressions and nonverbal behaviors into concrete communication with others and away from perseverative, repetitive expressions or self-stimulation. Similar dynamics can be practiced using other tools—making patterns with blocks, dominoes, paper—any object that appeals to a child's particular tactile needs and stimulates their interest.

Their appeal may be based purely on the functional level (e.g., texture, color, shapes) or prompt imaginary interactions. Bart's interactions with the art materials were initially on the functional level, but through treatment, they became tools for simple pretend play.

Furthermore, many of the approaches done in individual treatment can be modified for use in conjoint or group settings, both between the group leader and the group and between group members.

## ☐ Conjoint Treatment

Two high-functioning, first-grade girls—Becky, with long, straight, black hair and a commanding little voice, and pixie-haired Mindy, a rolypoly, more withdrawn little girl with some moderate speech impairments—are paired together for a conjoint social skills mini-group. The pairing of these two girls resulted from observations that both girls were able to turn-take with adults and expressed and acted (albeit unsuccessfully) a great desire to have friends, especially a "best girlfriend." However, they were having great difficulties sharing social attention, initiating appropriately, and sustaining successful play interactions with peers. Their parents were acquaintances and were eager for the girls to work together. Parental motivation is always an important factor.

Both girls liked to draw and when assessed, drew elaborate stories that they eagerly recounted. They both came to their first session eager to draw a story for the therapist. For the first several weeks of conjoint work they were allowed to create their separate imaginary stories and take turns sharing their pictures and recounting their tales (primarily to me). Sharing my attention was initially very difficult for both girls, and prompted a struggle for control (loud protests and interruptions) and demands for exclusive attention. These behaviors were restrained from producing utter chaos by a behavioral reinforcement system of friend's rules. Yet, this very struggle held the seeds of motivation to successfully turn-take and share, for, failing to turn-take and share, as they increasingly became aware, resulted in their not getting any attention. The girls were coached and supported to share with and attend to each other (as well as me), ask appropriate questions, and perform such basic social skills as presenting their picture so that their groupmate could see it. Their pleasure at this new source of attention (from a peer) proved exciting and over time became a motivating factor (Figure 4.6).

The content of the girl's stories were increasingly reflective of their interest in each other's stories. (This is in contrast to their lack of

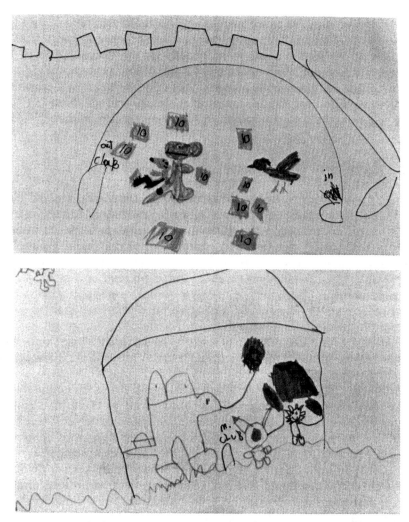

**FIGURE 4.6.** Both drawings have the same title, "My story has Pikachu and Yoshi too," as two girls interact in small group. The parallel process supports social interaction.

interest in any verbal sharing about facts or events outside the session). Primarily, the girls began to copy elements of their friend's story into their own, and they became more verbally interactive, asking questions about what is happening, offering suggestions, and (with mild coaching), giving compliments, which resulted in beams of pleasure from the recipient.

The drive toward more socially-successful behavior was augmented by the list of friends rules that the therapist co-constructed with the girls, where they earned stickers (an attractive reward for theses girls) for successful compliance of the rules and success at a challenging friend skill (such as being nice and a good sport when the other goes first). Since both, especially Becky, strongly desired to share first, this was truly a significant achievement—a success that was enthusiastically shared with the parents at the end of the session, along with other social gains and a summary of the group's activity of the day.

Figure 4.6 displays their first attempt at the directive, "We will draw a story together" by taking turns. I initiated a story that started on a single piece of paper, then exchanged. Each girl first selected her "own" color of marker. The co-creation of the story motivated the girls toward a remarkable level of attentiveness and cooperation. They were thrilled as a story took shape about four little girls on their way to a party who got lost in a woods with star trees and almost missed a party. Although it is rather poignant that the girls selected the title "The Lost Girls Who Missed All the Fun" when, upon completion, they were encouraged to name the story. However, they were able in the process of the joint creation of the narrative, to explore feelings of isolation and disappointment, as well as feelings of commonality and friendship, themes of sharing, and the meanings of presents and of birthday parties.

I inserted and shaped some of these themes during some of my turns to contribute and punctuate certain elements of the girls' story to encourage cooperation. In addition, I modeled appropriate time frames for turns. Both girls, who initially were prone to extend their turns until prompted by me, began to appropriately give each other social cues ("It's my turn now!" "Hurry up please!"). A new story was begun the next week, and again, the week after.

Additionally, Mindy and Becky were asked which friends rule they wished to excel in each session, and so the perseverative activity of drawing stories was continued, but a range of goals were explored, such as turn-taking, reciprocal conversation skills, offering and receiving compliments, and resolving areas of conflict. Autistic features particularly problematic to both girls, such as the tendency to talk at peers, the desire to control outcomes, to always be first, and identifying the difference between imaginary stories and stories from life, were all in play. These traits were interrupted in a way that reinforced their pleasure in a social activity and provided them with an experience of social success.

## Conjoint Work Between
## Minimally Verbal Teenagers

Armando, a 14-year-old boy, was referred for social skills interventions. He presented with all the criteria for autism, with very minimal speech consisting of formulated one- or two-word responses to simple direct questions and perseverate outbursts, and with severely delayed academic functioning. My misguided invitation to Armando to an ongoing social skills group was a disaster. It resulted in loud negative perseverations of "No group! No group!" and stunned the other group members. Individual interventions were instead utilized for about a year.

Initially, Armando's discomfort with me was so severe that I allowed him solitary engagement with the materials provided. I found, though, that nondirective turn-taking activities in creative tasks with popsicle sticks, plasticine, blocks, and toy models,[2] stimulated Armando's interest and willingness over time to engage in reciprocal interactions. In addition, I focused on punctuating, reflecting, and responding to Armando's behavioral communications, such as connecting them to apparent feelings in the immediate dynamics in the room, for example, labeling and treating his runs around the room as his communication of excitement and pleasure with a finished project. Armando (especially when whispered to) became more verbal, as well as less socially inappropriate in his behaviors. I periodically asked Armando if he would like another peer to join us. Repeated streams of, "No group! No group!" finally changed to a whispered yes.

Peter (with whom I had also been working with individually) and Armando together graduated to conjoint treatment. Peter, delayed developmentally in many ways, though without a diagnosis of autism, began his treatment, like Armando. He was essentially mute, but with receptive language abilities. He differed from Armando in his expres-

---

[2]I used toy models as well as puzzles. Armando hit a point of not wanting to come to the session, and we were able to identify model building as something that he was interested in and motivated to engage in with me on task. He was allowed to start his process in his customary, solitary way. Within 15 minutes he was pacing and perseverating "No group, go home!" under his breath due to his inability to figure out how to manipulate the pieces successfully. While setting limits towards further escalation, I reminded Armando of my presence in the room and his options of asking me for help or doing the task together. Armando's natural frustration served as a significant motivator for him to do the task together instead of by himself. Most of the children I have worked with benefit at times for being allowed to consciously chose whether they work together or independently. They often, still to my surprise, choose the more social choice, and are more cooperative and eager to interact for having had the choice offered to them.

sive language potential. Peter was selectively mute due to his severe social anxiety. Only his parents had ever witnessed his potential to be a chatterbox. Peter in individual treatment was unwilling to talk, interact with me, or engage in any joint art activity for months. I allowed, even encouraged his avoidance of verbal engagement. Communication was initially almost entirely nonverbal (points, nods, smiles as well a graphic mirroring) despite his receptive language abilities. My goal was to join at his level of functioning and reduce his anxiety.

When conjoint treatment was established, reciprocal interactions between the two boys was often paltry and only subtly apparent. There was no conversation, and they were unable to sustain interactions without my facilitating the activity, and successful in turn taking only occasionally in short intensive spurts. There were sessions which consisted almost entirely of parallel play. However, Peter sometimes playfully mirrored Armando's rote verbalizations, which caught Armando's attention, and there were moments of boisterous cooperation (in jointly knocking down block towers). Their time together was about sharing space while engaging in their own respective activities and interacting intermittently through art activities.

## Questioning the Efficacy of Treatment

Peter and Armando bring up the question: How can one identify the level of meaningfulness and usefulness of this level of interaction, or rather at times, lack of social interaction as we generally define it, to clients with such severe social delays? Despite almost nonexistent overt communication between the two of them, both parents reported that the boys eagerly came to group. Peter, talked endlessly through the week to his mother about Armando. Armando punished me with aloofness when Peter was absent and offered goodbyes to Peter without prompts. Armando's clock watching in the session dropped dramatically. These boys had only minimally generalized their gains outside the session, and those changes were generally limited to the home environment. Yet, I would argue, their quality of life was improved by these positive experiences, and further, that their willingness for and interest in further social interaction (albeit in supported settings) was stimulated. A treatment plan for both boys was to slowly increase the complexity of social interactions between them, including eventually adding another peer, to make a "real group." Art activities were key for these boys for whom language was often an insurmountable barrier of expression, giving them a meaningful avenue to interact with the world and each other.

# ☐ Small Groups—Using Art to Moderate Interactions

With latency-age boys with social difficulties, with autism or not, expecting a sustained focus to a joint task with peers miss understanding their challenges. The goal is to encourage and support whatever level of interaction the children can sustain, for whatever length of time that provides a closure of success. This may mean several changes in group activities, and periods of parallel or even solitary play, perhaps a special activity time to help the children modulate the stress of social interactions. For some groups, I ritually begin with a self-directed drawing where the children are encouraged to draw something meaningful to them and then share their production and any associated stories with the other group members to any degree they are able. Their peers are then encouraged to ask questions or make comments on the topic. This semi-structured check-in and protoconversation serves to both smooth the transition into group and help the group members begin interacting with each other.

Many latency-age games, especially with boys, are competitive. However, competitive play is too a great challenge for many of these children with autism, who often find a game pointless if they are not going to win. Joint art activities can be a forum for these children to interact cooperatively without the pressure of competition, and practice the necessary initial skills of sharing outcomes with others. Art activities, such as building with blocks or making a party sign, can be constructed to support the successful experience of turn-taking and the parallel skill of attending to the actions of others (sharing space, sharing objects, taking turns being leaders and followers, and resolving conflicts). Conflict and frustration can quickly derail a group member's interest —so often, the simpler the activity the better. Furthermore, it is important to allow a child to retreat from the hub of the group activity and work separately while continuing to support the child in a way so that he or she may reenter when ready. Their product is included in the group product, such as allowing the child to construct a house that can then be connected to the group tower, or to make a party symbol that can then be cut out and added to the group sign. Inclusion of the artwork is a respectful way to acknowledge the difficulties of shared tasks for some, while simultaneously working toward peer interaction.

For those children who are eager to meet the challenges of the rules, structure, and the risk of defeat in competitive play, time-out periods of parallel or solitary art tasks help modulate the associated tension and stress. One little girl has learned to time out herself and go do a drawing when she is getting out-of-hand from the stress of a board game. For those who have greater ambivalence toward structured games, encouraging creativity in having them help design a game (several clever Pokemon based games have emerged), define the rules, and teach the game to the group, is a way to motivate them to then participate and keep to the rules they have set. I have found that children are more able then to accept the outcome of not always winning. Resounding praise for a child's creativity and sportsmanship in a survivable (for them) and meaningful context provides incentive for later generalizing these competencies.

Chaos is a frequent danger in elementary-school and junior-high groups, when combined with the usual childhood energy, social anxieties, difficulties in reading social cues, proneness to sensory overwhelm, and lack of social skills. Ebb and flow of group process to maintain each child's ability to put up with all the stress of peer interaction and reap the joys of having friends, requires much attention to group dynamics and flexibility in facing the group's fluctuations. Involving parents at the end of each group by having the group members share something about the session's activities and then punctuating both group and individual successes in making and keeping friends, also serves to generalize success outside the group.

## ☐ Adolescent Groups

Adolescents with high-functioning autism and Asperger's may be able to be coached on specific social competencies with didactic teaching, coaching, role playing, and the use of videos (Cartledge & Milburn, 1995; Mishna & Muskat, 1998). However, I have found that adolescents with a diagnosis of autism, who are socially avoidant or awkward, have very likely developed finely-tuned defenses against experiencing social inadequacies. They may have become increasingly isolative or aloof over the years, or may have developed aggressive coping to counter peer rejection and teasing, therefore are not, at least initially, able to absorb didactic coaching. Yet, I consistently find these teens extremely desirous of group acceptance. As structured settings are generally found to benefit this population, they often have been highly dependent on others for years to initiate activities, except those in their preferred areas of interest. These adolescents frequently look to the group leader for structure. Paradoxically, as typical adolescents, they also resist adult authority. A careful balance of structure and intervention, which encourages client-led activities while offering didactic teaching and supporting successful social interaction, is often difficult to sustain. The utilization of activities of different degrees of structure allows for a focus away from the highly-charged interpersonal interactions. At the same time, it allows and supports joint attention and reciprocal engagement. Coaching, such as in reading cues, is more successfully soliciting attention from peers and getting their needs met in the group. Later on this approach can be done indirectly and be depersonalized through the vehicle of the ostensive task.

## An Experience of Teamwork—The Popsicle Tower

A small group of three male teenagers had been working together for about six months. Concepts of team activities versus individual projects were explored both verbally and through simple single-session activities. A new idea of doing a "bigger" project together was introduced and the teens were given a range of materials to use and build with. The group unanimously decided on popsicle sticks, which were a novel material for this group. The group was then given a cardboard "base," a box of popsicle sticks, and a bottle of glue. The only rule was to take turns, building one stick at a time.

In the first session of this activity, the group, with regular coaching and reminders, was able to sustain effective turn-taking. The result was three separate mini-structures beginning to materialize on the edges of the cardboard base.

The next week, a new challenge was given that each popsicle stick must touch at least one stick placed by another group member. This new rule produced groans and raised issues of control and territoriality. There were cries of "Don't do that!" and frantic efforts to adjust the popsicle sticks laid by other peers. I encouraged discussion about whether the group wanted a rule of "No moving someone else's popsicle." We shared aloud the pros and cons of this rule (e.g., "I can't move your popsicle stick, but then again, you can't move mine."), and each group member began to see their individual gain in this rule. The group decided to add it to the other two rules. The group slowly became more self-regulating as the threesome became more curious and attentive to each other's choices and how the joint activity was increasingly developing (Figure 4.7).

Continued issues of control led to further discussion and more cognitive exploration of ways the group members could influence peer choice while maintaining the group rules. I diagrammed options that arose on a large piece of paper—they could make suggestions, ask favors, make trades, as well as tease, threaten, or insult each other. I nonjudgementally reflected these options as they occur in the group

**FIGURE 4.7.** An adolescent group struggles with the challenges of a shared task, as demonstrated in "Popsicle Tower."

process and also offer alternative strategies for their consideration. For example, they could try to plan ahead together or try to sabotage each others plans. Meaningful didactic education on concrete strategies and their relative effectiveness was offered at this point to the group, this was possible due to the group's increasing investment in the outcome of the activity.

## Expectations

I have observed that many children with autism desire meaningful social relating. The crux of successfully living and working with an individual with autism lies in sorting out the differences in how they and "the rest of us" define meaningful social and interpersonal interactions. Without the understanding and respect of others for these crucial differences in meaning, interacting with a person with autism results in frustration for all parties.

The question that must be asked regularly when dealing with social goals, is "Whose goal is this and who does it serve?" A frequent social goal that I have established for children coming to work with me, is "increase eye contact." Certainly, in our western culture regular eye contact with others is an expected part of effective communication, as well as a means for the observer to glean the emotional subtext of the conversation or interactions via the communicative expressiveness of our eyes. For one, our preoccupation with eye contact is partly cultur-ally based—many other cultures have different ideas about eye con-tact. For example, some Asian cultures consider it inappropriate and disrespectful for children to make eye contact with adults.

Many children with autism find eye contact extremely overstimu-lating, and asking for such a child to attend to our words (which is already difficult for them) with the added demand of eye contact, may be an unfair and unreasonable expectation. I have found some chil-dren to become more motivated to make eye contact if they are shown that it is a great way for them to tell whether someone is listening to them—which is a more relevant reason for these children than a reason based on our needs for connection. A way to move from mini-mal eye contact to greater eye contact is through the art expression. If the art is looked at by both parties, then brief eye contact can flow from the discussion of the art. Gazing at a mutual object first estab-lishes a comfort zone, this leads to gradually tolerating more of the discomforting interaction. Our culture has a bias for words to be the key means for social relating and has been moving away from rela-tionships based on doing things together (building barns, sewing quilts) and toward relationships that are more about sharing thoughts and emotions. Furthermore, we are increasingly learning about the true multidimensionality of our minds and spirits, and our biological needs for multidimensional relating. Many individuals with autism relate better through symbols and metaphor and through the sharing of tasks, than through emotionally-laden discussion. Perhaps we can best join them in this way, to the benefit and growth of ourselves as well as our clients.

In addition to a language bias, our culture also has a bias toward sociability. There tends to be an assumption that something is wrong if a child prefers his own company to that of his peers. The social child is more generally considered the better adjusted one. Respect toward a child with autism, to my mind, means at times respecting a need or desire for solitary time and play, even within the group setting.

## ☐ Conclusion

Groups are often utilized as logical means to teach social skills, par-ticularly when the nature of the client's need lies in their difficulties with social interactions. However, groups are only as useful as they benefit each group member. Working with children with autism, who globally have difficulties relating successfully with others, serves to punctuate this truth. Furthermore, groups of two or three may be functioning optimally at that size in regard to the member's needs. I have found the use of art to be a profoundly powerful tool in my work with children with autistic spectrum disorders. This is an area rich in possibilities, both clinically and theoretically, in the field of autism and with populations whose diagnoses or delays result in fundamental social deficits or differences.

Art, in the broadest sense of being a created or co-created object endowed with meaning, can be a bridge to others for individuals with autism. Art provides access to communication for these individuals with language difficulties, or other deficits that handicap their left brain abilities to communicate and interact. It can provide a meaningful, safe, and comprehensible arena for social connection, communication, and shared engagement where they can be successful with peers in a group setting. A group can provide these children and adolescents with a rare experience of social pleasure. Art can provide an avenue for social relatedness for a more severely-autistic or handicapped individual who simply cannot process or tolerate the stress, confusion, and anxiety prompted by the stimulation of more normal (i.e., verbal) means of social engagement. Mutually meaningful relationships can be built and social competencies developed without a word being spoken. Visible language can break the barrier of isolation and frustration. It must not be overlooked.

# ☐ References

American Psychiatric Association (1994). *Diagnostic and statistical manual of mental disorders* (4th ed.). Washington, DC: Author.

Attwood, T. (1997). *Asperger's Syndrome: A guide for parents and professionals*. London: Jessica Kingsley.

Baker, M., Koegel, R., & Koegel, L. (1998). Increasing the social behavior of young children with autism using their obsessive behaviors. *The Journal of the Association for Persons with Severe Handicaps, 23*, 300–308.

Cartledge, G., & Milburn, J. F. (1995). *Teaching social skills to children and youth: Innovative approaches*. Boston: Allyn and Bacon.

Grandin, T. (1995). *Thinking in pictures: And other reports from my life with autism*. New York: Vintage Books.

Gray, C., & Garand, J. (1993). Improving responses of students with autism with accurate social information. *Focus on Autistic Behavior, 8*, 1–10.

Katz, I., & Yellen, A. (2000). *Social facilitation in action: A behavioral intervention therapy for individuals with autism, Asperger's Syndrome and other related syndromes*. Northridge, CA: Yellen.

Lewy, A., & Dawson, G. (1992). Social stimulation and joint attention in young autistic children. *Journal of Abnormal Child Psychology, 20*, 555–566.

Mishna, F., & Muskat. B. (1998). Group therapy for boys with features of Asperger Syndrome and concurrent learning disabilities: finding a peer group. *Journal of Child and Adolescent Group Therapy, 8,* 97–114.

Prokoviev, F. (1998). Adapting the art therapy group for children. In S. Skaife, & H. Huet (eds.), *Art psychotherapy in groups: Between pictures and words* (pp. 44–68). London: Routledge.

Tiegerman, E., & Primavera, L. (1984). Imitating the autistic child: Facilitating communicative gaze behavior. *Journal of Autism and Developmental Disorders, 14,* 27–38.

Trevarthen, C., Aiken, K., Papoudi, D., & Robarts, J. (1998). *Children with autism: Diagnosis and intervention to meet their needs* (2nd ed.). London: Jessica Kingsley.

# ☐ Suggested Readings

Autism Society of America, http://www.autism-society.org.

Gray, C. (1994). *Comic book conversations.* Arlington, VA: Future Horizons.

Mundy, P., Sigman, M., Ungerer, J., & Sherman, T. (1986). Defining the social deficits of autism: The contribution of non-verbal communication measures. *Journal of Child Psychology and Psychiatry, 27,* 657–669.

Restall, G., & Magill-Evans, J. (1994). Play and preschool children with autism. *American Journal of Occupational Therapy, 48,* 113–120.

Sigman, M., & Capps. L.(1997). *Children with autism: A developmental perspective.* Cambridge, MA: Harvard University Press.

Wolfberg, P. (1999). *Play and imagination in children with autism.* New York: Teachers College Press.

Aimee Loth Rozum

# Integrating the Language of Art into a Creative Cognitive-Behavioral Program with Behavior-Disordered Children*

More and more children, the majority of them boys between the ages of six and twelve, are being referred to mental health clinics for being out-of-control, hard-to-handle, and unable to follow directions, when parents and schools complain of poor attention levels, distracting behaviors, problems with peers, low self-esteem, and poor performance. These children usually have a long history of behavior problems and have been shuffled along in school without meeting the educational standards for their grade level, often with a reputation as a problem child. By the time the ordinary support systems are exhausted, these children have failed academically and socially for many years. The

---

*The term behavior-disordered is used here to include children diagnosed with attention deficit/hyperactivity disorder, oppositional defiant disorder, and children with poor social skills that are linked to depression, anger management, and socioeconomic stressors.

I would like to recognize the clinicians that developed this group including Rita Coufal MFT, ATR, Kasia Daum MFT, ATR, Paul Garcia, LCSW, and Heather Thibodeau, LCSW.

label of failure has been internalized, which results in very low self-esteem, compounded by compensatory aggressive, self-destructive impulses. These boys and girls arrive at a clinic with a multitude of problems and burdens.

How to treat these children has become a topic of growing concern in the academic and mental health communities. A primary goal is the abatement of negative behaviors that prevent the child from achieving success in the social, academic, and interpersonal spheres. However, many strictly behavioral programs do not give voice to the child's experiences, which are the motivating factor behind the behaviors. The challenge is to devise a model that teaches these children new behaviors and addresses the traumatic experiences of their lives (Barkley, 1997).

Classic art psychotherapy has long been considered an introspective process, based in dynamic and analytic principals (Kramer, 1971; Naumberg, 1966). However, new thinking is expanding art therapy theory, blending social constructivist and narrative and cognitive approaches (Riley, 1999, Malchiodi, 1998). This more contemporary thinking leads to expanding the application and use of art with various therapeutic modalities. One such application is integrating art expressions with the highly directive, structured, and time-limited approaches of cognitive-behavioral therapy. This union may seem incompatible but, in fact, can be used with great success both for the group and the therapist. Parallels are found in the work of Damasio (1994) in his discussions of the need for both rational and emotive qualities of thinking as basic to the ability to make good decisions.

This chapter outlines a rationale and structure for group treatment that combines art (a language to share experience) and cognitive-behavioral interventions (tools to master problem behaviors) into a working group model.

## ☐ Group Treatment with Behavior-Disordered Children

Group treatment is a highly effective modality for children with behavior disorders. These behavior problems, which are traditionally addressed in individual treatment, may succeed in exploring emotional issues linked to disruptive or aggressive behavior. However individual work does not provide opportunities to practice self-regulating skills in a monitored environment or allow the therapist to see the behavior as it happens. Children with behavior disorders experience failure in their social roles. They are referred to treatment because they have persistent conflicts with their peers and authority figures; they cannot sit still in class, have problems staying focused, and, in general, have difficulties managing their everyday lives. These youths usually have no trouble sitting still and concentrating when they are by themselves or in individual sessions. Problems arise in social settings where the child has difficulties screening out distracting stimuli, or is highly reactive to perceived cues from authorities and peers, and often a combination of the two. Problems in social roles, regardless of the cause, are best treated in a social setting (i.e., group) (see Figure 5.1).

The appeal of group treatment is that all the identified problem behaviors can be attended to simultaneously. Group treatment provides an opportunity to respond to behavior as it happens. Participants develop skills in conflict resolution, communication techniques and the ability to self-monitor their own behavior. Group also helps the child experience, externalize, and examine behaviors and relationships (Rubin, 1984) Most important, a well-run group also affords the children an opportunity to succeed. By the third or fourth grade, children with behavior disorders have been yelled at, punished, and failed for three or four years. They are convinced that they are no good, that somehow their problems are due to laziness or some other

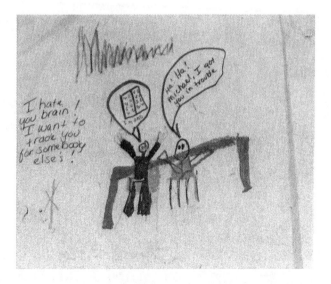

**FIGURE 5.1.** A 10-year-old boy, diagnosed with ADHD, feels that his brain has become his enemy. In his drawing, he says, "I hate my brain. I want to trade you for somebody else's." In a text balloon, his brain says, "Ha! Ha! I got you in trouble."

flaw that they cannot overcome. Over time, the adults in their lives become more and more frustrated and angry when they do not respond to whatever parenting and discipline methods the family prefers. After a period of time, rather than consider new techniques and seek support, the adults abdicate responsibility and blame the child. After this rejection, the children experience a new traumatic loss and may give up, which leads them to gravitate to peers with similar problems, low expectations, and hopelessness. The only people who are satisfied are the adults, who feel justified in their withdrawal, since the child couldn't be helped and was headed for the bad (see Figure 5.2).

## Goals and Expectations

A successful group will focus on the children's progress. In many cases, it may take weeks or months for a child to master the defeating anticipation of repeating past experiences of failure. Many sessions should be spent building up a child's confidence, reducing shame, and depersonalizing mistakes. In group, the clinician sees exactly what happens when the child makes a mistake, gets angry, and escalates. In a group of behavior-disordered children, this is a regular and expected occur-

**FIGURE 5.2.** A 12-year-old boy with poor impulse control is unable to stay on task.

rence. However, each episode can provide the child a chance to practice de-escalation and mastery of feelings.

## Symbolic Reparenting

The greatest challenge in conducting behavior groups is the task of reparenting each child. The therapist becomes the adult who shows the child that frustration can be tolerated, that mistakes can be made while self-regard remains intact, and that strong feelings can be modulated with out damaging effect. The therapist functions as the "accepting parent," supporting the child, providing structure, and rewarding the effort. The therapist must always be consistent and, with a co-leader, provides a secure parenting dyad, which allows the child a safe space to fail. In conjunction with safety, opportunities are offered which enable the child to then slowly succeed. A child may be too self-conscious or insecure to practice new skills alone or in the presence of authority figures such as parents and teachers. A peer group provides a secure space where it is more comfortable to try out new techniques as well as new-found confidence, and experience positive peer support (Rubin, 1984; Riley, 1999).

## ☐  Why Art Works

Running a successful group for this population is extremely challenging. It requires experience, willingness to experiment, and a particular personality and style of therapy. It also requires considerable planning of activities, taking into consideration the member's tolerance for stimulation, their individual attention spans, and the group's therapeutic goals. Most, if not all, children's groups incorporate some kind of art making because children are attracted to art activities. Given paper and markers, most youngsters will be occupied, for at least a short period of time. The challenge is to use the art in a meaningful way that is not merely an activity and provides some therapeutic benefit to the child and group as a whole.

## The Functions of Art Expressions

The use of art can serve many important functions for the child and the therapist. Careful observation and examination of the artwork can give the therapist a great deal of information about the child's basic functioning level. For instance, the art can provide useful information regarding the child's developmental level. When a few pieces have been collected, the therapist can check to see that the child is meeting expected developmental milestones, such as the use of baseline, perspective, and the characteristics of the human form (Lowenfeld, 1982). The art can then be evaluated on a regular basis for signs of change, both positive and negative. Often a therapist can see signs of stress that are not necessarily being verbalized. In one case, observing the art of a young male with a budding psychotic disorder, the therapists were able to have a sense when the youth was beginning to decompensate, even before other signs became evident. Interestingly, this happened most frequently with collage work.

"Josh" would create a benign-looking piece and then begin to describe it in a way that showed his increasingly loosening associations. In another instance, a young girl's artwork showed that she was significantly delayed for her age. She could not follow a simple directive, her work was repetitive, she could not utilize the art materials in a creative fashion, and she usually resorted to copying someone else's work. During sharing "Lisa" could not expand or describe her work. This illuminated what turned out to be a clear case of pervasive developmental disorder, and although she enjoyed the social aspects of group, she could not contribute to it, or, in fact, gain from the group. This was very difficult to explain to her mother, who felt that Lisa's enjoyment was justification enough for her to remain.

The therapists had to again explain the goals of the group, the distinction between behavior goals and socialization, and the importance of each member contributing to and challenging the others.

## Art Making: Personal Growth and Group Process

At a personal level, art making affords the child an opportunity to feel successful, contribute meaningfully to the group, and practice a safer mode of expression. Many children must overcome learned inhibitions about art making and the idea that things should look a certain way (Rubin, 1984). A belief that a drawing is not good unless it is photo realistic is instilled at an early age, the result being that the child's natural creative impulse is squashed early. Many sessions may need to be spent re-educating the group about art making and the importance of creative expression. Social pressures also come to bear, since children (especially boys) hate to fail in front of each other. A positive nonjudgmental atmosphere encourages peer interaction and positive feedback, and provides the facilitator a way to further support a child's self-esteem.

At a behavioral level, art making tests a child's ability to handle stimulation in the form of materials and group activities. A therapist can observe the child at individual and group tasks. Can the child work as a team member? Is he able to take turns? Can he participate in planning and discussion? Does he succeed better alone? Is his art affected by group involvement? Does he gain support from his peers or feel intimidated? Can the child manage free access to materials or does he become distracted and disruptive? Some children with attention problems become so distracted by a few markers that they can spend 20 minutes fiddling with the tops and never start the project.

Art making also works to build group cohesion, and becomes a way for a disparate group of children to find a common ground and build a distinct identity. My experience has shown that children become more sensitive to one another as a result of creating things together. As the group progresses, the members become aware of the characteristics of each other's art style and come to support each other. In one instance, a boy had a hard time making animals, yet loved including them in his art. A fellow member noticed this and gave him encouragement as well as technical support. In this way two youngsters, from very different backgrounds, came together and formed a special bond. Likewise, the art making gave members opportunities to be generous with one another by sharing materials and ideas.

## ☐ Growth, Development, and Containment

In group there are always two processes going on: The child grows and changes both as an individual and as a group member, and these can often develop simultaneously. Individuals utilize the resources in the art and each other to build relationships and solve conflicts. The art gives them opportunities to practice problem solving and talking about their feelings. Because a difficult topic can be expressed nonverbally and then with the help of the staff and other members, the child can begin to practice finding words to give voice to the problem (Smitherman-Brown & Church, 1996).

Along with problem solving and bonding, art making acts as a container. Behavior-disordered children are often very aggressive and volatile, and can carry a great deal of anxious energy with them. It is inevitable that this will be released in the artwork. This release can serve a positive or negative function and the therapist should be aware

**FIGURE 5.3.** A problem-solving drawing: Dad is angry with son for demanding money; Mom says, "No! No!"; Son tries to find a better way to ask parents; Son changes his approach and says, "Thanks for the five dollars."

**FIGURE 5.4.** A boy dealing with his feelings of abandonment. (A) Stepfather, mother, and two brothers; (B) Asks his married brother for attention, "Don't you care about me anymore?" But his brother rejects him by supporting his wife who says, "Leave me alone!" (C) Biological father, stepfather, and mother. (D) Stepfather and mother drawn together while the boy stands alone, "I'm all alone. I have no one to be with."

of and prepared for both. The making of imagery can be a positive and harmless outlet for pent-up aggression if the child's basic integration is not threatened by it. One way to tell if the release of emotion is healthy is the general feeling of relief that follows the exercise. The youngster will feel better having let loose a little, or shared something frightening or powerful. It becomes dangerous if there are signs of disorganization or distress, indicating that important defenses might have been swept away following the release of feeling (Kramer, 1993) (see Figures 5.3 and 5.4).

With Josh, the child with psychotic disorder, the art making had to be monitored closely. Efforts were made so that he felt safe and contained and the staff helped him to monitor his own responses. In fact, Josh became adept at recognizing when he was getting off track and the staff helped him get it together by slowing down and making changes to his artwork that made it feel more contained. Josh then could feel in better control of himself and his feelings.

## Necessity for Structure

In general the content of the children's art products should not be controlled. In an unstructured art group the children would be allowed to make whatever they wished. With a behavior-disorder group, specific directions are given and the children are expected to produce art within the guidelines. Although this may seem to hamper creativity, it is important to remember that the art making serves the goals of creativity and skill building. One way this is illustrated is an example from the latency-aged boys group. Jonas, a 10-year-old boy of above-average intelligence and good insight, would tend to perseverate on violent themes, make up stories, and create complicated artwork with violent content. It became clear that allowing him free expressive rein only exacerbated his behavior issues and so we limited his use of violence and helped him find alternative ways to express his ideas. He continued with his pictures of mass destruction, but was able to limit how he described them. In some cases we insisted that he create something with no violent themes. Like Josh, Jonas was able to recognize when he was getting "amped up" (his words) and that there was a connection between his artwork and his mood.

## Societal Issues

In today's culture, boys this age are exposed to a barrage of violent images from television, video games, and movies as well as on the streets and in the news. Therefore, it is to be expected that their art-work will reflect this influence. Also, as preadolescents they are very involved with the task of mastery, of themselves and their environ-ment. These themes show up in depictions of near-death battles involv-ing tanks, monsters, aliens from outer space, and heavy weaponry. The question always arises whether or not to try and curb this output of violent imagery. The therapists decided to make a general rule to restrict the excessive expression of violent images and themes, and to make an attempt to have the boys process the imagery, looking at both negatives and positives. They found that persistent use of violent imagery was more common in the boys with severe behavior prob-lems and ADHD symptomology. With these children, the use of vio-lent images and words was limited and tied to their point system. It was determined that allowing them free rein contributed to a further disintegration of behavior and overrode any defenses or behavior modi-fication techniques that they had learned.

## ☐ Cognitive-Behavioral Goals and Structure

The above discussion has focused on the uses of art with behavior-disordered children within the context of a group model. To further the exploration, the model will be explained from the base of cognitive-behavioral techniques and theory. The goals of the group are self-mastery and improved interpersonal problem solving. As mentioned in the introduction, the children are referred to treatment for impulse control, aggression, and social problems. A successful group will create a situation where the child has an opportunity to observe, master, and practice positive coping and interpersonal skills as the situations arise (Kendall & Braswell, 1993).

Cognitive therapy is an active, time-limited approach based on the theoretical rational that a child's affect and behavior are largely deter-mined by the way in which he or she structures the world. Cognitions are based on attitudes developed from previous experience (Beck, 1979). With behavior-disordered children, there are usually deeply held be-liefs that they cannot succeed and an expectation, that they will fail at even the simplest tasks. With cognitive and behavioral techniques the child learns to master problems and situations that were once consid-ered impossible. This is done by a two-fold approach: The child ob-serves positive problem-solving techniques and coping skills, practices them, re-evaluates and corrects negative thinking, and utilizes the support of positive modeling provided by staff and peers.

A focus is maintained on the here-and-now, to deal with the situation and feelings of the present moment. This helps the child stay focused and not slip into negative thinking and expectations based on past experiences.

## ☐ Program Structure

### The Referral Process

When schools and parents run out of options the children are often referred to a mental health clinic for medical evaluation and therapy. The vast majority of these children are latency-age boys. There are many reasons for this, but my experience has shown that many behaviors that are tolerated in smaller children become problematic as the child ages. In addition, as the child enters second and third grade, academic demands require greater sustained concentration and compliance. It is at this time that the behavior-disordered boys are referred. An exhaustive clinical intake should be made, including family history, and school and psychiatric records. If possible, psychological testing should be done to rule out learning disorders, mental retardation, psychosis, seizure disorders, and any other organic factor that may affect behavior. Once this intake and testing has been accomplished and a referral to group has been accepted, the caregiver can be brought in and educated about the group.

### Parent Interview

After a child is referred for group treatment, the first and most important step is the parent-family interview. The child's individual or family therapist should have discussed the general idea and goals of group treatment with the family; however, the meeting with the group team begins the treatment process. At this interview the group structure and goals are explained. Each section is outlined and the child and family hear about the importance of art making in the group process. At every opportunity an effort is made to remove art making from the realm of crafts or fine art. Art expressions are presented as a valid way for the child to practice social skills and appropriate articulation of feelings. Punctuality and regular attendance are stressed to both parent and child. The parents are asked to speak on any special concerns, as well as talk about their child's strengths. At this time the parent is given a schedule for monthly meetings with the team to discuss progress.

Consistency is stressed. If a child misses group more than twice, even with a call, a parent meeting will be called to discuss the absence. In addition, there is a 15-minute grace period from the start of the group, and anyone coming later than that is not allowed to participate. It seems cruel to turn a child away, especially since he relies on a parent for transportation, but once turned away, it rarely happens again. Parents and child understand that this is a firm limit. Also, it reinforces the other families' efforts to be prompt. The child becomes aware of the expectation that the parent, as well as the child, will be involved in the group.

## Group Schedule

The group outlined here has been in existence for over 10 years. It began with three staff and nine children, and eventually became two staff with no more than five children. The staff has always consisted of at least one art therapist and a clinical social worker. This combination has worked well and protected the art as a focal part of the treatment planning. Despite pressures to increase the number of participants (and increase the billing) the group has remained limited to five members. Five members allow maximum staff interaction and assure that on any given day at least three members are present.

The group is ongoing and open-ended, with the average length of a members' stay being one year. As a child graduates, a new member is brought in. If possible, it is important to resist attempts to limit group treatment time. Children with this constellation of problems have developed them over a long period of time, and the issues are not resolved overnight. A break-in period of two or three months can be expected, as the child learns the expectations and culture of the group. This leaves the remaining seven or eight months to learn and integrate new skills and esteem.

The group runs once a week, after school, for 90 minutes. It utilizes several different spaces in the clinic, allowing the participants to practice skills similar to those needed in school, such as moving through public spaces, sitting down and getting up from tables, and waiting in line. Group starts in a community room, moves to an open area for a snack, then moves through the clinic to the outdoor sports area, back to the open area for a cool-down period, to the art room, and then back to the community room for scores. During these transitions, members practice walking in line, not being distracting or distracted, maintaining behavior in public, and holding doors. This structure, although it takes up more room space, is very important since it allows the group to attend to many basic social skills.

### Group Schedule

| | |
|---|---|
| 3:00–3:30 | Staff meets to plan group, set up snack and art. |
| 3:15–3:30 | Members begin to arrive. Informal interaction time. |
| 3:30–3:45 | First community meeting. |
| | a. Staff announcements |
| | b. Check-in and share |
| | c. Set goals |
| 3:45–3:55 | Snack. |
| 3:55–4:10 | Sports (basketball, handball, etc., depending on space). |
| 4:10–4:20 | Cool down. |
| 4:25–4:45 | Art. |
| 4:45–5:00 | Scores and dismissal. |

(Another version of the schedule allows for more involved arts or activities programming from 4:00–4:45. This works well with extended art or drama projects.)

## The Therapist

Most students in a clinical training program are given some instruction in conducting groups. They are seldom given specialized training in behavioral techniques or cognitive models. The remainder of training is sometimes hands on but not always, with a more senior clinician. A beginning therapist learns by the sink-or-swim method and quickly discovers if he or she likes running groups or not. He or she might be more inclined to have a positive experience if they were educated in ways to control and structure a group of implosive and disordered children. A skilled and successful group therapist must be creative, interested in using art as a means of communication, comfortable with the unexpected, able to set firm limits, and in the case of children's groups, comfortable with the role of leader.

## Challenges

Behavior-disordered children can be, and are, very provoking. They challenge requests, refuse consequences, and are very sensitive to perceived criticism. It is the facilitator's role to help the child learn to contain feelings, to express them appropriately, and to accept adult authority. This requires the facilitator to be completely consistent at all times and confident in the leadership role. Even more important, the facilitator who expects respect must in turn be respectful of the child. Children who consistently experience powerlessness will often respond by exerting any kind of power, whenever possible. Because they do

**FIGURE 5.5.** Two group members create a termination drawing for the departing therapist. (A) Creator shows a supportive family and high intelligence; (B) Creator has great difficulty focusing; his best effort is to color each letter as a representation of the five members of the "grope."

not feel successful in traditional areas, they often become expert at sensing hesitation or uncertainty in adults, using it to their advantage. This leads to challenges and confrontations and the more flustered or angry the adult becomes, the more power the child feels, even through the results are ultimately negative. These behaviors can make group work frustrating and unrewarding. As a result, many clinicians will not work with this population.

In behavior groups the therapeutic use of modeling is paramount. A new child in the group watches the behaviors and reactions of peers and staff. The therapist serves as an active model and demonstrates the processes used in successful problem solving. There are two types of modeling, *mastery* and *coping* (Kendall & Braswell, 1993). The mastery model displays rapid and correct performance without difficulty or frustration. A child seeing this model can become easily discouraged. The coping model is more effective, where the therapist models how to cope with and solve problems. The therapist uses the same formula taught to the children and they witness using it to solve conflicts, respond to challenges, and so on. The therapist also encourages the group as a whole to model to one another, which is less threatening and makes the work seem possible in the eyes of the child who is struggling.

Power struggles are a common occurrence in group work, with both positive and negative outcomes. With behavior-disordered children the goal is always to help the child navigate such situations. In this instance the art becomes a powerful ally for the therapist. The use of art can work as a bridge between the child and the therapist, as well as the child and the group. In behavioral groups the facilitator rarely has a chance to step from the leader role and it is here that the use of art can be seen as a mediator. The therapist, in providing materials, offers something special and removed from the usual routine and expectation. The art materials offer the child a new way to express relationship with him or herself and the world around them. Because of this, the art therapist can never truly be a neutral figure or a blank screen. The therapist becomes a crucial component in a path of discovery and healing, and through attentive and respective attention to the art provides the child with an experience of being deeply understood. In this way, the person of the therapist, in conjunction with the art materials, becomes an important therapeutic tool (Kramer, 1993).

The art can also help build a connection to a difficult child. For instance the group had a particularly aggravating member named Ezra. He was very bright, but was burdened with a speech defect, which was much more pronounced when with his peers. He had poor social skills and severe attention problems. He was also almost perversely concrete in his approach to life. He was forever catching the staff in small inconsistencies, pointing out to his peers the smallest missed detail in their description of a movie or video game, and in general being very annoying. He was a hard child to like and, when he was having problems with behavior, I often found myself less patient than with the others and fought an occasional impulse to be punishing or demeaning to him. The team struggled with Ezra and spent a great deal of time discussing him and the challenge he represented. We struggled to overcome feelings of dislike and annoyance. It was not until we paid more attention to his art that we could begin to understand him.

Ezra's art, unlike his presentation as an intelligent and highly verbal child, was very impoverished. He rarely used more than one color and never depicted any organic life—there were no plants or flowers or sunshine, and the only animals or people he ever drew were being torn apart in battles with monsters or aliens. Even these drawings took him a great deal of effort; it seemed impossible for him to settle down to work. He would waste time making comments about others' work or fiddling around with the materials. We could only allow him one or two markers at a time, and even this did not help him to focus. He covered up his difficulties by adopting an attitude of defiance and nonchalance about the work. He acted like he hated doing art and didn't care. He often belittled his peers.

Ezra's physical presentation was at odds with the self he showed through his art. His work showed no swagger or virtuosity. Instead, it indicated a little boy whose inner world was swirling with aggression, violence, and helplessness. His parents and teachers had expectations of him that far exceeded his abilities, and his peers ignored him or made fun of him. In his art we could see a small boy in battle with terrible, overpowering forces, alone in a barren landscape. Seeing him this way made us more sensitive to him and helped us with our countertransference. Had we not had the benefit of the art, we would not been able to see the small child inside the annoying nine-year-old.

## ☐ How to Use Art in Behavioral Groups

### Difficulties

A major challenge for the use of art is time. There rarely seems to be enough time, even if the group is dedicated to art therapy, let alone if a therapist is attempting to coordinate art time with other activities such as sports or games. If the team decides that art and imagery will be used, then a commitment must be made when planning to allow adequate time for creative work as well as time to process. A rushed art section does nothing but reinforce the notion that the work is unimportant. These children are able to process their art expression in very meaningful ways. Because many of them have difficulties with verbal skills, the therapist can again play an important role, leading the child through the exploration. Time is needed to help the child talk about what was made and also for others to make comments or share similar experiences.

## Successful Planning

The following issues must be taken into consideration when planning art directives: number and composition of group, tolerance for media, the setting, therapeutic goals, and time.

As mentioned earlier, a behavioral group should not have more than five members with no less than two staff. When thinking of an art task, consideration must be made for how many children are present and how contained they are. Due to the low self-regard that usually attends behavior disorders, it is important that the child be given as much opportunity to succeed as possible. This is not to say that a therapist must make sure a child never experiences failure. However, children with ADHD and oppositional defiant disorders fail repeatedly, usually by their own hand (being disruptive, missing directions and cues, etc). They will also fail at their attempts at art making, usually from these very same behaviors, which can prevent them from accomplishing the task entirely. So when a directive is designed, the children must be considered and the most impaired child is catered to, since the more creative and contained child can make good work from any material.

Following closely on the consideration of group composition is the consideration of media. Therapists who use art should be coached in their understanding of media. Many therapists limit the materials used to markers or crayons, due to a lack of training and a lack of comfort with art making itself. In general, I try to avoid too much use of school-associated art materials such as markers, because I find that children tend to be more stereotypical and less creative when using them. However, a benefit of markers is that they are a firm media. They do not run or smear and they produce clean, even lines. With some children, particularly those with severe behavior or attention problems, it is best to start off with such an easily controlled medium. The therapist can offer one or two markers at a time, offering more as the child can manage them. The softer media, such as chalk, pastels, and paint, require more self-control to use. There is a difference between the use of materials with a general art therapy group and with a behavior disorders group. In a regular, unstructured group, part of the process would include seeing how the child uses the materials, and if a child became over-stimulated by something it would be part of the process. However, with a behavior group the goal is to teach control and mastery using very small steps. Materials such as pastels and paint are introduced slowly as the therapist sees that the child can handle them and will not decompensate or become over-stimulated.

## Caveat

A common mistake and one that I have made myself, is to focus to much on structuring the environment to control behavior that the art sessions become rigid and uncreative. For months I resisted using anything messy out of the fear that the boys would become so engrossed in the tactile stimulation that they would not be able to focus and things would dissolve into a free-for-all. Finally, I decided to let them make masks using plaster strips. I planned well ahead to control the process and began with much trepidation. I was rewarded by being proven completely wrong. The boys found the process of applying the strips to each other fascinating, and more surprising, were very soothed by the sensation of having their faces enclosed in the cool plaster. The most hyperactive and reactive child in the group relaxed as if he were at a spa. They were highly motivated to return the next week and decorate their works, and made revealing and beautiful representations of themselves.

I would not recommend a project like this with a new group or a new therapist. Part of the success was due to the fact that the group was well aquainted with each other and the program, so the external controls were in place. Once a group is established, it is fun to see what they can do, and more stimulating for the staff as well as the youths. The goal should always be to encourage expansion and mastery of the self and the materials. This inquiry requires work from both the child and the therapist.

## Environment

A major challenge to using art is having access to an appropriate space. Ideally, there should be a table large enough to accommodate five children and two staff with elbow room, storage space for material and art, and a sink for clean up. Most staff will find some combination of the above, some much less. The one item that is not negotiable is the table. Space is needed for the art making and a group table promotes the practice of community skills such as sharing space. In some circumstances the floor can be used, but only in an emergency or as a special treat as a release from the more confining space of table and chair. As well as promoting a group situation, a large table affords opportunities for larger and more creative projects.

Art materials should be kept from view to lower distraction, and only those to be used set on the table. If storage is available, materials can be brought out as needed, otherwise, a carrier or basket can be kept next to the leader's chair. It is best to give each child a set amount of materials with the instruction that they may ask for more or trade with other members. The conservation of materials serves the following purposes:

- It lessens the chance that materials will be abused.
- It lowers stimulation so that a very distractible child has a better chance of concentrating, and the exchange of materials with staff and peers keeps the group involved with one another, rather than each member working in a separate space.
- Lastly and perhaps most important, when art materials are shared the children can experience a sense of nurturing each other, experiencing pleasure and sharing in the positive outlet of feelings.

Any person who has run a group knows the feelings evoked by the question, "What should we do today?" An experienced art therapist can create directives on the spot based on the needs of the client at that moment. While this is my preferred approach, it is a mistake for behavior groups. Preparation and planning of directives in line with therapeutic goals is a must. Creative tasks planned at the last moment often have that unprepared feel. An exception is when the staff has access to a well-stocked supply cabinet from which to gather materials. Most therapists will be transporting materials to and from the group room, and so will have to plan ahead.

The planning of directives is not a science, but it does become easier with experience. For the beginning it is best to prepare a file of directives and make certain that the materials are available in advance. A month's work of projects can be researched and planned. Many art therapy textbooks will contain a chapter on group work and case studies showing directives. With experience, the therapist will be able to consider what the goal is for the group and design an appropriate directive. For instance, the "Architects" directive was born when I was thinking of ways to help the boys practice working collaboratively. In another instance, I wanted the group to talk about their backgrounds and neighborhoods and so the "Neighborhood" directive came about. (Each therapist has favorite directives, and I have included a list at the end of the chapter of those that have worked well for me with this population.)

The issue of time is an important one and an ongoing struggle in all therapeutic work. Occasionally a session stalls before the time is up, but usually it is the opposite, especially in group work. It seems that someone or some project is always cut short.

In behavioral groups the management of time is very important. One goal for the members is time management and planning, and in order to help the children do this, the staff must be organized and prompt. When the art is left to the end of the group there is the risk that things will be rushed and, besides the members being unskilled at handling pressure, it sends a message that their product and sharing in unimportant. Also, a rushed or distracted child runs a greater risk of decompensating or becoming more disorganized and experiencing failure.

In running a boys' group for three years, the one thing I have learned is to allow more time for art making and to plan directives more carefully so that they use the time allotted. A minimum of 30 minutes must be planned for more complicated projects. It is crucial to watch the clock so that each member is allowed five minutes to share their artwork (older children should be given more time). Often a child cannot finish the directive in time, but they must be given an opportunity to share about what they had planned to make. This reduces the experience of failure and the child is not punished for running out of time. Too often I have seen therapists say, "Well, you ran out of time," and the experience becomes more like losing points on a test for missed questions rather than an opportunity for growth, which is what the art is about.

When a directive is given, announce how much time the group will have, encourage advance planning before pen goes to paper, and then give regular prompts so no one is surprised (see Figure 5.5).

## ☐ Conclusion

Behavioral groups are challenging and fun for both the members and the staff. Combining behavioral techniques that help a child manage behavior with art interventions that are designed to attend to communication skills and positive expression of feelings, attends to the whole child. This kind of group is more pleasing and rewarding for the therapists because it provides a meeting place for two very different therapeutic approaches, which can be integrated with great success. I consider art intervention a sort of "secret weapon" in a mental health climate. It is a creative tool that counteracts other groups that are focused entirely on the elimination of unacceptable behaviors in the shortest period of time, with no consideration for the past history or current interior landscape of the client. As an art therapist, I welcome my colleagues who are interested in introducing art into their practice, and encourage them to find good art therapy supervision to assure they are working safely and responsibly.

---

## Suggestions and Directives

### Hello
Trace members hands on the paper and decorate however they want. When finished, cut it out. Then share to say hello to the new person, and glue all the hands together on a large sheet of paper.

### Hello Collage
Have members pick two or three pictures out of things they like or want or are good at. Glue them on paper and decorate it. Share the pictures.

### Hello Card
Make a card to say hello to the new person. Members should say something about themselves and about group.

### Island
Tell members that their schools are sending them all to an island to do a science project about dolphins. They will be gone six months. They should decide what they need and draw it on the island.

### Neighborhood
Design and build a neighborhood. Decide what will be needed and draw or build it.

### Pass-Around Drawing

Each person gets a piece of paper and one colored pastel. Each person makes one mark and passes the paper to the next person, who makes another mark, and so on. When several turns have gone, call one last turn when the papers rotate back to their original owners. Share.

### Group Banner

Decide a name or theme for the group. Each person draws a contribution on a piece of paper and all the pieces are then glued to a banner.

### Group T-Shirts

Decide a name or a theme and then each person gets a t-shirt to decorate with that name/theme. These can be worn for group or sports, etc.

### Puppets

Each person makes a puppet of any character they want. Use socks or bags, or the heads can be molded from drying clay and then bodies added out of fabric. Each member can share about their puppet. They can then be used in role-plays or theatrical productions.

### Masks

Decorate a pre-formed mask or make masks from fast drying plaster strips and decorate. These can also be used for dramas and role-plays.

### Clay Animals

Make four animals out of clay. Now make a place for them to live, using a box.

### Tissue Paintings

Using tissue, have each person make a painting of a place they would like to be. (You will have to show the children how to put the tissue on the paper using a thin mixture of glue and water.)

### Architect

Spilt up the group into one group of two and the remaining together. The larger group is a team of architects, hired by the two people (smaller group) to design their house. Use a large piece of paper for the blueprint, and some pencils. (Staff will need to help with organization.)

**Animal Kingdom**
Each member makes one animal and then the group gathers to make an environment.

**Goodbye Poster**
Each person is given a small sheet of paper cut so that when all pieces are joined, they will fit on to a larger piece. Each member is asked to make a goodbye picture for the graduating member. When finished, they are shared and glued on to the larger piece, making a poster for the departing child. The graduating child works on a single drawing, which is left for the group and displayed with the pictures of past graduates.

# Materials List

The following is a basic list of materials:

Colored pencils
Washable markers in various sizes
Oil pastels
Oil infused clay (does not dry)
Air drying clay
Chalk pastels
Paint daubers
Tempera/Acrylics
Watercolors
Craft sticks, plain and colored
Collage folders
Paper in various sizes, colors and textures
Glue sticks
White school glue
Safety scissors
Pencils
Paper plates of various sizes for supplies and to work on
Boxes and containers for supplies and as environments
Paint brushes
Wipes and paper towels
Fun supplies to expand directives
Fabric scraps
Sequins, buttons, fake jewels
Pipe cleaners
Feathers
"Found" objects such as twigs, leaves, small stones

# ☐ References

Barkley, R. (1997). *ADHA and the nature of self-control.* New York: Guilford Press.

Beck, A. T. (1979). *Cognitive therapy and the emotional disorders.* Middelsex, England: Penguin.

Damasio, A. (1994). *Descartes' error: Emotion, reason, and the human brain.* New York: Avon. Books, Inc.

Kendall, P., & Braswell, L. (1993). *Cognitive behavioral therapy for impulsive children.* New York: Guilford Press..

Kramer, E. (1971). *Art as therapy with children.* New York: Schocken Books.

Kramer, E. (1993). *Art as therapy with children* (2nd ed.). Chicago: Magnolia Street.

Malchiodi, C. (1998). *Understanding children's drawings.* New York: Guilford Press.

Naumberg, M. (1966). *Dynamically oriented art therapy: Its principles and practice.* New York: Prune and Statton.

Riley, S. (1999) *Contemporary art therapy with adolescents.* London: Jessica Kingsley.

Rubin, J. (1984). *Child art therapy* (2nd ed.). New York: VanNostrand Reinhold.

Smitheson-Brown, V., & Church, R. (1996). Mandala drawing: Facilitating growth in children with A.D.D or A,D.H,D. *Art Therapy, 13,* 252–260.

# ☐ Suggested Readings

Beck, A., Rush, John, A., Shaw, B., & Emery, G. (1997). *Cognitive therapy of depression.* New York: Guilford Press.

Epperson, J., & Valum, J. L. (1992). The effects of stimulant medication on the art products of ADHD children. *Art Therapy, 9,* 35–41.

Lowenfeld, V. (1987). *Creative and mental growth* (8th ed.). New York: Macmillian.

Naumberg, M. (1987). *Dynamically oriented art therapy: Its principals and practice.* Chicago: Magnolia Street.

# A Condensed Guide to Creating an Adolescent Group: Art Tasks that Address Developmental Interests and the Changing Role of Adolescent Therapy

At one period of time during the 1970s and 1980s, groups were the preferred treatment mode for adolescent youth. Mental health money was available and outpatient clinics had success when they added an active, expressive form of therapy to their services for teens. Art therapy was a group activity that worked therapeutically and kept the adolescents returning to group. As an art therapist, I had the pleasure of leading groups with difficult children, but ones who were not so damaged as to be extremely hard to reach. For the last decade and into the new millennium the picture has changed. Mental health has reduced services to the adolescent who is having family and adjustment problems and focused only on the most recalcitrant group of teenagers. Adolescent group is a growing service, growing in residential centers, youth reclamation camps, hospital day treatment, and juvenile incarceration centers. Outpatient clients have limited their services to adolescents by providing small groups in foster homes and attempting to bring in the families to ensure a support system. The gang culture has replaced the therapeutic peer group with a more structured, powerful, and restrictive group that has, in many cases, also replaced the family.

Many adults wonder if the youthful population is becoming so attuned to violence, drugs, and rebellion against society, that as a society a real crisis is brewing? Or, are the youthful members of society demonstrating the rent in the family fabric that has been coming into being for many years? Therapists have no clear answers, but they do have a most difficult treatment challenge that calls for an approach that can break through the stone-like defenses of the soon-to-be adults.

There are many therapy jobs with these youths for skilled group leaders, particularly those who are creative, but there are good reasons why these jobs remain unfilled. This section will explore the challenge of serving these adolescents, the value of making interventions at this age, and some approaches that have been more successful than others.

# ☐ An Instant Survey of Adolescent Development

The drive toward individuation is primary in the changing development patterns of puberty. Achieving some notion of "Who am I?" is the constant quest and narcissistic focus for the years between childhood and adulthood. It is an attempt to define when childhood stops and adulthood begins, a rite of passage that must be experienced by each man or woman in their own manner. How to achieve this passage is the primary dilemma. With the neglected child who has unmonitored television as their "significant other and caretaker," and street culture as their principal source of exposure to values, adulthood comes early—an adulthood that misses appropriate opportunities to solve many areas of the developmental stages that makes real adulthood a successful achievement.

To have any notion of the adolescent that is in treatment, therapists need an understanding of both the possible internal damages, and even more, the external stressors that have shaped the child. The adolescents of today (the ones in the mental health system) are often the products of their toxic environment. In the face of the discouraging background, the therapist must explore with adolescents how they have preserved their particular abilities and talents; their resiliency, and capacity to empathize—and most importantly, who are their role models and how do they envision their gender-defined roles. It is not helpful to dwell on hopelessness and depression, in spite of circum-

**FIGURE 6.1.** An early adolescent's rendition of himself as a powerful alien.

stances that elicit those feelings in the therapist. There must be faith in the resiliency of youth (see Figure 6.1).

How can therapists discover whether the teen is congruent in their internal and external growth developmental processes? They could be working with a teen who looks like a fully developed woman of 18 and find an underdeveloped 13-year-old inside. Knowing at what age to gauge the therapeutic conversation is vital knowledge, and is not going to be discovered in the usual talk-therapy ways. This is only one example of the discontinuity of development that will be a major concern throughout treatment.

Drawings that project the maturation of the inner child will be of the greatest help to the therapist to assess the "real" boy or girl sitting in the group session. Just ask a teenager about how others perceive them and how they perceive themselves, and take a clue from there. A suggestion that has to do with years and numbers are acceptable to the teen since it does not suggest pathology. A question that also leads to a fairly fail-safe response is, "Draw how old your parents see you, and how old you would like to be seen?" This leads to discussions of being infantalized and being parentified. Many households, particularly with a single parent or working mother, depend on the older children to parent the younger siblings. The conflict comes when parenting and infantilization are both operating at the same time. The parents expect that when they are home a certain set of rules apply, although there are usually a different set for when they are out. "When I am away be responsible, when I am home do what I say." This form of mixed message is not unusual. The adolescent can clearly represent these contradictory positions and find relief in doing so. Other home-society-peer group conflictual messages are the subject matters to which teens respond. The newspaper is a great text to shape the group to their concerns and realities.

## ☐  Developmental Strengths to Engage

Adolescence is a developmental process that brings diverse traits to the forefront: intellectualization as a defense, a narcissistic focus, resistance to adult rules, a spurt of high creativity, and the ability to think both concretely and abstractly. For the therapist to know this only on an intellectual level is not useful unless these traits can be used to reach the client. With the modality of art as the language of group, some of these developmental stages can be integrated into a framework for art expressions and dialogue. For example, it is important to bear in mind that the dominant view of the world focuses mainly on the self, a strong narcissistic filter of any event is related primarily to how it appears to affect them personally. Knowing this trait can make life easier when suggesting an art task. "How do *you* view this event?" "How do *you* believe rules should be set?' "Represent *your* solution to these _____ ."

Using the developmental trait of narcissism to reach the adolescent, and then being open to taking their statements seriously, is helpful for both youth and therapist. Going through the psychological door of the adolescents' struggle to find their own identity must be done with finesse, and the visual statement is often the most graceful way to achieve this goal.

Creating an art statement is a projection of self, it is safe, it can be justified intellectually, it is not understood by an adult unless explained, and that explanation is controlled by the adolescent. Art expressions "fit" the teen process.

## ☐ Where Do We Find Our Adolescent Groups?

Without addressing the issue of the environment of the groups and exploring the context of treatment, we cannot proceed to match art language to the present-day teen. With the exception of a few private practice groups that have survived through the talents of their leaders, and the reparative children's groups in special programs, most of the adolescent groups are held in settings where group therapy is a mandated part of the institution or the probation department. Some residential centers make art therapy groups a part of their schedules, as do therapeutic schools and drug rehabilitation programs. There is more or less capable attention given to the forming of the groups, and the necessary pre-group screening is essential. Juvenile court-ordered groups are even less concerned with therapeutic change and are focused only on behavioral adjustments. The one place that disadvantaged youths can find groups where they have a choice to attend, and do, is in domestic violence shelters and walk-in adolescent centers for the homeless (Malchiodi, 1990).

These facts are important because the discussion of using the language of art in adolescent group needs to be based on the reality of the present-day market. (For a larger view of adolescent group refer to Riley's *Contemporary Art Therapy with Adolescents,* 1999). Too often the youngest therapist in the field finds their first job or training with court-ordered teens. The youths may not actually be in jail, but their mandated treatment feels the same to them. The rate of burnout and depression in therapists in these settings is dramatic. Therefore, the following plans will attempt to address the real world of the mental health services in the urban areas of the United States.

## ☐ Groups for Adolescent Youths: Some Beginning Considerations

Psychological theories aside, it makes no sense to mix older teens with younger teens, and as already noted, premature adolescence may start

even as early as 10 or 11 years of age. In spite of their precocious entrée into this stage, these children are not dealing with the same issues of the fully sexualized and experienced adolescent. The therapist must make every effort to screen the members of a group, at least for chronological age. Ideally there should be three levels: preadolescents (about 12 years of age), midadolescents (13–16), and older teens (17 and up). In due time the immature or developmentally delayed teen will become obvious and adjustments will need to be made, but the therapist must start with some frame.

In addition, there should be as few members as possible in the group. Character-disordered, acting-out boys cannot be handled safely in a group larger than four or five, with two therapists. While this rule has been broken many times, little can be accomplished if there is no order or security in the room. Be sure that there are no dominant gang affiliations that would explode in the session, and try for same-sex groups to reduce sexual tension. Later, if the group members are socialized to therapy, these structures can be modified.

## Structure

For the first meeting a limited amount of media should be available. The notion of being able to make some marks on a page will probably be scoffed and denigrated. In spite of this bravado, often the real fear is incriminating oneself with a concrete product that can be used against them. The therapist must make very clear that the art is theirs to keep or leave, that there are no interpretations made or even considered, and the art tools are there to make therapy a little less toxic. To be convincing, the therapist must really believe this statement. Personal and biased interpretations will leak out if they are in the therapist's awareness. This is not hard to do when the adolescent is the master illusionist and the therapist's fantasy of what the drawing might mean is usually incorrect. What is on the page may have some meaning in their society, it may just be a stereotype image or, more likely, a horrendous product that is calculated to "pull our chains." Blood and gore everywhere and knives, guns, and dope challenge the therapist's empathy (see Figure 6.2).

The teenagers are given the paper and a few felt pens, pencils too if they ask. These familiar tools are comfortable and do not pose a threat. The request to draw or write anything they wish is so open-ended that it is hard to resist. The question inevitably will be asked, "Why are you having us draw?" The answer, "It is a way to spend our beginning time together and get acquainted. Therapy can come later."

Be content if the teen has put anything down on paper—the first round has been won. The visual communication has been introduced. Looking at these angry images, think about how painful it would be to have these visions and emotions dominating the thinking processes.

These wild drawings are often intensified in group, as each member tries to cap the other and be the "winner" of the "beat-the-therapist" contest. If there is some humor in accepting the art and really seeing it as a form of art, the teen will sense acceptance and be able to continue the group process the following week.

In a girls' group the introduction to art talking may be more difficult. Girls are more critical of their work and more sensitive to exposing weaknesses to the other members of the group. Asking for a magazine picture collage of, "What do girls your age find the most annoying?" may be a good start. It allows them to be critical, it asks a general (not personal) question, and gives space for them to make a statement without artistic investment. In their eyes, cutting out collage pictures is not a challenge to their abilities.

In both cases the therapist has an immediate base to begin to compare some traits of the teenagers in the group. The content will be less important than observations such as organization of the page, freedom of line, or liberty taken in modifying inventively the collage pictures—all clues to the individual traits of the adolescent. Clues are

**FIGURE 6.2.** Depiction of adolescent violence in, "Going to the Mall."

**FIGURE 6.3.** "An Island of Our Own," a drawing created by an adolescent group of girls.

all that you can expect with this population until some trust is formed, and that may take a long time (see Figure 6.3).

## Next Step

After several meetings, where the invitation to make a product is left open, as in the beginning, there is a shift in focus. In the past several sessions new media, or at least a broader color selection, has been introduced. Casually placing, for example, oil pastels, or a basket of plasticine balls, on the table is a subtle invitation to explore some expressive tools. If the group has shown some interest, the relationship is building, although it would be too early to expect this to be acknowledged.

Reading the background history of these teenagers one wonders if they have any trust left, seeing that so many adults have hurt them and abandoned them at every turn of their childhood. Knowing that recapturing the capacity for trust and attachment is more than a conscious decision, it is a struggle to revitalize a diminished neuronal path in the brain, gives therapists more patience and understanding. The encouraging new information is that neurons can regenerate, so there is some hope that additional paths of thinking and emotions can be created.

Recently, I was discussing the clients at a residential center and it appears that the population has become so very seriously damaged that sociopathic youths are sharing rooms with autistic boys or girls. The capacity of these adolescents to relearn basic trust is bound to take a prolonged period. Fortunately, there are still some places where a teenaged person can remain for a fairly long period of time. Treatment should be based on more than psychological theory; the time has come to incorporate psychological and neurological information into treatment approaches. In addition, the search for pathology and the language of pathology should be discarded in favor of a realistic assessment of external stressors.

## Moving On

In the next stage of group process the members are often willing to start making a project. Building with wooden sticks and glue guns and making alien worlds of cardboard and other construction material can catch the imagination of many of the adolescents. The older youths may make very complicated "machines," or they may prefer to begin a cartoon script, or some ongoing project of their own. The girls may turn to fashion design and other creative projects that reflect their interests. The gender-defined roles in the adolescent community remain archaic. Although the girls are often very tough and physical, they still see themselves through the eyes of "their" men.

A very creative therapist, Sara Roemer, who was faced with a weekend assignment to provide art therapy to unruly boys in a residential center, did a remarkable project. She provided cardboard cartons, which were placed one above the other and glued together, into a tower. These were named totems. Several age levels were invited to make their own totem poles by painting each box with a symbol (or something they invented). The result was a competition between groups to make the most amazing totem. The results were gratifying. Groups were formed that worked together; the groups were proud of their totem poles; they personalized them; and they identified with them. Boys that had shied away from the art therapy group became involved and considered joining a group. The artwork remained in the hall for a long time and the agency used them for public relations. What started as a project from desperation, resulted in an experience that had many positive reverberations.

Perhaps the reader is wondering where is the therapy in all of this? The therapy is through the fact that the adolescent is present—that the resistance is minimal and they are offered the opportunity to solve problems by making art, which is a positive experience in contrast to their defeats and lack of problem solving in society. There is a bridge between the activities in one area of life that can be translated into other spheres of living. Art is a healing activity, and knowing that gives therapists courage to be inventive themselves and encourage creativity without concern for a more traditional treatment plan. There is a time for art as therapy; there is a time for art as an illustration of problematic issues. The adolescent will make that transition when they are ready.

## Transitions

During this phase of treatment the therapist will be rewarded if a variety of media are brought to group. Different objects, textures, shapes, and colors appeal to different members. As the group becomes involved in their tasks, they are open to discussing issues that are of value to them. Asking questions around the concept of "respect" is a productive move. Many of the adolescents in Los Angeles are of minority cultures, and their hierarchies have structures and rituals that an outsider cannot assume to know. The therapist could ask, "Could you show me (illustrate) what respect means to you? For my generation I think it was not the same." "If a person loses respect, is it possible to regain it?" "How does a boy's (or girl's) life change with or without respect?" "What advantages do you have if you have respect? What do you lose if it is gone?" "Do you think that your parents have the same notion of respect as you and your friends have?" "Does coming to therapy add or detract from your respect status?"

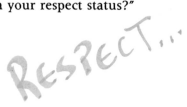

**FIGURE 6.4.** The "Island" where six participants in an adolescent group could have had anything they wanted.

An entire group can be spent on each of these questions. Members will compare their drawings, and talk among themselves about this core issue. If there are youths of different cultures in the group, this can be the first opportunity to look at differences and sameness in belief systems. Often the primary message to many young men is a composite of their fathers' message (even if the man is long gone) and the current adolescent value standard. In one recent case, a 16-year-old believed that it was wrong to steal, but it was all right to receive stolen goods, "because you hadn't really done the stealing." This was a direct message from his father who was a fence. If he was a thief he lost respect; if he only received the goods, he retained respect. For the young man to reject the concept of stealing and fencing goods would be the same as rejecting his father. He had not been able to individuate sufficiently to keep the father and discard the behavior.

It is not easy to remain in a nonjudgmental place during these discussions. However, if the group presses for an answer it is essential that therapists share their own beliefs, explain why it seems to work, but do not impose it on the group. (Note that each member should have been informed of the legal limits before they enter group. If it is perceived that there is a threat to self or others, allow them be a part of the reporting. *Never* go behind their back.)

## Maintaining the Group

Adolescents who are traumatized from early childhood, or start out life with a deficit due to neglectful prenatal care, such as cocaine or alcohol addiction in uteri, often have short attention spans. To retain the group focus the therapist must find a variety of ways to sustain their interest. Alternating from art as therapy to art as activity is one way to focus on problems and then focus on creativity. Each way of using art expressions influences the other without having to make it a point. The youths will begin to see meaning in their creative art products and art in their problem solving illustrations. Adolescent group allows all forms of creativity to be useful and the therapist can cast aside preconceived notions of how the art is supposed to be used (see Figure 6.4).

Art tasks that provide a group project, such as a group drawing on one large paper, are a symbolic vehicle for group cohesion. Many of the approaches described in the first chapter are applicable to adolescent group, particularly after they have established a group persona. The most successful technique for adolescents is the suggestion by the therapist to look at both sides of a problem. This stage of life is filled with ambivalence, and therefore, the artwork should reflect that state. The pro and cons are always available to this age since that is their worldview. For example, "What messages from the adult world do you choose to keep? What messages do you reject?"

## "Marking-In"

If the therapist has a room that is used every week, a graffiti wall mural might be started on a wall of the room and left there. The wall becomes a sign-in place where just a quick symbol or personal mark indicates that the adolescent is in group. The wall is not discussed, the symbols are not interpreted, and the accumulation of marks from week to week are a presence in themselves. This mural attests to the permanence of the group, and the individuality of each member. The words are not censured, and the violent images are tolerated. It is a place where the teen can clear immediate feelings and never be criticized.

The therapist can use this wall mural as a gauge of the temper of the group. Some symbols may trigger anxiety, such as suicidal ideation; therefore the behavior of the group member can be monitored for safety. It is also an amazing experience to see the mural become more and more covered with marks that indicate that something is really going on in the therapy. The content may not be revealing, but the continuity is important.

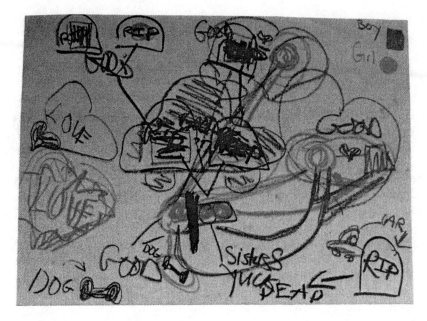

**FIGURE 6.5.** An adolescent boy draws the family "Genogram." He is the center, represented by a car and his relationships in the family are represented by "good" or "yuck." The lower right corner shows how his father died in a car accident.

## Gender-Defined Roles

Art expressions about women's roles and men's roles will keep the group's attention, as well as questions about sex, responsibility for pregnancies, abortion, and many other social dilemmas. With these over-exposed youths, the subject matter can be as open and questioning as the therapist is comfortable with. Do not underestimate the ability of even the most laid back teenager to be critical of the social system and of adult customs. At times they even can reflect on their own culture.

All of these issues are the subjects of the art directives that a leader may be seeking. It is counter productive to have directives that skirt the real-life issues of the clients. Art expressions use metaphorical communication; there will be plenty of opportunities to explore intra- and interpsychic difficulties that emerge from the personal world and concerns of the teenager. Teenagers can draw, and if they choose not to, they can use the collage box of pictures very well. Graffiti demonstrates the artistic inventiveness of the teen when their larger pieces are looked at. They may be slow to start, but rely on their creativity to become available (see Figure 6.5).

## Continuing or Terminating

The question of terminating a group is influenced by many factors. The primary consideration should be for the well being of the group members. Unfortunately, in the settings which have been the primary focus of this chapter, this decision may be made by administration, not the therapist. If the funding limits treatment, the group should have been structured along a brief therapy model (Cade & O'Hanlon, 1993). Short-term therapy is preferable for adolescents, since they move from stage to stage and the issues that are problematic change with their development. However, with severely damaged youths the treatment should last as long as possible. Often the residential centers will keep a group available for the length of time the child is in residence. For school-based groups the summer break is often the closing point. Whatever the circumstances, the closing of group should entail rituals.

One of the "truths" of therapy with adolescents is that "they will leave before you leave them." In spite of this tendency for the teen to re-experience abandonment (which often is a major distressor) when the therapist announces that group will close, the group should be encouraged to plan the last several weeks of being together.

It is useful to borrow from White and Epston's (1990) technique of sending a message to the next group that advises the new group how to handle their problems and project a more positive change in their life. This can be done by providing a large sheet of mural paper and having the group work together to send a message with words and pictures. In a group of angry, older adolescents the therapist may be discouraged to see that the group message is not encouraging. This reflects the youths' life experiences. However, if the group has had a sense of cohesion and community, the art expressions may be quite different.

Younger adolescents are more inclined to cooperate with this idea, and often their mural can be surprisingly wise. The greatest impact from group interactions is with the younger-age adolescent. Their internal processes are more in flux and they have suffered for a shorter duration. If the placement or family has made supportive changes, and the group has reinforced the youth's capabilities, the prognosis is guardedly optimistic. Working with the early adolescent group may be more chaotic, since there is a great deal of hyper behavior, but it is rewarding to see their receptivity and their eager use of any positive change in their lives.

Having discharged, in the mural or in other visual products, their (unsaid) disappointment that group is closing, it is appropriate to have each member draw or make a collage of an evaluation of the other members' positive qualities and any change they may have seen. There should be a "gift drawing" for each person from each member. Adolescents can be generous toward one another, and this is the time to direct their focus in this manner.

Every member will be gifted by a drawing from each of the other people in group, and the therapist may join in and contribute. These drawings are significant as a step toward saying goodbye and ending on a personal note. It is a very rare occasion that even the most hardened teen will openly destroy these gifts. Some youths have seen their therapist later in treatment and recalled the value they placed on the affirmation they received from their peers. In addition, it is always fascinating to find that there is almost complete recall of the images. The impact of the visual representation seems to remain available long after many of the other events have faded from memory. The power of a statement rendered visually has been observed many times. Art therapists use this knowledge to increase the efficiency of therapy and bring into the therapeutic relationship the personal illustrative language of the client.

When the last day of the group comes around, it is a difficult time. To let the group decide how to end it may not be very successful. For example, one time a boy brought in his father's pornographic movie; that was unacceptable. Another time the teens brought in music that was so vicious the clinic would have been horrified. The best solution may be food, but thought through carefully, not a child-like party. (It is amazing how the testing never stops.) Take orders and buy the preferred sodas, pretzels, popcorn, and other snacks. Do not be surprised if the orders are "oh, anything" to a laundry list of goodies, way out of budget. It was very clear that the parting could not be emotional, and that the adolescent shorthand for good bye was all that would happen.

When a difficult group has terminated the therapist may often feel sad. They may have a desire to see that these young people have a better chance in life, and question if the group had made a difference. No matter how challenging the members were during the group, there are always a few moments when the injured child slips out and is known. It is that child to which the therapist warms, and hopes that life will give the boy or girl a second chance.

I will end with this quote from a girl who joined our adolescent group at 13 years old. She is now 16 years older and I have the pleasure of keeping in touch with her now and again. She wrote this reflection at my request.

> I've just finished watching a tape of myself at 16 talking about some of my artwork I did in therapy. I truly believe if it were not for the art therapy process, I would not be who I am today.
>
> Group art therapy helped me because I was able to see my peers having similar problems and expressing them in different ways. Red and black colors, as well as arrows and brick walls were my signature drawings. Through group participation, I gained a different perspective of the use of colors and began to sporadically incorporate them into my drawings to tell myself there was a light at the end of the tunnel.
>
> Art was my vehicle of communication. Even though there were times my message wasn't getting across to my therapist, I was getting it out of me and my head. Once it was down on paper, it became easier to see my troubles weren't so scary and that knowledge allowed me to begin to open up verbally.

*Thank you, Kelly.*

## ☐ Summary

The preceding tone of this chapter has a major theme that is hard to hear through the noise of adolescent behavior. The core concept in adolescent work is the knowledge that multiple factors are in play as the child makes the transition to adult. One of the factors that the therapist can draw upon is the ability to create. If the opportunity is offered without interpretive strings attached, the teenager may well become involved in a task where the use of media and free expression leads the way to establishing a relationship. The therapist with media at hand is an adult who offers a gift. The choice of drawing over talking is not a problem for the adolescent, and drawing in group is even more acceptable, since it reflects a peer activity.

There are often questions from professionals about what art directive to ask the adolescent. Throughout this chapter adolescent concerns and stressors have been discussed—*these concerns become the directives.* Asking adolescents to externalize their concerns through a visual product is usually the only directive a therapist needs. At times with a younger group who are too active to settle down, it is helpful to create group projects. The suggestions should reflect the developmental age and the gender of the early-adolescent youth group.

Working with adolescent groups is not easy, and the therapist needs all the help that can be mustered. It is wise to read about basic adolescent development (Ponton, 1997) and art therapy with adolescents (Riley, 1999). There is new information about adolescent brain development and fresh neuro/psychological speculations. The more a therapist knows about this period of development the more suggestions for acceptable topics that may be the subject matter of group expressions can be offered.

Finally, hold on to a sense of humor, and the art products do help in this area. Children have such a remarkable ability to make visual statements that jolt, educate, and amuse, that the art product often saves the day. If the therapist is left with a stack of drawings from a non-verbal teen, be (somewhat) content that something has transpired in that therapeutic hour.

The language of art is an essential addition to adolescent group. At one extreme, the adolescent thinks the therapist is not a therapist because he or she allows free drawing, at the other extreme the teen recognizes that the art is helping. The letter from Kelly, quoted above, is testimony to the adolescent inner processing that therapists may suspect but never know for sure is going on. I have had enough years working with this population that I have faith in the process.

# ☐ References

Cade, B., & O'Hanlon, W. H. (1993). *A brief guide to brief therapy.* New York: Norton.

Malchiodi, C. (1990). *Breaking the silence: Art therapy with children from violent homes.* New York: Brunner/Mazel.

Ponton, L. E. (1997). *The romance of risk: Why teenagers do the things they do.* New York: Basic Books.

Riley, S. (1999). *Contemporary art therarpy with adolescents.* London: Jessica Kingsley.

White, M., & Epston, D. (1990). *Narrative means to therapeutic ends.* New York: Norton.

# ☐ Suggested Readings

Demasio, A. R. (1994). *Descartes' error. Emotion, reason, and the human brain.* New York: Avon Books.

Dickman, S. B., Dunn, J. E., & Wolf, A. W. (1996). The use of art therapy as a predictor of relapse in chemical dependency treatment. *Art Therapy, 13,* 232–237.

Emunah, R. (1990). Expression and expansion in adolescence: The significance of creative arts therapy. *Arts in Psychotherapy, 17,* 101–107.

Feen-Galligan, H. (1995). The use of art therapy in treatment programs to promote spiritual recovery from addiction. *Art Therapy, 12,* 46–50.

Freeman, J., Epston, D., & Lobovits, D. (1997). *Playful approaches to serious problems: Narrative therapy with children and their families.* New York: Norton.

Haesler, M. P. (1996). The absent father: Gender identity considerations for art therapists working with adolescent boys. *Art Therapy, 13,* 275–281.

Leader, E. (1991). Why adolescent group therapy? *Journal of Child and Adolescent Group Therapy, 1,* 81–93.

Malchiodi, C. (1998). *Understanding children's drawings.* New York: Guildford Press.

McNiff, S. (1981). *The arts and psychotherapy.* IL: Charles C. Thomas.

Minuchin, S. (1974). *Families and family therapy.* Cambridge, MA: Harvard University Press.

Osman, B. (1997). *Learning disabilities and ADHD: A family guide to living and learning together.* New York: Wiley.

Soo, E. (1986). *Training and supervision in child and adolescent group psychotherapy.* In A. Rister and I. A. Kraft (eds.), *Child group psychotherapy: Future tense.* Madison, CT: International University Press.

Sugar, M. (1997). Adolescents and disaster. In L. Flarety and H. A. Horowitz (eds.), *Annals of the American Society for Adolescent Psychiatry.* New York, NY: Analytic Press.

Vick, R. M. (1999). Utilizing prestructured art elements in brief group art therapy with adolescents. *Art Therapy, 16,* 68–77.

Walter, J. L., & Peller, J. E. (1992). *Becoming solution focused in brief therapy.* New York: Brunner/Mazel.

Worden, M. (1991). *Adolescent and their families.* New York: Hayworth Press.

# Working with the Elderly Population with a Serious Loss of Cognition: Visible Communication as a Mode of Memory Retrieval and Other Functions, Such as Self-Regulation and Social Intercourse

This chapter describes a day treatment program for elderly persons who are experiencing a loss of mental functioning, a condition that is named dementia. Some of the members of this therapeutic community that have an illness, Alzheimer's disease, have suffered strokes, are deeply depressed, or are just experiencing the extremes of normal aging. The activities and groups that are structured to counter the advances of memory loss and physical deterioration will be discussed, as well as the support groups for caretakers and spouses. The rationale for using art tasks will be defended by examining some of the neurobiological information available for laypersons. Information that suggests a holistic approach to treatment involving all the senses makes a positive difference for this population.

The groups using art therapeutically are deconstructed to help the reader understand the rationale for creating group activities along lines that parallel the loss of neurological processes. Recognizing the patterns of deterioration provides therapists with background material on which to create opportunities that encourage the opposite effect, stimulation versus passivity. The form that therapy takes when working with the elderly is tailored to meet their capacity to integrate information; it is a specialized form of therapy and the concept of insight and growth is not appropriate. Rather, the goal is to maintain and sustain the abilities that are functioning well and attempt to delay further deterioration as much as possible. Landgarten (1981) is very clear that, ". . . in-depth work on lifelong unresolved material is contraindicated for the aged. Issues of conflict, guilt, rage, separation and loss are dealt with to a therapeutic degree. However, deep investigation tends to activate anxiety and deepen depression" (p. 252). Jenson (1997) combines music, movement, and art in her treatment of Alzheimer's patients. She focuses on the client's strengths (i.e., emotional memory, primary sensory function, social skills, and procedural memory skills). She remarks that a sense of humor often remains lively. It is also a very helpful and caring mode to make connections with the elderly. Shore (1997) explores the notion of wisdom in the elderly, and gives examples where the struggle with the art process gave the client a parallel process to struggle with their personal issues of aging.

There are many activities discussed in this chapter that could be generalized for therapy groups serving persons with a variety of illnesses. Aging is normal, but some illnesses of aging are not. With the "graying" of America, it is time to create skills that will address this significant shift in needed mental health services.

## ☐ A Day in a Program for the Elderly with Dementia

Looking around the room filled with activity and movement, at first it is hard to tell that much of the interaction is between the staff and the client-members of this day treatment program rather than between the men and women in attendance. After a brief period of adjustment, the visitor can appreciate how interaction and conversation is modeled and encouraged: client → caretaker, client → staff, client ↔ client.

In this day program for elderly clients who are suffering from deterioration both mentally and physically, every hour of the day has been constructed to delay further onset of dementia and physical deterioration and forestall premature institutionalization. Each hour is a small triumph or a sad defeat.

A program such as this requires a dedicated staff that treats the members with respect and wisdom. There are many staff members who are trained in aiding elderly clients. There are also activity specialists who conduct hour-long multidiscipline group activities, such as movement, dance, word association, bingo, bridge, and studio art, and special entertainers who are not scheduled regularly. The social workers and psychotherapists see the clients either casually, on a one-to-one conversational basis, or assist group members to focus on an art project, a word retrieval exercise, a movement activity, or take a short walk with one or two people. The art therapists have a special role in creating small groups to foster friendship and social skills among the members or help a new member to integrate into the general environment. In addition, there are helpers who are either personal caretakers that come with their employer, or less skilled caretakers that do everything. The ratio of staff to elderly is three to one.

Therapists using art tasks are successful in achieving their goals of socialization, dealing with anxiety of loss, the painful awareness of confusion and memory loss. They succeed because they are often able to tap into mind-brain associations and skills that are not available when the client is asked to intellectualize or verbalize material. Art therapy reduces stress by providing tasks and projects that are pleasurable and nonthreatening for this population. The other expressive arts and "art for art's sake" also play a vital role in the positive experience these clients have when they spend their day in this program. It is difficult to evaluate which of the many activities should be called therapy, and which are named by another title; the composite interaction is the true therapy (Spaniol, 1997).

## ☐  Some Basic Facts

This book does not intend to offer the reader a medical, mind-brain primer on dementia. It is a subject about which much has been written and said with greater clarity than could be replicated here. However, it is useful to keep some facts in mind to avoid frustrating both the client and therapist. Dementia is a common disease that affects the majority of aging people who need environmental support. These men and women require either a day treatment program or intensive home care. Treatment outside the home is preferable, if it is well planned and tailored to the functioning level of the elderly person. A program away from the home also provides relief for the primary caretakers and reduces depression in the home as the afflicted member declines. As a result of this support system, premature institutionalization of the elderly person is averted.

Alzheimer's disease is characterized by changes in the structure of the cells of the brain, and is identified by neurofibrillary tangles, neuritic plaques, and other degenerative processes. The chronology of the disease goes through stages, generally called early, middle and late stages, and marked by certain losses in behaviors and abilities to use cognition and communicate. In the early stages, the awareness of memory loss, misplacing objects of value, or recent memory loss of topics is common. Since most people on occasion experience these same problems after middle age, the early diagnosis is often missed. Partly because of the deterioration, and partly because of the anxiety these symptoms generate, there is often a noticeable personality change. Irritability, paranoia, delusions, and distractibility are often observable.

As the disease progresses there is a further decrease in knowledge of recent events, problems leaving familiar surroundings, and disorientation for time and place. In the late stage there are physical manifestations, disorientation of self, agitation, and delusions. At this stage the person must be aided in nearly all aspects of daily life.

There are three other forms of dementia that are not as well known, or as commonly used in the layperson's vocabulary: vascular disease (caused often by hypertension and successive small strokes), Parkinson's disease, and Lewy body disease all leave the victim with progressively diminishing capabilities.

For the therapist it is often sufficient to know that dementia is a syndrome of progressive cognitive dysfunction and severely impacts the functions of daily living. It is also important to remember that each person's progress is singular, and that knowledge of tools to improve the cognitive–linguistic abilities may be of significant importance.

A description of Alzheimer's disease taken from the University of California, Los Angeles Alzheimer's Disease Center publication: "Alzheimer's disease (AD) is the most common form of late-life dementia, causing general memory loss and other cognitive declines in approximately 8% of the people over 65. Research suggests that the disease process begins years prior to clinical confirmation" (p. 9). There is research of many sorts that employ imaging techniques of biological processes and utilize drugs that may retard the decline of brain functioning.

Autopsy studies of the brains of AD patients show characteristic brain cell damage or lesions know as neuritic plaques and neurofibrillary tangles. These lesions collect in brain areas involved in memory performance and in time interrupt the ability to cognate or employ short term or long term memory" (p. 9).

At this writing there is no known cure for this illness, however, there is an emphasis on early diagnosis and use of current interventions that have significant impact on the patients memory, cognitive abilities, troublesome behaviors, and functional capacities.

Alzheimer's disease is also called senile dementia, and is the major cause of presenile dementia, or dementia not associated with advanced age. The disease is most noted for speech disturbances, disorientation, severe loss of short-term memory, and leads to progressive loss of mental faculties, even though the victim often remains physically healthy (Compton's Encyclopedia Online, 1998).

A layperson's knowledge of how memory works is useful for the clinician interfacing with elderly clients. According to the American Online information (AOL, 1999), memory is a four-step process.

1. The brain must encode a message from one or more of the senses (sight, touch, sound, or smell) into a neuronal message to the correct centers of the brain.
2. The message must be repeated or considered important and related to things stored in memory in the past.
3. The message must be stored in either short-term or long-term memory. Repeated experiences that are important move into long-term memory.
4. The memory must be retrieved from long-term storage when one wishes to recall it. There is no way to estimate how many memories can be stored in the brain, but the old adage of "use it or lose it" seems to be correct.

The rationale for many of the group directives and activities that follow will be based on these premises. All the senses possible are used in the creative tasks repeated many times, with clues provided (visual, verbal, and kinesthetic) to help retrieve stored memories. There is high interactivity with the clients to create a positive environment. The groups are not able to act upon the illness of dementia, but they do challenge the progressive decline that will eventually dominate. The delay can be filled with pleasant experiences that calm irrational behaviors and give the families peace of mind when they observe their family member engaged in activities that they could not provide in the home.

## ☐ Multiple Opportunities

It is a challenge to cover all of the opportunities that the day treatment program (where I provide consultation) makes available to the elderly clients. Without exception, every opportunity is carefully constructed to provide stimulus that may aid in retarding the progress of dementia. The program is organized on an hourly basis, moving from one form of structured encounter to another. There are opportunities for individual conversations with therapists and caretakers at the beginning of the day, which serves as an evaluation of the general emotional stability of the member. It is also a time that socialization is encouraged and personal needs noted. Large group, which focuses on word retrieval and current event discussions, follows this time for socialization. It is led by a highly-trained speech pathologist who specializes in this field. She also has advanced training in the area of brain pathology and is able to assess and advise treatment of clients. The hour before lunch is set aside for physical exercise, led by an experienced leader. Music, singing, and body exercises are mixed with a variety of active directives. A short walk is taken outdoors, then lunch follows, which is served at small tables, to no more than four or five clients. Eating is another time for socialization.

The afternoon is art time—a studio experience. The art teacher is a master at providing art opportunities that are within the scope of the elderly and still result in beautiful products. There is also a bridge game, a religious group, a special interest group, and other groups that add variety to the daily program. None of this could be possible without a large and devoted staff, who are sensitive to the mood changes and needs of the members, and are genuinely interested in making their clients' world a more kind and accepting one.

## The Place of the Art Therapy Groups

The art-as-therapy groups are scheduled according to the needs of the members. They are conducted by art therapists and a marital and family therapist who is experienced in working with the elderly, and is exceptionally creative. I sometimes join in the group activities or observe through the one-way mirror. Supervision follows the group.

We have chosen to do several theme groups. Friendship and social communication for the higher-functioning members, as well as a modification of this same goal for those with greater loss of cognition. Group art therapy has been successful in orienting new members to their unfamiliar surroundings. Art therapy groups have been beneficial for members who are facing the holidays with trepidation, and is particularly beneficial in illustrating the narration and memories that are still available to the member. These groups will be discussed later in this chapter.

The description of the program makes clear that there is little time to do much more than is structured. Therefore, therapists must be prepared that their sessions will not always be arranged in the traditional manner. Time for group and individual work is carved out of the larger program, and the preference of the elderly individual for certain activities may preclude finding a convenient spot for consultation. This is truly a milieu setting, and the greatest gain is made when this is honored. Group with art is also a framework where the therapeutic interchange can provide the leaders and director of the program with information that could not be gleaned in the larger group activities.

What therapists need to keep in mind is that they are not dealing with a single form of deterioration of the brain. Alzheimer's is a disease, dementia is a process of aging, and many other cerebral accidents can damage the brain and physical functioning. Not every client has had the same history of functional loss, and some men or women who appear to be very frail are still able to communicate and contribute to the discussions. Looking at the elderly as a person suffering from an illness, rather than an aged person who is resistant, uncooperative, or is mentally capable of monitoring their mood swings but unwilling to do so, keeps the therapist in perspective. There is no argument that this is often a trying relationship, but each of us has to find a mental set that helps us through the hard times and frees us to enjoy the positive moments. Aside from learning a little about the physiological and biological processes of dementia, which helped me appreciate the behaviors I encountered, I have created my own vision of my clients.

## ☐ Looking Forward by Looking Backward: A Philosophy

As I look around the room I do not see the men and women just as they are today. Rather, I see them in their entirety. Here is a famous surgeon, who trained medical students and wrote important texts; here is a woman who created a powerful environmental society to protect endangered species; here a productive poet; there a graphic artist and cinema production chief. I am reminded of the woman who knew Anna Freud and as a girl studied in London with her, and I see the bon vivant in the fellow who dances as well, even now, as any man I have known. I see my clients through the lens of their life story which enables me to talk to *that* unique person and elicit a response that resonates with their past. If the reply to my query is not conventional (and it may indeed seem irrational) and if I know the previous accomplishments of my client–companion, I can find the shadows of meaning in the fog of confusion.

I take note that when the client, a retired psychiatrist who not only practiced but also taught at a university, parries my questions with a typical psychiatrist's response, for example, "Why do you ask this? Is it a concern of yours?" Even though he uses a substitute phrase for a cognitive answer, I understand that he is keeping his identity alive. His mode of communication is still operative and that makes him distinct from the others. It is with that core person I hope to work.

It is essential that therapists find their own vision, otherwise it is disheartening if one looks only at the present conditions and the decline that is inevitable. For this reason it is important that the therapist be aware of the history of the clients and their present relationships. Where do they live, and with whom? Are the stories they tell occurring in the here-and-now, or are they getting a glimpse of the important past events that still live in the present?

With the elderly that have dementia, either mild or advanced, the therapist provides better therapy if reality is suspended and they enjoy the journey with their client. That is not to say that careful attention is not given to the emotional and physical condition of the person who is there in reality, any discomfort must be attended to. However, to visit Anna Freud through my clients reality was a wonderful experience for me, and I was genuinely fascinated with the times and events that we discussed. It was also interesting to realize that we were having a perfectly logical, normal conversation when we remained in her time capsule, something this lady was quite incapable of doing during common conversational intercourse.

## Small Group

Many of the clients are, at times, anxious and unsure of themselves, and have trouble orienting to time and place. It is helpful to see two or three men or women in a small group and construct a task that is based on a positive theme and focuses them on a creative task. It is also realistic to understand that whatever suggestion is made, the clients will probably go their own way.

For example, two of my women clients had a form of friendship during the day program. They often sat together and usually had lunch jointly. This day one of the women, Alice, was quite agitated, while her friend Lucy was more stable. We three sat together at the art therapy table and I asked, "Could Lucy invite Alice on a pleasant afternoon trip to the country and stay in a lovely place until Alice was calm?" They agreed that they could take an art-imagery trip, and I set up a large piece of paper and drawing tools (both felt pens and oil pastels). I plotted some sections of the landscape and helped them get started, asking for their directions. What I did not count on was that "countryside and greenery" triggered Lucy's dominant obsessive story. She began to reminisce about her home on the east coast, how she missed it, how beautiful it was, how it was spacious and filled with friends and music. In contrast, nothing here in the west was the same, and nothing could compare with her girlhood home. (Her girlhood home was not anything like the dream-house she had created in her mind.) She became less calm and was picking up on Alice's distress. Their composite stress could escalate into real trouble.

Alice began to draw some shaky lines that she said were canals for boats, but Lucy wanted to represent her home, it's grounds, and all the flowers in the garden. My project was not going where I had imagined it would go. They each had entered their own visual world, a memory from the past that had impacted them so strongly that they could not generalize to meet the imaginary situation I created.

As often happens with this population, the therapist's flexibility is tested. I reached over and placed the collage box nearby and helped search for garden and house pictures and boats and canals of England (Alice's home). We made a pastiche of these disparate memories into a rather attractive outdoor scene, and both women were calmed. The collage became a container for their memories and the agitation associated with these memories in a way that was acceptable for them and decreased their anxiety.

## Discussion

What was the process here? A misguided attempt was made to provide an imagery-art opportunity to clients who could not use their imagination. These two women could only reproduce their limited but powerful memories and were then frustrated with an inability to recreate them exactly. Memory was not fluid, it was concrete. Therefore, when we went to collage (which is also concrete), a media which did not demand dexterity in drawing or special planning, the memories could be satisfied. Lucy's narrative was very structured and obsessive; Alice's was vague and needed to take a specific form to help her feel less confused. The art provided the tool to allow these two friends to experience a mutual task and a form of problem solving, as well as serving each other as an audience that was willing to listen to other's story with empathy. Often it is helpful to remember that even though these stories have been told endless times to the same listeners, the recipients do not remember well, and if they do they are tolerant of repetition.

Although this mini-group came to a conclusion that was unexpected, it was not unprofitable. The two women remained in conversation for the remainder of the day, and on the following week I had a tangible product to remind them of their time together. The artwork was used to stimulate recollection of their session and to assess if they could recall any of this experience. Lucy did remember (or said she did), but Alice had been too stressed to let this encounter remain in her consciousness.

Perhaps this limited goal seems so minimal that it is not valuable. I have questioned the value of these sessions, but when the art is placed on the wall and the art maker remembers the time it was created, then it becomes worthwhile. The rationale for continuing the art therapy is that the visual product stimulates a neurological pathway that words cannot. When different loci of the brain are activated by visual stimuli they reconstruct associations, these ensembles of neurons are unique and do not depend on verbal paths (Damasio, 1999). Reinforcing short-term memory is a goal that the entire team attempts to achieve through many different activities; art is one of the more successful ways.

## Long-Term Group

The program is fortunate to have a director who is a trained art therapist and values the advantages of this form of communication and the stimulus it provides. Once a week eight of the higher-functioning members join the three therapists in an art therapy group. This group differed from the studio art group in that it was shaped to reflect and encourage discussion about some common themes that stress these elderly clients over an extended period of time. Separation and loss are major concerns, as well as loneliness and anxiety about family members deserting them. The challenge that we confronted was to find a way to bring these issues to group without forcing them, and also be aware that often these emotions are taboo in many families, that painful emotions are not allowed to be discussed openly.

We found that at the beginning of the group simple media and collage was the most satisfactory for a group that ran less than one hour. At first, the members often became restless because of their emotional fluctuations and lack of the ability to stay attentive to one task for 60 minutes. However, as the group continued to meet, the members had greater tolerance for the hour, after three meetings we could have continued for more time if we did not have to compete with lunch time. Food is very important, and was often the subject of jokes and used as a metaphor for being cared for.

It may seem like overkill to have three therapists interacting with eight persons, but it was not. The members needed assistance in many ways. One woman had to have the directions given to her calmly and clearly in a one-on-one manner. If not, she became confused and mildly frantic. If spoken to intimately she then carried on and joined in the project. The next member, Bill, was hard-of-hearing, the therapist had to be sure the directives were conveyed to him, perhaps more than once. Peter, on the other hand, was more animated than necessary and began to tell everyone what to do and how to do it. Meanwhile, he did little himself. Susan understood the directive, but had trouble selecting the collage pictures because she has poor coordination. Harry was fully aware, but unless he received a little extra attention, he begins to be bored waiting for the others to start. Each member of the group benefits from interactions with the therapists. In addition, we listened for remarks that were not necessarily addressed to the group, but were valuable statements for all when repeated by the therapist or the client. The therapists moved around, helping those who needed it and admiring the work of those who addressed the theme. Every group is video taped and we sometimes laugh at the activity of the therapists, certainly not the conventional "therapeutic" interchange.

## Spontaneity and Laughter

In one group there were three therapists in addition to the eight members. A high school youth was doing community service at the agency, and was liked by the members so he "sat in." The theme that day was "What Do You Wish For?" There was interchange and some memories were reviewed, and some wishes were directly connected to the daily routines and caregivers. When Sophia took her turn to talk about her collage, she said she wished to dance—she pointed directly at Craig (the high school youth) who accommodated her with a spirited waltz as we all sang the Blue Danube Waltz! That was a group to remember —and it was remembered, on video, in the minds of some of the group, and certainly by the therapists. Laughter and movement are always sought after, the waltz had it all and was spontaneous. After that success we incorporated some sort of verbal noise making or movement reflective of the art in as many groups as possible.

There are many therapeutic settings where group therapy is the preferred mode of treatment, but with the elderly it is almost a necessity. For the persons suffering from dementia, the need for group contact is essential because many social skills have slipped away, friends have died, and family is either exhausted with attempting to communicate or have withdrawn their daily contact. By replacing the stimulus that most of us require from informal social intercourse with a structured group, the facility can duplicate the normal environment to some extent.

# ☐ Guidelines

The following are some guidelines for therapists who are doing their best to retard the progression of mental deterioration of the elderly client: Provide a consistent environment; reduce external stressors, find therapeutic opportunities that are based on simple, clear directives; and be flexible and responsive to the variable moods of the elderly group member. Group therapy justifies an emphasis on social exchange and provides a climate that invites personal stories. These conditions cannot be accomplished unless there is a plan and a focused format, implemented each week.

# ☐ A Structured Experimental Group

To test the ideas that we had about the efficacy of an ongoing art therapy group, we chose six members who were able to relate to one another to a limited degree. These men and women had different diagnosis for their dementia, including strokes, Alzheimer's, normal advanced aging, and major depression. Two members were generally anxious most of the time, two were depressed, and the others were mildly forgetful but sociable, and were adjusting to being away from their families during the day. The members shared the ability to conceal some of their memory loss and word retrieval by substituting words or shifting away from the subject. All had been successful in their lives, still had some family connections, and returned in the evening to their own home or to a residential facility (not a nursing home).

*The Composition of the Group.* An 82-year-old man, Bill, who had been a hospital director; an 85-year-old man, Harry, who had taught graduate school; a 79-year-old man, Tom, who had been an officer in the war and a journalist later on; an 83-year-old woman, Annie, who had worked a white-collar job, but had many financial hardships; and another woman, 75-year-old Mary, who had been a professional musician. The sixth member was a man who had been active in the business world and had managed a big company as CEO. I mention him individually, because he came into group as one of the most active members cognitively and physically capable. We lost him as a group member within weeks because he was one of the unfortunates who went into a rapid decline and could no longer function with the others.

*Creating a Theme Group.*   As a team of art therapists, we decided that we would create ongoing art tasks that would have a theme, an opening and closing ritual, a consistent membership, and a constant time and meeting place. We shared our theme of "Friendship" with the director and she saw to it that the theme was picked up in other groups during the week to reinforce our short meeting time of one hour, once a week. To provide a vehicle for artwork we chose to create a "community" as the base for the ongoing project.

*Preparation.*   Two large, white cardboards covering the table, created the drawing surface; felt pens, oil pastels, construction paper in small sizes, glue, scissors, and tissue paper were scattered around the edges of the board. The members were invited in and they chose their seating places.

# First Meeting

*Conversation.*   Every group starts with a short informal assessment of the emotional and physical status of the members. This is done by asking each member how they are and how the day had been up to now. The notion of making friends at this point in their lives was brought up as a question. Was it hard to make friends at this age? Had they found it easier since they were all together in a program? Did they still have friends at home? Would they like to make friends now?

*Introducing the Theme.*   The facilitators took the lead in suggesting building a community that could be created any way that would please the members and would reflect their choice. It was necessary to offer guidance and reassure the members that it was an idea open to their modifications. It is essential that any task start with some planning that will ensure success and satisfaction. This does not imply that the directives are rigid, in fact, suggestions from the members are much encouraged. After some hesitation the group settled on a theme of a "Friendship Community."

## *Process*

Annie cut out a house shape and pasted it down and drew an open door. Two members worked with torn tissue paper, crumpled to be flowers; others made marks that represented buildings. One member was afraid that she "wouldn't do it right," and so was guided to choose a collage picture to ensure her success. She chose a home in a garden. Each member was invited to talk about what would make a community "friendly," which led to the decisions that they needed paths to connect their homes. A pen was passed around, which was the "friendship" colored pen, and paths were drawn. Mary made a tissue paper bridge, and Tom drew stepping stones. Some members were able to stand or reach where they wanted the path to go, others used the therapist as their hand, and directed where to make the marks. It is helpful to keep in mind that the therapist is in the role of a physical and mental extension of the client. What they cannot do physically is acted out by the therapist, when cognition is lost the therapist picks up the train of thought until the member recovers. We are aware that often the elderly use word substitution when the word or thought they search for is unavailable. Following their intent rather than depending on logic is an important skill to develop.

Some of the comments made by the members were, "There should be rules for a community," and "We should take care of each other." A sign was made that read "Fences make good neighbors," and communication devices were made such as telephone lines from pipe cleaners (see Figure 7.1).

As the session drew toward it's close everyone admired the beginning of their community and planned to continue the following week. After the members left, the art therapist team discussed the interactions and came to some conclusions about tasks and interactions we would encourage the following week.

We planned to continue the theme and brainstormed about what would be the next step.

## Second Meeting

Following the same conversational opening protocol, we observed that the group members did not clearly remember the created community from the previous week. However, they did begin to recall the process when they focused on the artwork itself, which had been set up on the table. Visual stimulus seems to tap into a form of awareness that rises from different memory sources than strictly verbal recall. This is supported by some of the information about the brain and its function (Seigel, 1999). Since art therapists in this facility are not trained to do

**FIGURE 7.1.** The "community" in the process of construction: The houses are still not anchored down, and the mailboxes and other additions are still in progress. Many forms of media were made available.

more than observe and make layperson connections to neurological information, I will only recommend that it is worthwhile to peruse this area of reading, to enrich the therapeutic relationship with the elder population.

The preparations for the group followed the same procedure as in the first group, as did the conversation and assessment period. However, there was a change in the group process.

There seemed to be some recall of the friendship motif, and one of the members suggested that they make mailboxes and send messages. The therapists took this suggestion and enlarged on it by discussing the pleasure and disappointments that center on getting the letter that we hope for. Positive and negative feelings are encouraged since too often the geriatric population is infantilized with cheery remarks, instead of allowing the full range of emotions to be expressed.

***Rituals.*** We added a new beginning and ending ritual to the group. It came about spontaneously as we were starting this second group. While we were getting seated, Bill took the hand of his favorite therapist who was sitting next to him. She smiled and took the hand of the person next to her on the other side, and soon everyone was holding hands. We recalled the old game of passing a message, which then became pass an energy noise, and within minutes the arms and hands were moving in a circle as the "energy" moved around the group.

This may seem childish, and indeed it was in many ways. However, it was physically energetic, it allowed safe touching that older people often crave, it stimulated the emotional and cognitive centers to pay attention, and it aroused playful feelings and laughter. The best part is that it was created by the group itself.

*Material for Mailboxes and Other Additions to the Community.*    Cardboard tubes, such as found in paper towel rolls, were cut to the size each member requested. Colored paper was used to cover the roll, and some mailboxes were decorated with glitter, stickers, or drawings. Spindles and turned bits of wood, tongue depressors, and other small objects were available in containers on the table to inspire the art makers to become inventive and foster their creativity.

## Process

Each member put their name on their box after it was decorated, and situated it in the area they had developed the previous week. Tom had been working unassisted, and when he announced he had made a mail delivery car we were all amazed! He had taken a paper roll, placed it sideways, and glued small wooden disks on the four corners to create his car. This was one of the unexpected surprises that happened in our group. Tom usually seemed depressed and not attentive, but we learned that the way he appears is not necessarily the way he feels.

After the mailboxes were in place each person wrote a letter to every other member. The letters were brief, folded into a small shape that would fit into the mail car, and then delivered by the appointed "mail carrier" to the designated recipient. The receiver then read each person's message and reacted to what was written. It was a great success. One man said he couldn't remember the last time he had gotten a letter, and another said he never received so many good wishes in a letter in his life. The activity was lively, extremely interactive, and reinforced the theme of community and friendship. This task was manually easy enough to do, and required little assistance from the therapists. There was a need to keep the action moving, since after one person read all their letters, it was useful to say, "Now it is Mary's turn," and keep the focus on the interchange.

The community was growing visually and symbolically. The group ended with our ritual of holding hands and sending energy from hand to hand. We all commented on how rapidly the hour seemed to pass. As we left the room we reinforced the notion that we would meet again in a week.

## Third Meeting

As the group entered the room we noticed that they gravitated to the seats in which they had been sitting the previous week. Two members directed the others where to sit. The therapists also took their accustomed place. Conversation was easily started, and the therapists began to subtly encourage the members to ask each other how they were feeling and what had happened during the week. This question was usually difficult to answer, but the intent was social and appropriate.

The art project from the previous two weeks was recognized and commented on by all the members. The tangible stimulus was aiding their recall. The energy, hand holding, noise making ritual was also familiar and entered into freely. Comfort and lowered anxiety for two of the members was accomplished by the ritual because it demonstrated belonging and inclusion through auditory noises (not words), sensory touching (hands), and the familiar environment. This made it possible for two more anxious members of our group to focus and join us, when at the beginning there were doubts that they could maintain their composure in this situation.

***Preparation.***   One of the art therapists created houses by folding construction paper into roofs and pasting them on to small boxes, about five inches square.

## Process

Each person selected a house and proceeded to decorate it. Annie pasted a chimney onto the roof, with a red feather coming out of the top. Bill said that it looked like the house was on fire. It was interesting to note that Annie's depressed affect was not reflected in her art. Her art was usually dramatic, and her comments were often quotes from the past, "A stitch in time saves nine," and other similar aphorisms. She worked diligently on her projects, and needed less help than any other member. One of the therapists had walked with her earlier in the day, and without changing her gloomy facial expression she commented on how much she looked forward to this group. Annie educated us to not make assumptions about a person's emotional state solely by their expression. Old age imposes lines and facial changes on the man or woman that convey an emotion which is often just the process of aging, and we, as observers, project as happy or sad. Annie's home life was not supportive and that carried over into her days at the program. She found it hard to access a variety of facial expressions, since the sad look was appropriate most of the time.

Mary's house was decorated with flowers from a collage picture, Bill's house was called "Happy House" and had a poem written on the side, Tom said people were welcome in his home, "but not for too long." When asked what we would see if we peeked through his windows, he said "a woman." The houses were left on the community drawing but they were not pasted down. The group ended with the hand-holding ritual.

The time ran out before the interest and we took that as an affirmation of our experiment (see Figure 7.5).

## Fourth Meeting

The group came in and went to their established places. The conversation was interactive, and the therapists reinforced this social behavior. It is useful to remember that when conversation lags it is often due to some physiological or neurological difficulty. Perhaps Tom makes an overture to Bill and Bill did not hear him. The therapist must step in and repeat the statement and act as a necessary conduit. Annie may address Mary, but do so with her head down and with minimum affect. Mary thinks she hears someone address her, but she is so anxious she doesn't know where to turn. Again, the therapist has to adjust the sender and receiver circuit. These difficulties of the elderly explain why the ratio of therapists to clients is ideally one to three.

> I learned to pay attention to physical difficulties when I helped a student evaluate a group in a retirement home. A large group was scheduled, but an even larger group turned up, some thinking there would be food and entertainment. We did collages about their marriages (which was a poor choice), and each vied with the other to tell stories of their dead spouses. Each "dearly departed" was more wonderful than the next, all were tremendously wealthy, and every mate was devoted beyond imagination. After this trip into fantasyland concluded I asked the attractive, attentive woman on my right if she had enjoyed the group. (She had not contributed more than smiles and nods.) She agreed enthusiastically that it was "a wonderful experience, but since she was completely deaf she wondered what had been said?" I learned a lot from that experience. To ignore the physical problems and address only the psychological difficulties is unrealistic and unproductive. I am happy to say that my ego recuperated after some time, and I still laugh at my naïveté.

### *Process*

The community project was set up on the table as usual and the media placed around the table. After the usual starting ritual, a therapist suggested that each member send a New Years message for the person sitting on his or her right and on his or her left. (We were about to enter the year 2000.) This suggestion did not seem to take so we waited to see where the group directed their interest.

Mary spontaneously made a significant statement. She said she was terrified of her house (the art project). She was asked if being in group terrified her and she replied "no," but she was terrified of not being able to do what would be asked of her. The group reassured her that she did well, and her house demonstrated how she had accomplished the task competently. This revelation seemed to indicate that the most anxious member of the group had felt safe enough to share her feelings with the others. The feedback that she got from her group friends was comforting, more comforting than if it had come from the therapists.

The houses were then given names. Annie's house was named "My Mortgage." She had nothing more to say about this, which was in great contrast to the other positive titles on the houses. The group spontaneously put her house in the center of their community art work, and surrounded it with the other homes; it was a powerful statement (Figures 7.2 and 7.3). Annie sat and kept looking until we had to leave. Again, it was the visible, tangible offer of comfort that reached her. It was a statement that was strong enough to be stored in her memory because it activated a path to recall that differed from the usual verbal stimulus that, with her, was faulty and only partially functioning.

Finding a name for the group was projected as the task for the following meeting, and we closed with our usual ritual. This group had the feeling of therapy, more than we had experienced before.

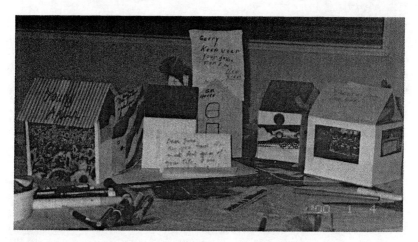

**FIGURE 7.2.** In a touching demonstration of caring and support, the group members move their houses to surround the house that was named "My Mortgage." The other messages were: "Young Again," "Keep Your Jokes," "Have the Best Year of Your Life," and "There is No Place Like Home." There is no necessity for words.

**FIGURE 7.3.** A close up of the houses of the community, clustered around the sad house named "Mortage." Other homes were "Happy House, Have Fun," "Peaceful House," and "Your Heart is Part of the Art" home. Collage, construction paper, drawing, and mixed media were used.

## Fifth Meeting

The group came together almost as normally as a group of persons who did not have to struggle with the challenges of dementia. We charged up with our generator ritual, and did not have to explain or encourage hand holding, everyone knew what to do. Mary still needed to be reassured, but only for a moment.

I have speculated, based on reading Seigal (1999), that Mary seems to suffer from highly-charged random stimulus that alters her brain to a state of high arousal. An appraisal–arousal process in which the brain evaluates and decides on the next step of activation normally follows this state of arousal. Mary may experience arousal and preconscience awareness that something important is about to happen without the benefit of the appraisal mechanisms that evaluate the stimulus as good or bad. Therefore, she is often in an anxious state for which she has no explanation. Her somatic sensations are alert, but her self-regulatory capacities are not functioning in a manner where she can calm herself (Seigel, 1999, 127–129).

Tom asked Bill to change his seating because he liked to sit next to him. Bill was pleased to do so. Mary sat quietly, a great deal of her fears diminished by the familiarity of the room, the membership, the ongoing art (community) project, and the reassurance of the therapists. Annie started to work on the area around her house without being asked. The houses continued to be circled around her home.

Preparation for this group was minimal. Cards had been cut of sturdy colored paper about the size of an index card. These were membership cards that would be created after we found a name for the group. These two projects had been agreed upon the previous week.

## *Process*

The idea of naming the group was recalled and contributions were written and read, with a unanimous vote for Bill's contribution. "Young at Heart, Doing Art." Everyone agreed this was a great name.

The cards were passed around and the suggestion was made that the membership cards be decorated or written on as the individual chose. The cards were embellished with collage, feathers, glitter, and other small objects that had texture and color. Mary's card sported a lavender feather with a collage image of people picnicking in the park. She seemed proud of her card and not so caught up in her feelings of inadequacy. Tom wrote on his card his joke—a joke he repeated in almost every group: "I draw flies," with a small bug symbol attached. Annie created a verse, "Young at heart doing art, let's never part," and printed it on her card. She was asked if she meant the group should never part or did she just enjoy the rhyme. She said she liked the sound of the rhyme.

During the art making, Tom and Bill reminisced about their childhood roots, since they had discovered that they had grown up in nearby cities in the same eastern state. Bill mentioned in the course of their conversation that his birthday was the day before. Tom commented on this to the group. The two men continued to talk and reinforce a friendship that had started in this group and had grown to where it was actively supportive during the rest of the day. This is an unusual occurrence of fellowship, since many of the members fail to acknowledge another member as a special person. Some of the men and women are withdrawn into themselves most of the time, unless they are specifically drawn into an activity. The entire program is constructed to combat the mechanism of withdrawal.

Bill then offered an invitation to his home (the created home of the community) for a party. The group leaders encouraged everyone to make food for the potluck party and bring it to Bill's party. Tom created a pizza of paper and bits of glued-on "salami." Mary offered yogurt represented in a magazine picture; Harry brought Bill his favorite keg of beer by a drawing. Annie's collage showed a picture of a strawberry, and she wrote the verse, "Strawberry pie; that's the name of my old guy." The group seemed pleased with the party they had created and closed group by singing "Happy Birthday" to Bill.

During group Harry, who is deeply depressed, expressed his discomfort at not being able to make a contribution to the party. He repeated his overriding concern that his family was too busy for things like this festivity. He seems at times to lose the distinction between himself and his obsessive ruminations about being left behind by his family. He feels lost even when he is in the presence of family members. On occasion he emerges from this gloom, can be a contributor, and be creative with the art. He always looks anxious and sad; so again, we cannot judge the person's internal state by relying entirely on his external affect.

It is noteworthy to compare the interactions between the beginning group and this later group. The movement toward greater interactive verbal and nonverbal narratives, the increased freedom of expression, and the introduction of humorous statements and verses are significant. These goals may seem small in other group situations, but with the elderly with dementia these gains are eventful. Group cohesion and free interchange are desirable with all populations, with this populace they are a rare occurrence.

## Continuing Plans and Activities

The next group was a further enhancement of the community. It was a beautification of the greenery by adding trees, flowers, and paths. Tissue paper was used to create the organic material, and wood chips helped make paths, and a turned spool became a water fountain. Harry surprised us by constructing a playground for children using a tongue depressor for a slide and gluing wooden sticks to form a jungle gym— a shadow of his past involvement with the schools. The therapists decided that the group was ready to move into more emotionally-laden personal issues. Each member shared a little of their concerns about loneliness and feelings of isolation, even from the family with which they lived.

Other themes for our group have proven successful as the group continues to consolidate. The members were delighted with a two part structured theme that involved boxes and photographs. In the first session the members were given small boxes that opened easily. The lids were attached which made opening and closing the boxes easy. These boxes were named self-boxes and the members were invited to write their name on the outside and decorate them with pictures or drawings that had something to do with themselves. When this task was accomplished we encouraged the group members to write memories and feelings from the past and in the present on small slips of paper and place them in the box. In addition, there was a basket of found objects on the table, and if any small items, such as a button or flower, remind them of some situation, they could place this in the box also. After the activity quieted down, the members shared with each other their treasurers in the box. A strong emphasis was placed on permission not to share the contents if the memory was private. Too often the elderly are not given the same respect for privacy that would be common place in most therapy groups.

The memories took on many shapes. There were crushed balls of tissue paper that had hidden messages written and then concealed by the crushing, there were small found objects glued together that were given significance, and there were magazine pictures cut and folded that had meaning for the member. It was a very active group and offered a progression of tasks and suggestions that we have found to be useful to keep the psychic energy flowing with a group that can be very passive.

The following session built on these boxes which were a metaphor for self and as a visual reminder of the group process. The members entered the room and found their places by finding their box. Then time was allowed to look inside and remember what the words or objects meant and exchange conversation. The therapists then offered an opportunity for the members to photograph each other with a Polaroid camera. There was a great deal of excitement engendered by this idea and the therapist in charge of the camera gave a demonstration of how to use it. With a good deal of assistance the members all entered into the activity and took pictures of each other. They expanded on the idea of portraits by asking the subject to express a certain emotion for the photo. For example, Mary would ask Bill to look happy, or Annie would suggest that Harry look scared. The picture taking caused laughter and appealed to the members' interest in themselves. At this age many elders are much more narcissistically focused than they were in their younger days.

The group concluded by pasting their portrait on the box. Where it was pasted became an opportunity for individuality. Some photos were on the side of the box, some were inside the lid of the box, and others were made to stand up by taping them halfway inside and out. In every case there was a strong sense of ownership and identification with this project. It developed that the group wanted these boxes in front of them for all the subsequent groups, they became a metaphor for stability and personal worth.

Another successful group theme grew out of the therapist's discussion of desirable goals for this long-term group. There was a consensus that it was time to encourage the members to feel safe enough to discuss some of the more painful issues of aging, and use the group as a protected place to open up to these feelings. Cards were prepared before the group convened. The words written on the cards were directly related to the life circumstances of this aged population: loneliness, sickness, family tensions, forgetfulness, fear, and many more serious statements of situations they encountered in life. The cards were scattered face down in the center of the table and the members were encouraged to guess what they were there for. There was little speculation. The therapists then brought up directly the issue that the really hard facts of aging were seldom discussed either in our group or in the general activity program. We thought that this group was well enough established to confront some of the difficult facts of aging. Each member reached to the center and picked a card, the card was read to everyone. The members were encouraged to swap cards if they did not like the one they had, or share it if two members felt they could relate to the emotion or situation described on the card.

The therapists were somewhat hesitant to challenge the group members on this level. There was concern that the trauma of aging would be more than the group could respond to in a manner that would be therapeutic. The results were reassuring and did not evoke emotions that were overwhelming. The therapists felt that most members were relieved to talk about sadness and loss, emotions that were considered too traumatic to discuss in their family.

Each person in the group could find some emotion that was active in their lives and they retained enough social skills to respond interactively with others. The issue of loneliness was particularly evocative, and the purpose of the group to foster friendship and counter isolation was again a major focus of the dialogue. To conclude the group on a more positive note, a pass-around drawing was done very quickly. Each member made a positive brief statement about each member and it was read aloud at the conclusion of the group.

We have continued to normalize the group and find group activities and goals that do not avoid the serious challenges of declining mental and physical problems of the members. By taking these chances we are rewarded with brief moments of wisdom and courageous remarks from the group that validate the dedication the therapists and the members have made in this collaboration.

The group will continue to follow the general format that has been structured, and we hope the membership will continue to remain the same. If a member becomes incapable of functioning in this group, we will have an opportunity to mourn the loss and not pretend that it has not happened. Too often the elderly are falsely protected against a reality that they are all too aware has happened.

## Discussion

The group described above is ongoing, therefore our conclusions are tentative. At this time, the desired goals have been met and we will press forward for more success. By adhering to the tenets that have proven helpful for the elderly client, we were able to create a group that was:

1. Sensitive to the member's reaction time declination;
2. Aware of the slower retrieval of memories or loss of associations and recall;
3. Patient with the slowing down of emotional intelligence and judgment;
4. Sensitive to the negative impact of stress and an unaccustomed environment;
5. Attentive to the presence of confusion and anxiety that accompanies the decline in neuronal processes;
6. Aware of the need for attention to health and mood;
7. Engaged with providing the necessary physical stimulation as well as mental challenges;
8. Committed to modeling and creating, energy and inventiveness through therapist interactions with members;
9. Courageous in bringing real-life subject matter into the dialogue;
10. Able to appreciate the strength of using metaphor and visual, tangible modes of stimulation and communication; and
11. Capable of using art in manner that provides an alternative vehicle for interactions and communication.

None of these attributes are as important as showing respect, and empathy, humor, and admiration for the brave group members that are facing one of the most traumatic declines that humans suffer—the loss of self.

## ☐ The Therapist

A difficulty that is not often discussed is the conflict felt by the therapists when they must accept the repetitious and slow pace that is necessary for success with these clients. The need to repeat, reinforce, and to help without infantilizing is a challenge. The indispensable quality of loaning energy and positive creativity to a group, in spite of the fact that the therapist knows the efforts might hold off the decline of the person's facilities just so long. The therapist has to find the courage to work toward goals that would be minimal in other settings, but tremendous in a program for the elderly with dementia. There has to be an ability to find rewards in unique moments, and satisfaction in the creativity it takes to provide stimulating opportunities that stay within the boundaries listed above.

## ☐ The One Way Mirror

At times one of the family members may watch the group through the one-way mirror. (Permission for observation is always secured at the initial evaluation interview.) Without exception we hear the same exclamation, "I cannot believe it is _____, he never acts like this at home. I see a completely different person. So animated, not depressed, more alert, what a change." For many family members, this is rewarding and encouraging, for others there is a tinge of anger or jealousy that we have the lively, agreeable person, while they have to deal with the other side of the personality at home. The greatest help that observation provides is the realization that bringing their parent (spouse or relative) to the program is not a form of rejection, but a benefit. How beneficial it is can only be appreciated by watching the transformation that is apparent in, for example, this group.

Not every family can visit during the day hours of the program, so we video tape every group that I have described above. Videos are made of other activities as well, so there is visual tracking of all the opportunities that are offered during the week. These videos can be seen with a staff person, and confidentiality is preserved. However, in this setting the families are often eager to share their positive experiences and educate other families about the help a good day program can furnish.

## ☐ Lower-Functioning Groups

Many of the members in the day program would not be capable of creating the art project described above. However, the principles that were listed are viable at every level of competency. The activities for a lower-functioning group have to be scaled down to meet the abilities of the members and has to rely more on tangible art objects to serve as symbols of group process. The less capable person requires a feeling of community and acceptance, even if they cannot clearly express this need. This level of dementia displays itself in multiple personality variances, which cloud the therapeutic picture and the ease of making a plan. The men and women often have radical mood swings, but my observation is that if the environment is safe, there is more euphoria than depression. Confusion is the greatest observable behavior, and forgetfulness is a given.

With these challenges, is it possible to conduct group successfully? I give an example that went well. The group was brought into the art therapy room and we spent quite some time looking around and remembering where we were, what we were going to do, and reassuring the members that we would take them back to the larger group in a short time. There was no resistance to this idea, and since most of the group had been in art activities they recognized the media laid out on the table. The project was a simple one that most art therapists have utilized at some time in their careers: the idea of making masks. Masks can be very creative and serve many purposes; our purpose was limited and tailored to the capabilities of the clients. I think it is worthwhile to repeat here that it is not necessary to have a long list of tricks to provide art opportunities. It is important to carefully construct the task to fit the dynamics of the group, the needs of the members, and the psychological and behavioral level of the clients. Simple does not mean stupid. Sometimes simple tasks allow for greater inventiveness and a more satisfying experience.

## Preparation

Bright red paper covered the table. It was sturdy paper that would not easily tear and had a surface that would accept pen or pastel marks. Paper plates had been prepared by cutting out two "eyes." Pens, craypods, jars of glitter, and small boxes of found objects were placed around the table in reach of everyone. The time allotted for group was also flexible. The attention span may be limited and a long group may be anxiety provoking. Fifty minutes may be tolerable, but it is important to announce as the closing time draws near that, "Group will conclude in five minutes," which adds to the predictable structure that brings comfort to this population.

## Process

As soon as the members entered the room and saw the paper plate masks they held them up and laughed and talked "through" them.

Some were talking to each other, and some were just talking. Immediately, it was noticeable that visual stimulation bypasses some of the anxious feeling that are evoked in a verbal group. Since every member of this group had more advanced disabilities in verbal expression, memory, and meaningful communication, to be offered an alternative mode of group was a great relief. The therapists had little trouble in encouraging the members to decorate their masks; they had more difficulty in limiting the flow of glue and the generous use of color that needed to be contained on the paper. It was a very spirited and positive art time. When most of the masks had been decorated in individual ways, the group was invited to tell a story or say hello to the other members. Each person was given time to hold the mask in front of their face and be the center of attention. This was successful in most cases.

The next step was to outline each member's hand, cut it out, and place it next to the mask. This resulted in an implied human form, since our eyes and mind instinctively supply the missing body parts. Names were added and lines drawn across the big paper to indicate connections. The finished product was attractive and was gazed at with a sense of pride.

The therapists were supportive in a different manner than in the higher-functioning group. They found meaning in the disjointed ramblings of one woman, and group connections in the shy man's few words. It is rather like orchestrating many instruments to create some musical sense of many sounds. The laughter was the cohesive force throughout the session. In particular, it was both amusing and frustrating when Miranda turned on her "gracious hostess" persona and directed the group to do various things that in her constant flow of words by themselves were recognizable, but in a sentence were jumbled together in ways that were a puzzle. However, her affect was so expansive and charming that one strove to make meaning out of meaninglessness.

We glued the masks and hands down and concluded the group (Figure 7.4). The members left without remarks, but smiling and thanking us for a good time.

## Discussion

We had little hope that any member of this group of six would remember the group even later the same day. That was not our goal. We posted the red paper with the masks glued in place, in the activity room and often remarked that Lucy had made this one and Michael

**FIGURE 7.4.** An example of the simple maks that were created, then glued to the group paper by a lower-functioning group.

the other. The creator would smile and pretend to remember, or perhaps did remember, we never can be sure. Our goal was to normalize and generalize group acceptance and group cohesion. It is probably true that these realities were ours, however, I cannot imagine working with these fine people and not engaging in a supportive dialogue.

The lower-functioning members work cooperatively with art tools better than any other mode of expression. The concrete object appears to anchor their responses and to contain their random reactions to stimuli. The art therapy group is designed to be alert to the flashes of reality that may surface and illuminate these moments. The group provides a more intimate exposure to relational activities than is possible with the larger program groups. It is also an excellent way to assess and evaluate the capabilities of the individuals. How each member responds to the art exercise can be compared to their previous responses. The lower-functioning group may have members who are in rapid decline and others who seem to have made some gains for some unknown reason. All of this information is helpful in providing the optimum program for each member.

With these clients the therapists are able to set limited goals. They are not as frustrated with hopes and disappointments as they are in the higher-functioning group. The more disabled men and women have enough obvious changes that their dementia is very clear, and only the most naïve would think otherwise. Therefore, tapping into the essence of their personalities is what remains, and that limits the grandiose fantasies that we all have about saving our clients. Satisfaction comes from knowing that a segment of the day has offered the client an opportunity to exercise strengths that are still in place and to be appreciated.

# ☐ The Studio Art Group

The art group is a core activity of the program and has great appeal for clients with all levels of functioning. The talented art teacher comes prepared with art activities that ensure success and result in some remarkable group efforts. By breaking down the art product into small segments, and giving clear directions, the results are beautiful. For example, the exterior wall of the facility is tiled with large, brilliant flowers. These were created by having designs inscribed on small tiles, and when assembled, they made large images. The surprise that has been exciting for all of the staff is the emergence of real talent in a few of the members. Free form paintings have become a driving force of the day for one member. He cannot wait for his art time.

Studio art is therapeutic. The therapy comes with the satisfaction, mastery, and admiration the artist gains from the art experience.

# ☐ Additional Groups

The program reaches out to all members of the family that are caring for a father, mother, spouse, or relative dealing with dementia. There is a group for spouses caring for their partner in the home or keeping the relative in a nursing facility. Each situation brings up special issues and unexpected joys and sorrows.

There is a group for children of demented parents—the so-called sandwich generation. It deals with how to give to the elderly while still caring for children in the home. This generational position is particularly stressful.

A group that has not yet been formed is for those who are recently aware of some memory loss, or other attentional difficulties. An early Alzheimer's group to ease the fear and provide information and stress reduction techniques, will be a positive service for the community.

In the supportive groups mentioned, the family members are good therapists for one another. They share resources, narratives, and emotions with people who understand in a way others could not. These groups also help the member who is attending the program, since they will return home to a less stressful emotional climate. In times of emergencies, hospitalizations, or death, the fellow members of the support group can make a vital difference to the acceptance of the trauma of loss. Perhaps the outsider believes that losing a burdensome spouse would be welcomed. In most cases the role of caretaker has become so imprinted on the well partner's mode of being, that when death comes to a spouse or parent, they feel a tremendous loss of identity. That is felt even though they also experience a release from

**FIGURE 7.5.** Two views of "Houses" in the community created by the elderly group in program for persons suffering from dementia.

a burden. Talking through these conflicting emotions is essential to moving on to acceptance of the reality of death and regaining a sense of individual identity.

There are many forms of death. As the severely stricken elder becomes unable to recognize family members and becomes unaware of surroundings and cannot respond verbally or rationally, they are "lost" to their family. These long-lasting "deaths" are often more tragic then the literal loss of life.

Art therapy is of use in these groups in the same manner that was described in chapter 1. Group process and group cohesion is aided because these groups are self-selected around a dominant issue. The groups are also open ended, this has to be attended to, as new members are integrated and old members move on.

The program also offers one other group, which was briefly mentioned earlier. The local high schools request their students to consider doing community service. During the summer the youth program is particularly active. Young students become volunteers for a few days a week. They make a contractual agreement with the program director and are given certain responsibilities. They are paired with one or two elders, and act as their friend and take their histories, which develop into projects. One young woman who was very talented in photography made a booklet for the program that was a portrait photo book with a brief biography of the member photographed. This project became a published book. This youth–elder program has received recognition at mental health conferences and in publications. The young people become very attached to their client–friend, and a form of grandparent–grandchild interaction is formed. This is a benefit for both.

## ☐ Summary

The fear of being overwhelmed with distress and sorrow when working with the client with dementia is understandable, however this concept is based on some misconceptions. Although problems with the aging and the elderly client are difficult, there is movement in the field. There certainly is a growing need for clinicians who bring a more informed mode of therapy and art therapy to this population. With the growing interest in psycho/neuro/biological/brain/mind processes, and mind-body explorations, the therapist can come to this population with a new perspective. Understanding the limitations and the possibilities of the clients with dementia clarifies the therapeutic structure. Within that structure the possibilities can be rewarding and a challenge to one's creativity.

Art becomes the primary mode of therapy and communication. Accepting this shift from a dominantly verbal cognitive stance, to an emotional-experiential stance is an exciting experience for people who are willing to let go of traditional parameters of therapy. The inclusion of the other expressive arts is also useful. In this manner providing an integrated therapeutic experience to the elderly client, the therapist is rewarded by having a wide spectrum of creative opportunities. The challenge is the reward.

A rather remarkable incident happened that reinforces my curiosity about how our mind works and our senses interface. One of the more alert men at the center, and one who had been very active in our group, had an ear infection that prohibited the use of his hearing aid. Mr. Jones was rendered completely deaf. He had over the last year become an enthusiastic and talented artist, using acrylics to create beautifully colored abstract paintings. Every day he impatiently waited for the studio art time. This day he could hardly make a mark. Little squiggle lines, made up of rather unpleasant colors was all he could do. He looked depressed as he said, "How can I paint when I cannot hear?" I had never considered how sight and sound complement each other. Thinking about dramatic events, such as this, makes speculating about the complexities of how we experience the world one of the advantages of working with the elderly.

The client with dementia is not the only person to be served in this setting. Relatives, both close and more distant, attentive caregivers, and all people who share the world of the elderly client are worthy of supportive therapeutic interventions. Finding a program, such as the one I have described, makes interacting with the elderly a positive experience. That is not to say that there are not countless moments of sadness, even anger, at the progression of deterioration that is to be expected. However, sadness does not necessarily equate with depression. Sadness is a normal reaction, which makes working with the client with dementia within the range of our normal spectrum of emotions and capabilities. Aside from sadness, there is joy, humor, and a spirit of collegiality with a team that is caring and patient with men and women that have contributed to the world.

For those who want to experience the full range of the human life span, I want to reassure them that it is worthwhile to pick up the challenge of working with the elderly with dementia.

# ☐ References

Aol.com/search/fastweb?getdoc+viewcomptons+A=534=0=Geriatrics. 12/27/99 America Online Academic Assistance Center. (1999)

Bayles, K. A., & Tomoeda, C. K. (1997). *Improving function in dementia and other cognitive–linguistic disorders.* Tucson, AZ: Canyonlands.

Compton's Encyclopedia Online (Version 3.0). (1998). The Learning Company.

Damasio, A. (1994). *Descartes' error.* New York: Avon Boosks.

Doric-Henry, L. (1997). Pottery as art therapy with elderly nursing home residents. *Art Therapy, 14,* 163–171.

Jenson, S. M. (1997). Multiple pathways to self: A multisensory art experience. *Art Therapy, 14,* 178-186.

Kahn-Davis, K. B. (1997). Behind the veil: Mandala drawings by dementia patients. *Art Therapy, 14,* 194–199.

Landgarten, H. B. (1981). *Clinical art therapy.* New York: Brunner/Mazel.

Seigel, D. J. (1999). *The developing mind.* New York: Guilford.

Shore, S. (1997) Promoting wisdom: The role of art therapy in a geriatric setting. *Art Therapy, 14 ,* 172–177.

Spaniol, S. (1997). Art therapy with older adults: Challenging myths, building competencies. *Art Therapy, 14,* 158–160.

UCLA Alzhiemer's Disease Center Publication. Winter: 1999. California University Press.

## ☐ Suggested Readings

Bertman, S. L. (1991). *Images, insight, and interventions.* Washington, DC: Hemisphere.

Blee, T., & Kaye, C. (Eds.). (1997). *The arts in health care: A palette of possibilities.* London: Jessica Kingsley.

Bush, J. (1997). The development of school art therapy in Dade County public schools: Implications for future change. *Art Therapy, 14,* 9–14.

Carni, S., & Mashia, T. (1996). Painting as a language for a stroke victim. *Art Therapy, 13,* 265–270.

Compton's Encyclopedia Online (Version 3.0). (1998). The Learning Company.

Couch, J. B. (1997). Multiple pathways to self: A multisensory art experience. *Art Therapy, 14,* 178–186.

Couch, J. B. (1997). Behind the veil: Mandala drawings by dementia patients. *Art Therapy, 14,* 187–193.

Deichman, E. S., & Kociecki, R. (1989). *Working with the elderly: An introduction.* Buffalo, New York: Prometheus Books.

---

The References and Suggested Readings include a group of books that are designed for the families and caretakers of a person suffering from progressive dementia. Self-help books that explain the progressive manner of dementia, and the methods that make this progression less painful, are a help for families that are faced with this developmental crisis.

There are numerous non-technical texts in the bookstores. I have listed a few that were recommended. The first choice is *The 36-Hour Day,* by Mace and Rubies. This choice was made by the director and staff of the Opica agency. There may be others that are helpful.

The second text is far more comprehensive and will serve the therapist and the family that wishes advanced understanding of problems and treatment, *Improving Function in Dementia and Other Cognitive–Linguistic Disorders* by K. A. Bayles & C. K. Tomoeda, (1997).

Doric-Henry, L. (1997). Pottery as art therapy with elderly nursing home residents. *Art Therapy, 14,* 163–171.

Dowling, J. R. (1995). *Keeping busy: A handbook of activities for persons with dementia.* Baltimore, MD: The Johns Hopkins University Press.

Drackmik, C. (1995). *Interpreting metaphors in children's drawings.* Burlingame, CA: Abbeygate Press.

Dunn-Snow, P. (1997). The gorilla did it! Integration of art therapy and language arts in the public schools. *Art Therapy, 14,* 50–53.

Dyer, J. (1996). *In a tangled wood: An Alzheimer's journey.* Dallas, TX: Southern Methodist University Press.

Engle, P., & Muller, E. F. (1997). A reflection on art therapy and aging. *Art Therapy, 14,* 206–209.

Essex, M., Frosting, K., & Hertz, J. (1996). In the service of children: Art and expressive therapies in public schools. *Art Therapy, 13,* 181–190.

Gregoire, P. A. (1998). Imitation response and mimesis in dementia. *Art Therapy, 15,* 261–264.

Gruetzner, H. (1992). *Alzheimer's: A caregiver's guide and source book.* New York: Wiley.

Harway, M. (1996). *Treating the changing family.* New York: Wiley.

Hodgkinson, L. (1995). *Alzheimer's disease: Your questions answered.* London: Wellington House.

Julliard, K. (1998). Outcomes research in health care: Implications for art therapy. *Art Therapy, 15,* 13–21.

Kahn-Davis, K. B. (1997). Behind the veil: Mandala drawings by dementia patients. *Art Therapy, 14,* 194–199.

Kahn-Denis, K. B. (1997). Art therapy with geriatric dementia clients. *Art Therapy, 14,* 194–199.

Kerr, C. C. (1999). The psychosocial significance of creativity in the elderly. *Art Therapy, 16,* 37–41.

Kiendl, C., Hooyenga, K., & Trenn, E. (1997). Empowered to scribble. *Art Therapy, 14,* 37–43.

Knapp, N. M. (1994). Research with diagnostic drawings for normal and Alzheimer's subjects. *Art Therapy, 11,* 131–138.

Lambert, D. (1995). *The life and art of "Grandma" Layton.* Waco, TX: WRS.

Malchiodi, C. (1999). *Medical art therapy with adults.* London: Jessica Kingsley.

Malchiodi, C. A. (1997). Art therapy in schools. *Art Therapy, 14,* 2–3.

Manor Health Corporation. (1996). *At the heart of Alzhiemer's: Guidebook to understanding and caring for a person with Alzheimer's disease.* Silver Springs, MD: Manor Health.

Miller, B. (1984). Art therapy with the elderly and the terminally ill. In T. Daley (ed.), *Art as Therapy* (pp. 127–139). London: Tavistock.

Oliver, R., & Bock, F. A. (1987). *Coping with Alzheimer's: A caretaker's emotional survival Guide.* New York: Dodd Mead.

Orr, P. P. (1997). Treating the whole person: A combination of medical and psychiatric treatment for older adults. *Art Therapy, 14,* 200–205.

Parashak, S. T. (1997). The richness that surrounds us: Collaboration of classroom and community for art therapy and art education. *Art Therapy, 14,* 241–245.

Prager, A. (1995). Pediatric art therapy: Strategies and applications. *Art Therapy, 12,* 32–38.

Ridker, C., & Savage, S. (1996). *Railing against the rush of years: A personal journey through aging via art therapy.* London: Jessica Kingsley.

Rode, D. C. (1995). Building bridges within the cultural of pediatric medicine: The interface of art therapy and child life programming. *Art Therapy, 12,* 104–110.

Rosal, M. L., McColloch-Vislisel, S., & Neece, S. (1997). Keeping students in school: An art therapy program to benefit ninth-grade students. *Art Therapy, 14,* 30–36.

Rosner, D. I. (1995). Medical art therapy: A window into history. *Art Therapy, 12,* 135–136.

Russel, J. (1995). Art therapy on a hospital burn unit: A step towards healing and recovery. *Art Therapy, 12,* 39–45.

Schexnaydre, C. (1993) Images from the past: The life review scrapbook technique with the elderly. In E. Virshup (Ed.), *California Art Therapy Trends.* Chicago: Magnolia Street.

Silver, R. (1978). *Developing cognitive and creative skills through art.* Baltimore, MD: University Park Press.

Silver, R. (1997). Sex and age difference in attitude toward the opposite sex. *Art Therapy, 14,* 268–.

Silver, R. (1999). Differences among aging and young adults in attitudes and cognition. *Art Therapy, 16,* 133–139.

Smitheman-Brown, V., & Church, R. P. (1996). Mandala drawing: Facilitating creative growth in children with ADD or ADHD. *Art Therapy, 13,* 252–260.

Vick, R.M. (1999). Utilizing prestructured art elements in brief group art therapy with adolescents. *Art Therapy, 16,* 68–77.

Wald, J. (1989). Art therapy for patients with Alzhheimer's disease and related disorders. In H. Wadeson, J. Durkin, & D. Perach (Ed.), *Advances in Art therapy* (pp. 204–221). New York: Wiley.

Yale, R. (1995). *Developing support groups for individuals with early-stage Alzheimer's Disease: Planning, implementing, and evaluation.* Baltimore, MD: Health Professions Press.

8

# Groups in Psychiatric Hospitals and Day Treatment Programs: Art as an Entrée into Unfamiliar Realities

Describing group treatment for persons who have been diagnosed with a form of psychosis is a difficult task at this time in mental health services. The population that requires specialized attention because of a diagnosis of schizophrenia, bi-polar or severe depression, paranoia, and other serious conditions that interfere with functioning in the world, are offered treatment within a broad spectrum of services. To present a plan for group therapy using the art modality depends entirely on the setting and the policy of the hospital or facility. To make some sense of the present day in-patient services, I will follow the programs according to their time line.

In some hospitals the "revolving door" policy of the 72-hour hold is the necessary time frame; in other hospitals funded by private insurance, state funds and Medicare, the treatment duration may last as long as nine months. There are places where long-term care still is provided. Veteran Administration hospitals and a few state facilities have programs that are not time limited, except by the discretion of the medical team. This chapter attempts to give some basic ground rules that apply in most contexts, and discusses how art as language can best be used with persons who are not in touch with reality and have limited skills in introducing someone to their created reality.

## ☐ Inpatient Groups

Vinogradov and Yalom (1989) suggest that there are certain features of inpatient groups that the therapist should anticipate:

1. Rapid changes in group composition.
2. Patients in brief treatment participate for only a few sessions.
3. Frequent meetings (often daily).
4. Little or no time for group preparation.
5. Presence of severe psychopathology.
6. Great heterogeneity in patient's pathology.
7. Rotating staff/lack of continuity in group leaders.
8. Myriad effects of ward milieu on group process.
9. Presence of extra-group socializing.
10. May be only form of psychotherapy available to patient.
11. May be only forum to address stress of hospitalization (p. 110).

In light of the above list, there appears to be few circumstances that provide the client with an opportunity to regain some form of stability. The onset of a severe psychological disturbance, often accompanied by hallucinations and anxiety are extremely distressing. There is the danger of suicide or deliberate misuse of drugs that require immediate interventions. Add to that the confusion of the hospital, the large staff and many fellow patients moving about, and one can imagine how, initially, the hospital appears to the patient as a place of danger, not a refuge. It is important for therapists to keep this fearful emotional reaction in mind as they plan for the group activities.

## ☐ The Brief-Brief Group: An Assessment and Supportive Function

In most hospitals there is an ongoing group that provides art therapy as the primary mode of expression. The group is usually open ended, since the short stays during assessment are based on the 72-hour model. Often the patients are in group because they are forced to comply with the daily activity program; they are not introduced to the use of imagery as a therapeutic tool. In addition, the group members may have very different degrees of psychopathology and behavioral symptoms. How can a group possibly survive these hurdles (Pepin & Wakefield, 1996)?

Although it is not fail-safe, the group for recently-committed patients can be held together with a judicious use of art as the primary mode of communication. The focus of the group is to help the patient learn to express their distress by communicating to their personal self, and occasionally to others. It may seem strange to communicate to the self, but through graphic expression the patient can make the first step to safely release some of their extreme feelings. The piece of paper and the group setting act as a container where some statement can be made in graphic form that would be too difficult or even impossible to express verbally. In addition, observing other hospitalized persons using this nonthreatening mode of therapy gives the individual the first sense of using the hospital to regain some sense of stability. Careful planning will equip the leader with a selection of themes that can be helpful to a newly introduced member, as well as the more experienced member, and to externalize the powerful forces that have become dominant (Haesler, 1997).

## Structure and Directives

To do an expressive art group in these circumstances the therapist must have media that is simple and easily controlled. The art tools should be limited and presented to each person in a small container. The paranoid patient would be stressed if they were forced to share their pastels, and the manic patient would be out of control if offered too many choices. From the moment of group assembly each move is thought through and structured. The structure does not have to be obvious, but it must be there.

The group members usually feel more secure if they draw an individual drawing. If the group is not too large they may wish to discuss their product, but more often the art will be left unexplained. The art suggestion to the group should have something to do with the here-and-now experience of being in the hospital. For example "What did you feel when you first arrived here?" "How can the staff help you?" "Draw three colors that represent your feelings the first day." Collage pictures should be available, as well as simple drawing tools, such as oil pastels and felt pens. Do not be surprised if many of the group members do some art that seems to have little to do with the therapist's suggestion. What the therapist has done is set a structure, taken responsibility for the goal, and demonstrated that all forms of representation are acceptable. The deviant expressions should be honored for being more important to the individual than the therapist's notions. In addition, with psychotic patients, therapists as never know if they are *not* responding. Their art language is their own, and perhaps not translatable to others.

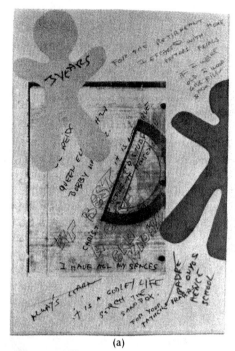

(a)

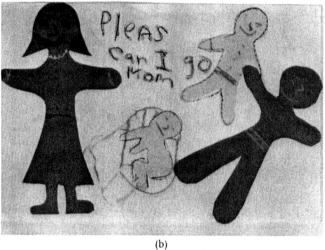

(b)

**FIGURE 8.1.** (a) Two examples of using pre-cut figures; with a baby, an adolescent, an adult male and female, with a 60-year-old schizophrenic male. Responds to the directive, "Recall stages of your life," with "It's a goofy life. For retirement, I escaped with the flies." (b) A 30-year-old male, diagnosed as manic-depressive, asks his mother, "Please can I go mom." Displays seeking permission at all stages of development.

The therapist should be secure in the knowledge that any form of externalization is a step toward self-regulation. To do even the most chaotic scribble the client has had to make some decisions. Pick up the felt pen, move the hand, and observe the shape that is created; choose to change the form, or leave it alone; write a title. Any product is testimony to still being alive in this world, and on some level in control of "marking a mark." The goals are minimal in these groups. Comfort derived from moving media across the page, and seeing attractive colors emerge, is sufficient for a patient that may only be in the group two or three times. This is a period to give pragmatic and ordinary life directives and accept abstract and unusual responses.

An outsider might ask, "Why bother with the directive if everyone does whatever they chose to?" The answer is that the therapist shows that they are sensitive to the impact of the milieu—that they regard the group as "normal" and have normal expectations, but knows that being in crisis is painful. The therapist appreciates that there are different levels of functioning and some members can be responsive to reality and some not, and that the art product often has a meaning to the creator that the outsider may never know. The art often has a calming effect. It can be a nonverbal comment or externalization, and the maker is secure in the fact that it can be honored unconditionally.

The therapist must lookout for members that become over stimulated with the colors, movement, and shapes that emerge on the page. These members should be observed and perhaps asked to fill in a solid from around their art. Agitated clients must be promptly attended to, and if sitting next to this person and instigating a containing frame around the images is not enough, they should be asked to return the next day when they will be less anxious. Bear in mind the context of the hospital where safety is everywhere, and this brief 72-hour stay is to provide medication and support and reduce suicidal intent (Hrenko & Willis, 1996).

## Therapeutic Advantage of a Brief Service Art Experience

Except in rare cases, the art helps patients to focus. In the act of making a product they may close out the surrounding environment and retreat into an inner world. This is not a goal that would be recommended in other circumstances, but here the major task is to help patients gather forces together and regulate themselves to the best of their ability. A pleasurable task that allows the interior thoughts to surface on the page where they can be observed and contained, is of great use. In addition, the staff can observe if the drawings become less chaotic, indicating that medication is effective. Or the opposite, if the work indicates greater decompensation of form and control, some new approach may be indicated. There is more agitation than apathy displayed in these intake groups, and the goal of containment and support makes the structure of the group very clear (see Figure 8.1).

The therapists often become distressed themselves in a parallel manner. Therapeutic training emphasizes the therapeutic relationship as the most valuable tool of therapy. In these brief-brief groups there is little, if any, chance to establish a relationship. Therapists should not exclusively confine their hours to this type of group. It is not unusual for therapists to find that the patient's disorganized and sometimes demonic images have been absorbed into their own image bank.

As mentioned earlier, it is important to consult with a therapist friend and externalize these images and deal with the overload. To work only in crisis interventions with extremely disturbed clients can lead to early burnout.

**FIGURE 8.2.** A Plasticine figure representing "Personal Feelings" from a 32-year-old female who was sexually abused.

# ☐ Long-Term Art Groups for Hospitalized Patients

There are two types of art groups offered in long-term treatment of hospitalized patients. One is for higher-functioning patients and one is for lower-functioning patients. The goal is for the lower-functioning group to move up to the higher-functioning group. The next move is to join the community and a day treatment program, or to become a functioning member of society. Chronicity is an issue in assigning the proper group for the individual, and the constant attention to the patient's needs is necessary in order to avoid keeping them in a group that is no longer appropriate. The following discussion will explore the these groups.

All of the inpatient groups share some of these goals, according to Vinogradov and Yalom (1989).

1. Engage the patient in the therapeutic process.
2. Teach the patient that talking (and making art expressions) helps.
3. Teach how to spot maladaptive interpersonal behavior.
4. Decrease patient's sense of isolation.
5. Allow patients to be helpful to others.
6. Alleviate hospital-related anxiety (p. 113).

I will offer a selection of activities that employ art to achieve the goals listed above (see Figure 8.2).

## Lower-Functioning Group

Patients whose self-regulating aptitudes are in disarray, and whose cognitive abilities are not online, should not be pressured to express their feelings in a manner that suits the normal patterns. The confused or frightening dialogues that are in the mind of many of these patients are out of most people's experience. One cannot imagine what one has never known. For this reason, an open studio approach may be best for these clients. Not because this is a "lower" form of art in therapy, but because creating an art product is often the first step to organizing mental processes. For many of the reasons mentioned above, a free environment where the art product is admired for itself alone (uninterpreted), is often the first hospital experience that is directly connected to a personal and creative statement. There is pride in achievement, and stimulation of self-worth when the art is admired and a focus of approbation. McNiff (1999) has spoken about the value of a nonverbal and verbal dialogue with the created product. The therapeutic process is instigated through the personal vocabulary of the creator.

Holtom (1978) describes the opportunity to do expressive work in the hospital: "The art department in a psychiatric hospital is often an asylum within an asylum. That is to say it is a refuge from the depersonalizing maneuvers of a large institution and its agents. It also provides people with the space to express inconvenient or unspeakable feelings" (p. 163).

An unwelcome, but necessary, component of the chronically-hospitalized patient is the effects of medication. Certainly the wide range of pharmaceutical drugs are becoming progressively less toxic to the consumer. However, there is often a dulling effect and a repression of imagery. This is good if the imagery is frightening, but it is a loss of creativity. Perhaps, as art therapists, my colleagues and I are sad to lose the exceptional art that has emerged from patients classified as psychotic. Their art speaks to the observer in ways that stir emotions and reactions in a unique manner. Books and exhibits of "outsider art" are an attraction for the general public as well as mental health providers (Figure 8.3).

When the term "open studio" is used, it is not that there is literally a studio with easels and a selection of paint medias. Few facilities have this available, and if they do the approach is often a drop-in policy. These are very useful and successful art studios, and the patients that benefit from them, are not classified as in group therapy in

**FIGURE 8.3.** An example of "Outsider Art," purchased at a hospital fundraiser. Artist unknown.

this text. Open studios are often run by artists and require a specially-trained person. The work done in these studios is therapeutic, but the fact that there is no assigned group at any particular period of time, falls out of the frame for this discussion (Henley, 1995).

However, the open studio format can be incorporated in groups that are assigned to meet at a specific time, with a specific group of members. Often uninitiated staff sees these groups as purely an art class. This perception leads to overcrowding and disrespect of boundaries. Staff may come unannounced into the group meeting to take a patient to another appointment. The staff may wish to sit in and join in the art project. All of these interruptions discourage group cohesion, which is difficult under any circumstances. Consultation with administration and education of the milieu is absolutely necessary for establishing the needed structure.

The groups with lower-functioning patients should provide a theme for each meeting. Clear and uncomplicated themes that are directed toward integration of thoughts and expressive of feelings are successful. "How are you today? How would you like to be most days?" "How did you feel when you were visited yesterday?" "Have you helped someone today?" "Show how you are reacting to your new medication." The directives are in the present, and they are concrete. It is also useful to display drawings from the previous meeting to establish visually that the group is ongoing and that it is permanent and safe (Lieberman, 1996).

## *Commonalties Shared by Hospitalized Groups*

In the groups discussed above, and with the higher-functioning groups, the notion of helping another can be fostered though art tasks that ask the group to make a product that demonstrates support of a member in distress, or make a solution-focused image that is intended for the entire group around a milieu problem.

The overcrowded group ceases to function as a forum for problem solving or resolution of reactions to being hospitalized, or even of reducing the fear of isolation. With too many people assigned to a group, there is greater chaos and the most disturbed members will withdraw into themselves as a protective measure. The alternative of exploding with escalating violence can be the result of too many stimuli. Art conscious therapists should use their expertise to counteract oversized groups. They can separate the group into smaller groups of six and give each subgroup their own art project. Sometimes, it is even helpful to make the task a nonverbal one, thus calming the group in a more radical manner. This choice would have to be used judiciously.

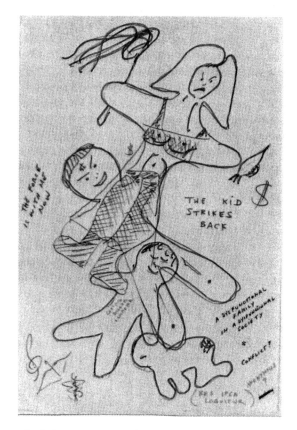

**FIGURE 8.4.** A dual-diagnosed woman depicts the stages of life with her abusive mother. "The force is with me now," "The kid strikes back." "Dysfunctional family in a dysfunctional society."

Often, if the directive is interesting to the smaller groups, they will be less verbal and concentrate on producing the product (see Figure 8.4).

If the groups within the group are able, they could have a spokesman report on the activity. If the group is higher functioning, the task could be a group task to which all the members contributed. There are many variations on this theme; however, the task oriented art expression is the creative focus that helps to regulate the interactions of a group.

## Higher-Functioning Inpatient Groups

These groups in a hospital or a day treatment program are structured in a similar manner. The members have retained or regained some ability to process their thoughts and emotions, and are preparing to move away from the protective environment of the hospital. They are being encouraged to communicate more clearly, express positive feelings, be aware of their mannerism and social skills, listen and form friendships (Vinogradov and Yalom, 1998).

The art tasks are created to make the goals of the group concrete. The patients are asked to make into pictorial form some of the tasks that have to be faced to re-enter the socioeconomic world, practical adjustments to the world outside the hospital.

For example, the group may make collages in which they imagine where they will be living after they leave the hospital. They would also be asked to make visible their feelings about moving into their homes or a halfway house. Reuniting with family after a psychotic episode is difficult on both sides. Doing art that confronts these problematic issues allows the patient to create the situation and then make dynamic changes on the visual product to indicate mastery and competence. What can be imagined can be translated into reality. It may take a long time, but imagination is the first step toward action.

It is important to confront and contain the tendency to revert back to wanting the nuclear family to come forth and solve their problems. With severely distressed people with psychopathological states of mind, an inordinate percentage of the adults still long for symbiotic attachment to their parents, primarily the mother. When they are preparing for a more active engagement outside the hospital, the "call" to the mother arises many times. This may indicate that their early attachment experience was inadequate, it also may indicate that the disease has reactivated more primitive longings to be loved and protected in the present as they may have been in the past. Chances are that their early life was not conducive to building a secure attachment and separation pattern, and their brain was impacted by these experiences. In the hospital setting there is no time to research these speculations. It is better to stay in the here-and-now and strengthen the skills that have survived and the coping skills that remain and can be improved. Many of the longed for mothers are either dead or out of touch, by choice or distance. The actual families of chronic psychotic people are usually totally exhausted financially and emotionally. They have little interest in entering the hospitalized person's life in an active way. It would be unkind to encourage the patient to fantasize that this would be a possibility (see Figure 8.5 a and b).

For this reason, the art tasks should reflect issues of case management. For many therapists this is the least interesting phase of group interaction. The goals are not to stimulate emotions or explore issues, but to muster the coping skills and pragmatic information centers in

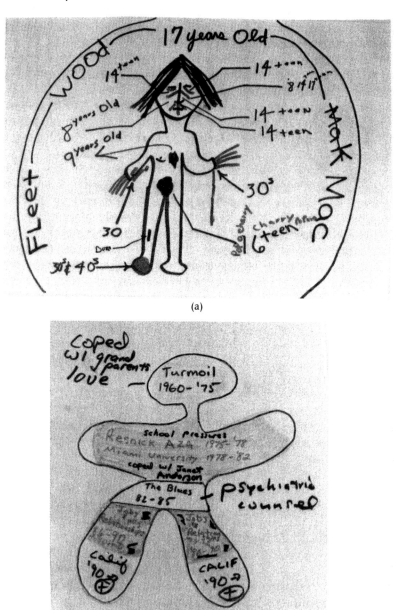

(a)

(b)

**FIGURE 8.5.** (a) A 40-year-old male schizophrenic on the directive, "Indicate your emotional injuries at different ages, where they were experienced on your body." (b) A 40-year-old male with major depression on the same directive. "Psychiatric confused," "Turmoil, school pressure, the blues."

the brain. In spite of these everyday issues that the group focuses upon, the art is extremely useful. By making these goals concrete, the patient must use their entire capacity for decision making and memory preservation. They can carry the conclusions for positive action in a more successful way if they have been active in creating and declaring the solution. The art product is formed in an active manner; it demands of the mind both the holistic thinking of the right brain and the cognitive decisions of the left brain. The physical motions of making the art, the ocular centers that record the product, and the verbal activity that explains the art product combine to make the problem-solving situation one that is imprinted in the learning center from multiple areas of experience.

There is a good chance that there may still be hallucinatory voices sending messages to the patient. Therefore, when more areas of cognition and decision making are brought into action, the better the chances the experiences of memory and integration of positive decisions have of remaining viable (Killick & Schaverian, 1997) (see Figures 8.6 and 8.7).

## Termination

The chances that there will be a formal termination in a manner that psychotherapists have been trained to expect is minimal. Termination

**FIGURE 8.6.** A male in his late forties responds to the directive, "What's on your mind today?" His "Death Wish" stems from his diagnosis of HIV.

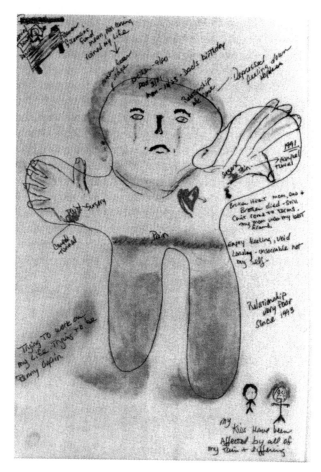

FIGURE 8.7. A 42-year-old female with bi-polar disorder indicates the pain in her hands and the situations that created the pain.

occurs when the insurance runs out, the facility has to make a turn over, or when the patient has reached a point of stability that the hospital feels the person can move on to a more open facility. The best termination ritual that can be performed in a hospital group is to bring the folder of the patient's artwork to them as a parting gift. The therapist can emphasize that this compendium of treatment demonstrates the commitment to growth that the patient has made. It also demonstrates that there are issues and potential areas of concern that have been addressed, but may indicate a place to begin a new outpatient therapeutic relationship. In other words, the patient can take their therapy with them (see Figure 8.8).

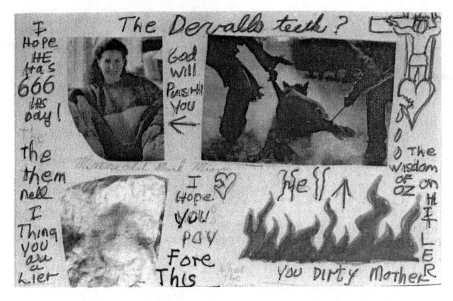

**FIGURE 8.8.** A 35-year-old male paranoid schizophrenic responds to the directive, "What's on your mind today?"

## ☐ Summary

When a person has had a major disorientation of normal brain functions and subsequent changes in behaviors severe enough that the family or mental health professional feels that he or she needs protection and intense evaluation and treatment, they are admitted to a psychiatric hospital. Group treatment is often the major therapeutic intervention available. The group is offered under difficult conditions, which are the result of financial restrictions and a policy of minimal psychotherapy and maximum pharmaceutical treatment.

The addition of art expression provides the patient with a mode of expression that is in contrast, and a relief from, the constant barrage of words, directed at him or her from the staff and from their interior voices. The entire experience tends to be frightening, at least at first, and the comparative calm of a focused task that calls upon a knowing that is generally not cognitive is a relief. The artwork may be incomprehensible, but it is a personal statement and does not need to be justified. There is a pleasure component built into media and color, and satisfaction in achieving a product that is accepted without interpretation.

In the environment of crisis interventions and extremely painful problems, a creative moment can be treasured to the time invested in its creation. The art can be carried in the mind as an image which has many levels of meaning—meaning which may reveal itself gradually as the patient becomes more clear and has time to enter a more functional state of being.

# ☐ References

Haesler, M. P. (1997). In K. Killick & J. Saverian. *Art psychotherapy and psychosis.* New York: Routledge.

Henley, D. (1995). A consideration of the studio as therapeutic intervention. *Art Therapy, 12,* 188–190.

Hrenko, K., & Willis, R. (1996). The amusement park technique in the treatment of dually diagnosed psychiatric patients. *Art Therapy, 13,* 261.

Killick, K., & Schaverian, J. (1997). *Art, psychotherapy and psychosis.* London: Jessica Kingsley.

Liebermann, M. (1996). *Art approaches to conflict.* London: Jessica Kingsley Publishers.

McNiff, S. (1999). The virtual art therapy studio. *Art Therapy, 16,* 197–200.

Pepin-Wakefield, Y. (1996). Artistic productions as a diagnostic approach to illness. *Art Therapy, 13,* 293–296.

Vinogradov, S., & Yalom, I. D. (1989). *A concise guide to group psychotherapy.* Washington, DC: American Psychiatric Press.

# ☐ Suggested Readings

Alter-Muri, S. (1994). Pschopathology of expression and the therapeutic value of exhibiting chronic clients art: A case study. *Art Therapy, 11,* 219–223.

Braun, L. N. (1997). In from the cold: Art therapy with homeless men. *Art Therapy, 14,* 118–122.

Engle, P. (1997). Art therapy and dissociative disorders. *Art Therapy, 14,* 246–254.

Frostig, K. E. (1997). Organizing exhibitions of art by people with mental illness: A step-by-step manual. *Art Therapy, 14,* 131–132.

Hanes, M. (1995). Clinical applications of the "scribble technique" with adults in an acute inpatient psychiatric hospital. *Art Therapy, 12,* 111–117.

Kaplan, F. F. (1998). Anger imagery and age: Further investigations in the art of anger. *Art Therapy, 15,* 116–119.

Rosner D. I. (1995). Medical art therapy: A window into history. *Art Therapy, 12,* 135–136.

Ross, C. (1997). *Something to draw on: Activities and interventions using an art therapy approach.* London: Jessica Kingsley.

Spaniol, S. (1998). Toward an ethnographic approach to art therapy research: People with psychiatric disabilities as collaborators. *Art Therapy, 15,* 29–37.

CHAPTER

Laurel M. Thompson

# Integration of Art, Movement, and Verbal Processing with Women in an Eating Disorders Program

This chapter uses a psychodynamic model to explore the relation between art, movement and verbal group therapy. This model is considerably different from the more post modern philosophies in the companion chapters. Psychodynamic theory influences how the therapist incorporates and integrates verbalization in an art therapy group, and makes decisions concerning levels of verbal and nonverbal processing. The art therapist's theoretical framework or goal for a particular group may influence the use of verbalization as a therapeutic intervention. This decision will vary depending on the involvement of the patient in the healing process of creative improvisation (Nachmanovitch, 1990): the use of art as a way to channel and structure feeling, the ongoing development of the image as symbol, and the readiness of the patient to use the artwork to foster verbal insight.

The group leader may choose to focus on the art image exclusively without verbalization because they believe the art making itself is the curative factor. Verbal insight may not be encouraged if the patient is using the art-making process as a means of structuring emotional organization or regulating affect. In some cases, the patient may not be able to articulate feelings verbally, either due to decreased ego skills or timing of the therapy process, and uses the art process and or product as an auxiliary ego. If patients are struggling to create symbols or complete an articulated image, it might be antithetical to disturb that process by talking. However, verbal exploration may be productive at times when the patient connects the nonverbal image with the insight that verbalization can bring. Which direction to take is dependent on the patient's functioning, the clinical setting, and the stage in the therapeutic process.

A common misunderstanding of the creative arts therapy process among analytically trained verbal therapists is that encouraging image-making is to encourage resistance or acting-out. Verbal articulation is seen to be the ultimate goal of working through: To use "action" is to act out. This is a historical viewpoint, derived from early attempts to put psychoanalysis in a scientific framework, thus looking at the "art" of psychoanalysis as suspicious (Guntrip, 1971). However, creative arts therapists encourage a working-through process, through non-verbal organization in addition to verbalization. The goal is not to forestall verbal insight per se, but to use the ability of the arts to differentiate and shape the material that cannot be expressed in words at the time.

In an attempt to clarify questions about the place of verbal work in art therapy specifically and creative arts therapy in general, work with women burdened with eating disorders will be examined in this chapter. The use of dance and movement therapy, art therapy, and verbal therapy with women with eating disorders highlights the issues involved in determining the effectiveness of integrating verbal and experiential modes of therapeutic intervention. The employment of these three modalities highlights significant differences in intrapsychic functioning with women with eating disorders and how it plays out in the context of group work. Group process can be seen to operate on individual, interpersonal, and group-as-a-whole levels (Rutan & Stone, 1984). Intrapsychic change takes place by focusing on individual psychodynamic forces. Interpersonal learning helps clients learn to be with others in the world through the microcosm of the therapy group (Yalom, 1985). Individuals learn about their own relationships by exploring their responses to others and avoiding the tendency to distance themselves from others by analyzing their interactions. The group is always more than its parts and the group as a whole is a powerful therapeutic agent. Through the use and function of kinesthetic, visual, and verbal modalities evolve and take on specific forms in conjunction with these different levels of group process.

# ☐ **Aesthetic Developmental Process**

Normal developmental process entails a move from a kinesthetic and movement understanding of the world to a visual one, and finally to an ability to understand the world through words (Sptiz, 1965; Piaget, 1969). Kinesthetic knowledge is reception, emphasizing a process of taking in from internal experience in order to know the world. Visual knowledge is perception, highlighting knowledge of the world though taking in of the environment and others. The use of movement and body experience can contact the most primitive areas of knowledge. In contrast, visual expressions incorporate the outside world to a greater degree, since it involves the translation of inner experience to the art, which is separate from the body. Verbal understanding of the world enables linear thought and abstract thinking. To achieve deep under-standing from multiple levels of knowledge and experience, kines-thetic, visual, and verbal modes are recommended.

Women with eating disorders are familiar and comfortable with process-ing through words, but if one listens closely, their words are often repetitions of knowledge that they have obtained by rote. "Fake in-sight" (J. Lavender, personal communication, 1998) is often verbal-ized, but this is often not insight based on any internal experience or knowing. Comparing work done in dance and movement therapy and art therapy clearly highlights that body knowledge is severely limited if nonexistent, but the ability to use visual imagery is strong. It seems as if the women are "restricting" body experience and "devouring" the art therapy process. It appears that the art process is closer to the earliest learning, in a developmental sense. Thus visual imagery might feel safer and easier to attain. It provides safety by distancing feelings and introjects of the internal world.

In contrast, dance and movement therapy highlights the paucity of body knowledge for these women. To go into the body is unknown, frightening, or overwhelming. To use and take imagery outside of the body is easier. Art provides boundaries around potentially threatening experiences. However, since there are limits to each of these modali-ties, and in the struggle to make meaning for women with eating disorders, I use art, movement, and verbal interventions conjointly in group treatment. The degree of structure in the art or movement directive is important in this context. Structured directives can lead to knowledge; the structure serves as an auxiliary ego. However, without unstructured directives, unconscious meaning and metaphors often stay inaccessible to verbal insight (McNeilly, 1983; Thompson, 1993).

Unexpectedly, the ability to use creative arts therapy deepened when

I led verbal groups in conjunction. Since verbal groups can be experienced as relatively safe (in that women with eating disorders can more easily defend in words), my leading the verbal groups and the creative arts therapy groups together enhanced the patients' trust—trust which is necessary to fully utilize metaphor and improvisation modes of experiential learning. The following case illustrations are taken from work in a five-day-a-week, short- to medium-stay day treatment program, in a private, outpatient day treatment facility for women with variations of anorexia and bulimia.

## ☐ Destructive Group Forces and Eating Disorders

It is important in any setting to focus on group process and interventions that foster therapeutic change. Factors such as cohesion, universality, interpersonal learning, and corrective emotional experiences (Yalom, 1985) are generally acknowledged to be positive mechanisms of change. In addition, the exploration of transference can lead to knowledge about patterns in relationships that are influenced by internalized significant relationships. However, destructive group forces also exist in groups, emerging from the nature of groups themselves and from the dynamics that develop from the mix of a particular group's composition. These anti-group forces arise from many factors, including the inherent difficulties involved in being a group member; feelings of neglect, deprivation and shame that a group member may experience in response to having to share group time; and the aggression and hostility experienced when the group and its members fail to contain feelings (Nitsun, 1996, p. 58).

The psychodynamic configuration of women with eating disorders contributes to forces that work against the creative potential of groups. The activity and reliance on food-related behaviors serve as adaptations to a lack of a reliable internal self and regulation of feelings. The clients control their eating to control their world, since there is not a locus of control inside themselves. However, being an active group member means that one must give up rigid controls over one's self in order to allow the group influence to offer new perspectives. This entails a lessening of boundaries to form connections that are alive, but also to allow change by responding to the ongoing interaction of those group members who are involved. For many people with eating disorders, the body becomes a split-off object, constantly compared to external standards, instead of a resource for interaction and evolution of experience. The body/self strives to remain autonomous, but in an isolated and depriving way. In relation to the use of the creative process and aesthetic organization, the lack of a fluid access to using kinesthetic or visual means of experience, this isolation can also be a source of anti-group phenomenon.

Anti-group phenomenon are a natural force in group functioning. When resistance emerges within the group, it limits new behavior and internalizations. The destructive forces need to be overcome and group members must look at their own part in the creation of them. The group can then become transformational, through the use of the group as a transitional object (Nitsun, 1996). The use of the creative arts can be used directly in this process.

## Stages of Group Development

Theorists of group therapy generally agree on three stages of a group's development (MacKenzie, 1994; Rutan & Stone, 1984; Schamis, 1998; Yalom, 1985). The beginning stage deals with issues of belonging and conforming to the group so that a safe place in the group can be established. The second stage is one in which group members strive to establish a place for themselves as individuals in the group. In the third stage, the group works on its tasks and issues, having established basic membership in and of the group.

The developmental challenges of a beginning-stage group contributed to the existing difficulties that I observed with my patients. Issues of conformity, trust, disclosure, and nurturance are issues of any beginning group, but these are also consistent core issues over time with women with eating disorders. The relative short-term therapy intensified these issues, as the group frequently stayed in the first stage of development. If the group composition and time in treatment coincided, the group was able to move into the second stage. This later stage, with its task of finding a sense of self in the presence of others, was also relevant to the women's ongoing issues. The ability of body experience to address experience of self, and the ability of visual art to explore issues of self in relation to the internal self, was important in choosing an appropriate modality.

## Sequential Integration of Modalities

Initially, I led only dance and movement therapy groups in conjunction with a meal support therapy (MST) group. Efforts to use movement, which stemmed from external cues and focused on relating to peers through movement, resulted in the group remaining at a superficial, defended level. The group, at best, relieved stress and anxiety in a palliative way. The atmosphere was one of suspicion, austerity, and wariness. Countertransference feelings about the group were felt as "lost," with feelings and thoughts dissipating into nothing or circulating listlessly forever. The group as a whole was a poor and inconsistent container, alternating from one of tentative holding to lack of substance.

When, in time, the group shifted to a focus on subtleties of internal experience, they began to facilitate an internal, meaningful experience. In the movement group any aspect of body experience was used—the awareness of muscle sensations through stretching; discrimination of the pain of a muscle stretch from emotional pain, to an internal pain that was alarmingly unidentifiable; and allowing the body to be experienced in a pleasurable way through the conscious relief of tension. The groups were cautious and very primitive in the sense that we were working with a fundamental sense of having a body in the world. The focus was on individuals in a very separate way. Meaning, beyond concrete, ego learning was not possible. The group was experienced now as a container and that allowed the formation of body experience as a transitional object. "Transitional objects are created by the infant in that an ordinary object is selected and given new meaning. The transitional object then becomes alive and is the first creative experience bridging the internal world with the external world" (Winnicott, 1971; Deri, 1978). The body, as a transitional object, was created by the women. They were imbuing new perceptions, sensations, and patterns with an aliveness that was not the norm for them. It was a creative experience; in Winnicottian terms this formed a bridge from internal to external. However, it was very transitory and short-lived. The relative lack and paucity of body experience at their disposal made it difficult to ascertain if these experiences had been internalized in any permanent manner. My own desire to find some certainty that the process was one of substance reflected the group process.

## Group Change

The group as a container had significantly, but subtly, shifted. From a faulty container that was inconsistent and fragile, a feeling of gentle consistency arrived. Individuals could now begin to make contact and articulate and strengthen experiences of self. Active work was done on an individual level, supported by a sense of the group as a whole. A container was created from a holding environment so that the body could also contain experience as a transitional object. Body experience was forming the foundation for a bridge to more authentic interaction with the external world. The contained and the container were in mutual relation with each other (Nitsun, 1996).

## Integration of Art and Movement Groups

After some time, I began to do art therapy groups in addition to the dance and movement therapy groups. The patients were not resistant to art therapy; in fact they looked forward to it. Where the group dynamic of the movement groups was one of fragility, tension, austerity, and isolation, the art therapy group dynamic was one of hunger, passion, and a feeling of not being able to get enough. Where the movement groups had been an excruciating 45 minutes, the patients in the art therapy groups had real difficulty stopping after 90 minutes. A short explanation of the qualities of different art materials at the beginning of the group was enough to start independent art-making in most cases. Over time, patients would move easily from needing more structured tasks to working on internally derived themes or tasks, reflecting an ability to make art from personal experience.

I quickly moved from organizing the group around one structured group directive to offering choices. I would offer a directive based on a previous group theme manifested for that day, which the women could choose, or they could construct their own. Their interest was held by the artwork and the group, although imagery was most often not understood on a conscious level. The women had real trouble discussing the aesthetic or emotional impact of their artwork. The art-making was helping to differentiate and articulate unconscious work, but an internal link to content was not often made.

The group functioned around individual work, but the larger issues were contained and absorbed. Interpersonal learning took place on a rudimentary level. Individual artists could present something about themselves through the nonverbal statement made through the artwork, or they could explain verbally. Individuals could comment on other member's work; however, they were guided to speak about how the artwork had impacted them, not a logical assessment. Group members internalized nonverbal statements about themselves. The group as a whole was strengthened, interpersonal interaction was made possible on a rudimentary level, and individual self-knowledge was increased. The distancing mechanism inherent in art-making made it safer for the group members.

Involvement in the movement groups changed. Instead of universally dreading the group, the patients made an effort to attend. The ability to engage was greater, although still reluctant, caused by the difficulty of contacting and staying with body experience. The women were able to explore a wider range of movement experience, including structured expressive movement, body image work based on body experience, role-play based on body attitudes, and partner work and related disciplines including relaxation and meditation. With the latter, some patients were able to practice these new skills at home, being able to generalize the material outside the group context.

## ☐ Discussion

These changes in both groups were connected: Not only were they due to safety because of increased familiarity with me, but the two different modalities were complementing and strengthening each other. The term "body trust" (Thompson, 1982) may be used to describe a phenomenological way of being in the body. This term does not refer to conscious feelings about body worth or knowledge about functioning of the body. It refers to a fundamental, unconscious belief that there are limits, boundaries, and resolutions of affect, phenomenologically experienced in the body. This trust is the product of repeated cycles of having a need and then experiencing gratification or resolution of that need in infancy and childhood.

A lack of body trust was shown in the movement group. The women were not able to complete movement phrases, had diminished movement quality, used a very limited range of movement response, and employed concreteness in the type of body experience allowed. They continually had extreme difficulty showing expressive movement and had limited ability to improvise. This configuration of movement responses was the reflection and vehicle of impoverished feeling, resistance to feeling, and inability to find new solutions. They did not trust that they could have an uncomfortable feeling and restore a sense of renewed balance.

This state shifted in my groups when the members were able to establish some sense of body trust through visual means. By using a visual modality, they were able to more easily experience cycles of resolved needs and regulated emotions. They were able to develop their ability to have this new trust in the presence of others without having to rely on outside criteria of shape, beauty, and size. Internal experience was discovered and used as a resource. However, this process was mainly internal and not accessible to advanced verbal understanding.

## Progress

After more time, I began to become involved in community meetings on a regular basis, and I also led verbal closure groups at the end of the day. The clients saw me in a multiplicity of roles. There were changes in many areas that were of benefit to people with eating disorders, a disorder that is extremely difficult to modify. For example, the ability of the patients to use art and movement deepened. The group process changed. The women were able to use body and visual imagery in other groups. They could refer to an experience in dance and movement therapy and use it in art therapy, and vice versa. They referred to art or movement groups in verbal groups to supplement the working-through process. All three kinds of groups began to take on the same milieu to a greater degree, and all three seemed to be a continuation of the others in dynamic and relatedness.

The group became a container that was varied, integrative, and sustainable over time and, therefore, stronger and more pliant. The group alternated between first and second stages according to issues and changes in group member composition. The group moved beyond its function as a global container and took on dynamic issues. Interpersonal and individual work was done within the group setting. All levels of group functioning, such as interpersonal and individual work, occurred simultaneously or as needed by the group at a particular time.

## Example of a Group Session

A group of three bulimic women met for an extended session after being in treatment together for several months. Lucy, who preferred writing, used an initial scanning of body experience as a starting point. She was able to link feelings of termination from the group to an abrupt ending of her relationship with her treasured nanny in childhood. Lucy worked in a profession that demanded verbal skills, but these skills did not help her with her emotional functioning. After grounding herself in her body experience, she was able to improve her considerable verbal skills in the service of an internal sense of self.

Betsy worked in art for most of the time, however the images did not make sense to her. The group feedback about the impact that the image had on them enabled her to decode the image. She realized that her art was about her enmeshed relationship with her mother, who was about to visit. By looking at and accepting the image as coming from herself, she was able to dare to acknowledge the anger she felt about her mother's attempts to keep her a child. She also was able to see the safety in assuming a child-like role. Betsy needed to let her imagery develop without conscious awareness of its meaning. The group helped her see her image in a new way, and she was able to accept that interaction to empower herself instead of oppressing herself.

Alicia needed to work with me directly in the group. She did a quick drawing, then shifted into deep work with body processing, work that enabled her to label a previously unarticulated bodily feeling as "incarceration," defining her eating disorder. From feeling totally hopeless about her ability to empower herself outside of her eating disorder, she was able to find a word that clarified her dilemma. She subsequently was able to further her exploration of this issue in a verbal group. Alicia needed the structure of working with me individually as an auxiliary ego. She could then shift her focus from body imagery to verbal description of the imagery, finding new meaning for herself. She used the art to establish a transitional space until I could work with her more intimately. Meanwhile, I worked to establish structured activities so that others could work more independently when Alicia needed attention. The boundaries and distance of the artwork helped her to hold her place in the group until she could find more structured, directed help, which focused on articulating her inner experience. Her hopelessness was increased by her inability to make sense of what she was feeling. We worked together to find some resolution of this hopelessness.

All three modalities were used interchangeably, and "fed" each other, as the group's needs dictated. Each of these women was able to move from one modality to another to do the work they needed to accomplish on that day. The choice of a particular modality was based on that modality's inherent characteristics and ability to contact the level of psychic functioning in which the issue lived. The group had evolved so that the members moved between working alone and working in direct interaction with the leader. By using creative arts therapy processing in addition to verbal processing, the women could move from unconscious to conscious, from abstract to content, and from inner to external experience. The developmental level of the group shifted from beginning to middle stage, moving from initial safety and conformity to establishing a sense of self in relation to others. The group's milieu was one of dynamic containment, ebbing and flowing according to the type of holding the women needed. Individual work could be done in depth. Interpersonal relations were supportive and furthered each other's work, both through contributing to the holding environment and also by learning from one another.

# ☐ Conclusion

The ability of the women in the eating disorders groups to take advantage of the creative arts increased as I conjointly led three types of groups using different modalities. One reason for this was undoubtedly my increased contact with them in the multiple group settings. However, more importantly, the women were able to explore issues using body experience and imagery, visual imagery and words, in a tangible and metaphorical way. All the groups shared content through discussions. In addition, they shared experiential processes in the struggle to make meaning through art and movement, and they shared their difficulties in engaging in the creative arts therapy process itself. They were able to share conscious and unconscious material through many differentiated avenues. The creative arts therapy groups helped them to clarify, differentiate, and give meaning to unconscious material, some of which stayed in their unconscious, but was also linked to each other through their mutual struggle in artistic work. Some of the work shifted from unconscious to conscious, linked through verbal insight. The depth of their work could not have occurred without the support of the work done in another modality. This success was aided by the configuration of nonverbal and verbal processing available to each woman in dealing with her eating disorder.

The purpose of this chapter has been to examine integration of modalities in group work, highlighting the particular properties of art therapy, dance and movement therapy, and verbal therapy. In this instance, work with women with eating disorders allowed an examination of inherent properties of each modality, due to the striking differences in functioning within these women. Because the women had such deficits in body processing, limited visual abilities, and familiarity with words, they needed to know the leader through verbal processing in order to feel safe enough to risk opening themselves to their nonverbal selves. As trust in the leader, trust in the process, and finally trust in their bodies grew, they were able to make new meanings for themselves. Their body selves could be used as a resource and not numbed, split-off, hated, or compared to others. They could use their visual selves to develop and enrich their internal worlds, instead of using visual functioning as a means of attempting to achieve an impossible physical ideal and to condemn themselves. They could also use their cognitive understanding to know and accept themselves, not to control and defend against others who might see their vulnerability. As trust developed in their bodies in a fundamental way, in their eyes as a link to the world, and then in their words as a safety net, meaning could be made.

This example of group therapy demonstrated that it is possible to deal with disparate functioning and to contain, support, and facilitate growth. The role of the individual within the group, the interactions within a group, and the group as a whole were intimately related and enhancing of each other. Characteristics of each modality shifted as the women gained knowledge of themselves. Problems stemming from eating disorders, as well as group issues of trust, disclosure, and safety, could be counteracted by the use of structure that lent them an ego when they needed it and loosened as they became more genuinely autonomous. Trust was established on many levels so that meaning could be made. By using kinesthetic, visual, and verbal knowing, the group can be seen as an amoeba, bending, turning, and shaping itself to meet and fill the needs of its members.

# ☐ References

Deri, S. (1978). Transitional phenomena: Vicissitudes of symbolization and creativity. In S. Grolnick, L. Barkin, & W. Muensterberger (Eds.), *Between reality and fantasy; Winnicott's concepts of transitional objects and phenomena* (pp. 43–60). Northvale, NJ: Aronson.

Guntrip, H. (1971). *Theory, therapy and the self.* London: Maresfield Library.

MacKenzie, K. R. (1994). The developing structure of the therapy group system. In H. Bernard & K. R. MacKenzie (Eds.), *Basics of group psychotherapy* (pp. 35–59). New York: Guildford Press.

McNeilly, G. (1983). Directive and non-directive approaches in art therapy. *The Arts in Psychotherapy, 10,* 211–219.

Nachmanovitch, S. (1990). *Free p[lay.* Putnam, NY: Jeremy Tarcher.

Nitsun, M. (1996). *The anti-group: Destructive forces in the group and their creative potential.* London: Routledge.

Piaget, J. (1969). *The psychology of the child.* New York: Basic Books.

Rutan, J. S., & Stone, W. (1984). *Psychodynamic group psychotherapy.* New York: MacMillan.

Schamis, C. (1998). Understanding the dance/movement therapy group. *American Journal of Dance Therapy, 20,* 23–36.

Spitz, R. (1965). *The first year of life: A psychoanalytic study of normal and deviant development of object relations.* New York: International Universities Press.

Thompson, L. (1982). *Body trust in the treatment of borderline personality.* Unpublished manuscript.

Thompson, L. (1993, November). Group art therapy: Towards an articulation of theoretical principles. Paper presented at the annual meeting of the American Art Therapy Association, Atlanta, GA.

Winnicott, D. (1971). *Playing and reality.* Harmondsworth, England: Penguin Books.

Yalom, I. (1985). *The theory and practice of group psychotherapy* (3rd. ed.). New York: Basic Books.

# 10
CHAPTER

# A Women's Group Created Around a Theme of Bereavement

There are a cluster of life events that affect the lives of women in similar ways. For example, the trauma of loss of a partner or immediate family member through death, separation, divorce, illness, distance, or mental disease. Bringing women together in group is the most successful approach to dealing with these emotional traumas. In some cases, group treatment follows individual therapy, in other cases group is an adjunct, and in many cases, it is the therapy of choice.

There are factors that stem from the basic nature of being a woman, and factors that society has grafted on to a woman's role, that have a major impact on her reaction to loss. Women's ways of solving problems in a holistic manner, and operating in a relational context, seem to me to fit Seigel's (1999) description of the ability of the right brain to understand metaphor, paradox, and humor (among other functions) as well as verbal representations. This method of experiencing life offers a broad spectrum of responses and an access to emotional content as well as rational reactions, areas in which women seem to excel.

Women have an innate talent to tap into emotional and rational thinking and find solutions that are creative. In spite of recognizing this multi-mode of "knowing," many therapies created by men impose structures and forms of finding solutions in a manner created by men for men (Gilligan, 1993). A woman's therapeutic group soon rejects the theories that are inappropriate for them, and turns the relational opportunities into a support, which helps the women move toward their own solutions.

**221**

Most women are inclined toward nurturing, an ability that has been reinforced through parenting their children or young family members, caring for their parents, and serving or working in the community. Even the most successful female CEO handles her role differently than her male counterpart. Her skill in bringing people and facts together often is the key to success. Therefore, in a woman's group there is less resistance from the members to become integrated into the group (Gilligan, 1993). Granted this is a generality, and there are many women who have great anxiety about trust, but they usually find their place in the group, particularly if the group leader is helpful.

A woman who is not concerned with seeking support in times of stress handles her loss in individual ways. However, the ability to retrieve resiliency in times of mourning is better accomplished with support than in isolation.

## ☐ A Group for Women Recently Widowed

The following description of a widow's group is offered as a model that can be transposed onto other groups dealing with externally imposed, life-changing, situations. This form of group is not structured to delve into intrapsychic problems from the past; it is created to aid realistic readjustments and restore function after a dramatic shift in roles or relationships. The groups are time-limited and the members are carefully selected to fit the purpose and goals of the group.

Groups with similar issues include widowhood, caretakers of partners or parents with dementia, groups of cancer patients or their spouses, groups of women who are battered or abused in other ways, and groups of women who have been recently divorced; in other words, women in situations where outside circumstances have been the major cause of trauma will benefit from this approach.

Hughes (1995) describes group in this manner: "Bereavement support groups are a form of magic. They are made up of people who have only their loss and pain in common. An alchemy takes place and the people form close emotional bonds. The mutual support and understanding helps them emerge in a more positive state of mind" (p. xiii).

In the examples that follow, the use of art expressions as part of the grieving passage accelerates the group process and provides the group member an entrée into material that is hard to face when recently traumatized by injurious events.

This chapter builds on previous chapters, and attempts to avoid repeating some of the basic advantages of art, group, and communication that has been previously discussed.

# ☐ Selection of Members for a Bereavement Group

Groups that are formed around a particular event in the life cycle are constructed differently than those that are dealing with personality disorders, or other psychological problems. For example, in the widow's group it is essential to place the members in a time frame. Women living without spouses for many years are not dealing with the same issues as those whose husbands or partners have died within the last six months.

Both groups are valuable, but in a time-limited frame, the approach differs. According to some authorities the loss of a mate is the number one stressor of all losses (Vernon, 1992). Addressing that loss and the accompanying trauma must be carefully structured.

Grief is a normal reaction to death of a loved one. Often the complicated and profound reactions are not understood, such as anger, disbelief, denial, preoccupation and guilt, dreams and sensory perceptions and nightmares, anxiety and resistance to change, and an identity crisis. All of these reactions are normal but may seem abnormal unless discussed with sympathetic others who understand by experience. A group of women who have encountered the same transitional difficulties is an ideal way to readjust to a major life-change (Walsh & McGoldrick, 1991).

In addition the socioeconomic circumstances of the women should be considered. It would place an unnecessary burden on a woman if she were the only one in the group who was in an entirely different financial situation. The poorest woman may have superior extended family support, and the wealthy woman may not have to thrust herself out on the marketplace to feed her children and herself. Difference is an issue that must be weighed by the facilitator. Sometimes it is helpful and dynamic, other times it can be isolating. It is obvious that money can make the material transition easier and lessen some threats of, for example, losing a home and facing dire poverty. However, richness can be evaluated in many ways, such as a loving family as opposed to monetary ease.

A balanced group offers the greatest possibilities for the members to help each other. While wealth does not make death easier to handle, it may help stave off the possibility of having to face multiple traumas simultaneously. It is important to bear in mind that this is a support group, and many issues of life management are better learned from others in the group than from the leader. A group that is well represented across the spectrum of socioeconomic levels provides the optimum resources.

## Pre-Group Interview

An initial interview can be most helpful to insure that the group will accomplish the goal of providing a positive experience: An experience that will lead to management of the trauma. In addition to gathering information, it is helpful to ask the widow to join with the therapist in creating a time-line map (drawing) of the events leading up to the demise and the people involved in the woman's life at this time. There may have been other recent losses that will make readjustment more difficult. There may be extended family and friends, and there may not be. Making these circumstances visible in a manner that resembles a linear form of genogram (sometimes called the family tree) individually created to reflect the narrative of the woman, is the first step to gaining insight and control over the external stressors. It also provides an instant blueprint of the possible resources in the family and community.

For clarity, this chapter focuses on a group created for widows whose partners had died within the last six months. The group met for 90 minutes every week for 10 weeks.

## Beginnings

The group was limited to eight members for a specific reason. The amelioration of trauma is accomplished when the bereaved person is able to tell their story of loss many times. Repetition provides a way to gradually gain mastery over the emotions that are provoked by the loss. The emotions are many, and only by telling and retelling can the "less socially acceptable" feelings be verbalized. If there were more than eight in the group, the time would always be a factor, and many would be left unattended.

The goals of the group were to assist the members through the mourning process, which according to Engel (1980) is an adaptation to loss. "Adaptation involves four basic tasks: accepting the reality of the loss, experiencing the pain of grief, adjusting to a 'new' environment, and withdrawing and reinvesting emotional energy"(p. 44). These goals were not verbalized by the group leader; however, as the situation warranted a personalized version of these adaptations, they were noted.

To begin the process of establishing comfort in this group, each member was asked to introduce herself and touch on the circumstances of their partner's death (i.e., a long illness, an accident, a sudden heart attack). No one was urged to share any more than they wished, and some members were too distressed to add more than their name.

At the end of the hour the leader asked the members to choose one collage picture that reflected an attribute of herself that she chose to share. Perhaps a representation of her hobby, sport interest, career; any picture of themselves without their lost one. The collage pictures were then assembled in the center of the group and remarks were encouraged about sameness and differences, as seen in the collage images.

The rationale was to underscore the commitment to group; that the woman is a group member; and that she will return. Each group member is a precious human being as an individual, with or without a mate. Some women feel diminished when they lose their "couplehood." These implied messages will not be verbalized unless someone in the group chooses to comment. At this stage, it is better to let the composite image created by the joining of the collages make the statement.

It is also useful to glue the individual collages on a larger sheet and have that on the wall the following week when the group reconvenes. The collage bears silent witness to the future cohesion that is desired.

During this first group session, it is important for the leaders to find as many threads of common interest, circumstances, and attitudes among the new members as possible. That does not mean a search for sameness, it means an exploration of areas of connection. The goal is to weave a

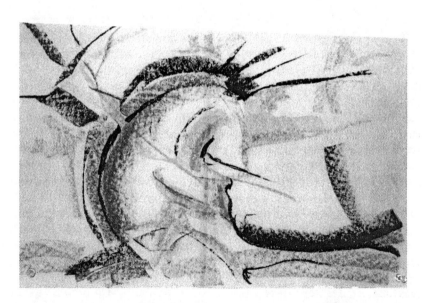

**FIGURE 10.1.** A 63-year-old woman's drawing with the broadside of oil pastels, representing the "confusion and break-up feelings in my life. Everything is moving, like a whirlwind."

fabric of trust that will be both protective and secure enough to invite comfort of expression and honesty.

## Second Group

This group is an invitation to tell the story of the death in greater detail. How the partner died, where, who was present, and was it an expected or a sudden death? With a membership of eight it will probably take most of the time to share all eight stories. Always allow the shy member, the highly defended member, or the member in denial to choose to delay their narrative.

White (2000) has formulated a method of encouraging clients to tell, retell, and respond to retelling by another retelling, until the texture of the story is rich with additional observations. This technique works in the widow's group in this manner: First the widow tells the detailed story of her relationship and loss; another member of the group then retells her story with her own words, but not adding any extraneous material of her own; the first woman then retells how she heard the retelling of her story; and the group reflects how they appreciated the experience. This expanded mode of "telling" turns the "thin" story into a "thick" story, an approach that would be a great enhancement to a bereavement group (see Figure 10.1).

It is helpful to have golf-ball size pieces of Plasticine in a variety of colors, in baskets here and there in the room. As mentioned before, the molding of clay provides a comforting activity for the fingers, which has a calming effect. Stress reduction is important in the first stages of group formation.

As the stories are told and retold, and as the members are encouraged to express their emotions, without specific encouragement, the clay will change shape and size. For some, the clay will be a product of the automatic movements of the fingers, for others it will be torn apart, reformed, and take on a reflective process of the conversation, although attention should not be diverted from the narratives to focus on the clay. The created object is simply a visible mirror of the dialogue; an activity that activates neuronal connections and facilitates expression. When it is time to leave, the pieces of Plasticine are assembled on a tray-base and stand silent witness to the group's emergent personality.

When the next group reconvenes, the members will be able to take an observant stance, recall the stories, and be reminded through the clay forms that they created in the past meeting. Activity while sharing an emotional event helps to anchor the telling and the interactions if it fits harmoniously. Shaping clay without making a specific product is a self-soothing device which also seems to make speaking less difficult.

## Third Group

The group members are encouraged to share with each other some practical knowledge. Where to find services for probate or related legal issues, or government services can be most useful. This conversation can be made into a game by having each member write their resource on a card. Place the card on the center of the table, and others can withdraw the card and replace it with theirs. Making physical (the cards) the aids to problem solving makes the daunting jobs a task that all the members of the group can try to solve together. Even unsolvable situations seem less frightening if many people confirm the reality.

A game, as described, is never created the same way in any group. For some, the cards are more words than pictures, others are solely pictorial. Some groups have created a box where the cards are stored, and it is understood that it is an ongoing repository for helpful ideas. Group members can be excited when they have made a discovery that helps another woman, or could help everyone.

For some therapists this type of art is not regarded as art—making abstract concepts concrete is one of the strengths of art. I know that naming a product by the label "art" or "tangible expressions" does not make it more or less valuable. A group leader's responsibility is to work toward providing expressive opportunities that match the dynamics of the group. In the early stages of a group, such as the one we are describing, the subject of grief is volatile and emotional. There is no need to offer opportunities that elicit additional emotional responses. Art expressions are often pathways to troubling material stored in implicit memory, and with the proper stimulus can come flooding back into consciousness. This retrieval process may be appropriate later on, or it may never be right for a group that is in need of closing down, not opening up. There should be a rhythm between the art and the process of the group, a rhythm that reflects and integrates with the therapeutic advances and retreats.

## Fourth Group

For most groups the fourth meeting often is the beginning of interactions that are on a more intimate level. The last three groups established that the group has a shared experience of death and a permission to react to this death in individual ways. They have had a sympathetic audience where they could tell and retell their dominant stories of the loss. They found acceptance and comfort so that they could also examine practical dilemmas and exchange pragmatic advice. The unspoken fear of group actions and reactions had been soothed by the reality of the other group members. Each woman had her particular difficulty dealing with her life and is respected for it.

The leaders have a good deal to do with this basic formation of trust. (Leader and leaders are spoken of interchangeably, since some therapists prefer to work with a "co," and others prefer to be solo). Until now the leader has been more directive then will be needed later. Gentle control and support is useful in the early stages of a widow's group. Some women require some protection from normal curiosity, some are mute and must stay mute at the beginning; other women have a tendency to dominate the conversation with their concerns and not give up the center. In a longer-term group, or a group assembled for therapy, the group interactions can be guided to solve these problems. However, in this example, the agreement is short term and the group has not contracted for therapy. However, the bereavement group always proves to be therapeutic. In this situation, the responsibility for setting limits and creating a therapeutic environment should be the leader's.

The addition of art expressions to the vocabulary is interpreted by the members as an indicator that the group is not therapy. As mentioned before, it is always interesting that people entering therapy for the first time cannot conceive of a therapy that is pleasurable. Imagine drawing instead of weeping—actually it usually is drawing *and* weeping that is such a relief.

Until this stage of group development, most of the work of the group and the leader has been in preparation for the next six sessions.

## Fifth through Ninth Groups

Anger and disbelief should be anticipated in the next cycle of mourning. For many women the expression of anger and rage toward their spouse leaving them is an area that is prohibited by the polite rules of society. The opportunity to make expressive marks on paper with media, such as pastels or paint, allows unspoken feelings of abandonment, accusations of irresponsibility and desertion, and many other emotions to flow onto the page. In some cases, verbalization flows simultaneously, in other cases, the silent expression is enough. Tears drawn on the paper, or real tears, are appropriate. Some tears are anger, some self-pity, and some loss and sorrow. All aspects of loss are acceptable, for every member of the group has experienced all of these feelings to some degree (Roberts, 1991).

Having an "anger–sorrow–grief" art task as a directive makes it possible for members to use each other's artwork as their own. They can identify with the representation created by another woman, and in some cases, the other person's art acts as a catalyst to access emotions that were unrecognized. The art expressions become support vehicles in themselves, although they were not created for this purpose (see Figure 10.2).

Again a symbolic holding container is useful. Overwhelming anger can be partitioned (actually cut-up the anger drawing) into "do-able" sizes; the container will keep the overflow until the smaller portion is able to be handled. Metaphors and symbols are very necessary at times when words and emotions are too raw to express. By using metaphorical symbols, the group members understand and a language is created that can talk about the untalkable. Facing trauma small steps at a time is healing.

## Photo Collage

Following the high emotional period, which will appear and disappear in almost every group, there are some touching memory themes. The group often decides to bring in pictures of the spouse in his or her

**Figure 10.2.** "We were like the sun and the moon."

youth and in older age. Pictures of children and homes are also shared. The group seeks to find a family environment in the sessions, and to bring in the reality of the deceased is important. These photos can be a centerpiece of a memory collage. The collage should be mounted on good sturdy paper because it often is a treasured momento of the group and the partner, and taken home after the termination of the group.

To facilitate the use of collage, which may be the preferred mode of making images for many women, the collage box should be well stocked. It is time consuming to go through magazines and tear them out in the sessions. There should be many pictures of many subjects, readily available. In some groups, the members are willing to bring in pictures and contribute them to the group collection. For others the use of collage becomes a hobby, and they continue with making composite images at home.

## Homework

There have been groups that have given themselves homework. For example, a group discussed, with deep sorrow, the loneliness of the half-empty bed. The cold half of the bed reinforced the absence of the loved one. As a group they made a pledge to move over to the other side of the bed, or occupy the middle of the bed, during the week between group. This move was "practiced" on paper by a drawing, and the expected distress was also put into visible form. The next group talked extensively how this move symbolized their necessary acceptance that they were single, that the death was irreversible.

A second distressing action that may be decided on for a homework task, is to remove the spouse's clothing from the closet. This is such a powerful metaphor that often it cannot be faced until more time has passed.

The leader cannot anticipate how the conversation will be directed at this stage of group development. The women will take the direction in their own hands. For some, home routines stir memories, for others it is vacations or missed opportunities. How many of these issues are common to a group is impossible exactly to foretell. Because of this uncertainty, the leader should be tuned into her or his creative talents to help these themes become concrete.

## Art as Healer

The following group is often devoted almost exclusively to doing art. All forms of media should be available as the group members lose themselves in the artistic process. Some paint, some draw, one woman created a shrine, and others reworked their photo collage. They renewed and refreshed themselves through the creative process. They know they are surrounded with others that understand, and no words are necessary.

## Social Component

Throughout the group the women were encouraged to exchange telephone numbers, meet outside the group time, and plan outings for the future. The rules of group therapy did not apply for this support group. At times, another person who is in a similar position is a comfort even more than family members. Family is also grieving, and the widow gives comfort as well as receiving it. For her children she often tries to contain her emotions to better soothe theirs. With a contemporary, who also has recently lost their partner, the complexity of emotions is more acceptable. For some women, widowhood is a release and the beginning of a new freedom. To be able to talk about this change with someone who appreciates that this is not "bad" is therapeutic.

Under optimum circumstances the center where the therapy is conducted may have a meeting room where the group members can meet over coffee to finish up the discussions started in group. If there is no place on site, then a coffee shop nearby could be a finale to the session. An hour and half for eight women is not always sufficient time, and the goal is to combat loneliness and isolation, therefore, extra "talk time" is seen differently than in other situations.

This suggestion is not in accordance with the traditional beliefs of how to run a psychotherapy group. This is a support group with different goals than a group created to explore personal intrapsychic tensions. This more psychosocial philosophy is a shift in thinking that must be embraced by the leader of a bereavement group. In any circumstance, if a group member signed on for one reason, and they are expected to perform in another manner, the client will be dismayed and leave. That is why the beginning interview is so essential for any group. Therapy should not be a mystery; it is a contract that has its perimeters like any other contractual format.

## Termination

Termination is difficult. Although it should be planned for, discussed, and anticipated several weeks before, it is still a painful process. The best solution is giving artwork to the members as a gift. Each member creates a goodbye image for each of the other members of the group. A small painting, collage, decorated photo, clay form, or any hand-created piece would be appreciated. Because it is time consuming to make eight pieces, often the work is done at home and brought into the final meeting. Exchanging the gifts is touching, and the accompanying expressions of gratitude and connection are deeply moving. The therapists freely enter into the process and recall moments of triumph, and sessions that were life changing. Each member of the group is singled out by the therapist and reminded of her strengths and abilities, and her growing competencies to take on the new role that life has forced upon her.

Saying goodbye is often tearful, however the tears are affectionate, sorrowful, a mixture of emotions, but usually not coming from the original state of hopelessness.

## Aftermath

For some widows a short-term group is not sufficient to help them resume life in a functional manner. For these women it is the responsibility of the therapist to have a referral list of therapists who deal with bereavement, community resources, or other groups that focus on a more specific approach to developmental changes and mourning. Often family therapy is a positive choice, and families can become the best support system. Friends and outside activities should be encouraged to guard against withdrawal and loneliness.

For some, enrollment in an art class has proven the next step in individuation. To become absorbed in the creative process is a major experiential component when making art, this can be the healing path for many (Allen, 1995).

## ☐ Therapist's Issues

There is a danger that the therapist who is engaged in group work centering around issues of loss, grief, and death will find the emotions are so powerful that they can be "catching." To remain empathic, stay close and distant simultaneously, is quite a task. Making reflective artwork away from the site is recommended as a protection against secondary traumatic reactions (Riley, 1997). Placing the emotional overload on paper or canvas can keep the leader in perspective and able to continue to serve the client.

This is true in other circumstances as well, where the emotive content is overwhelming, such as severe illnesses (cancer and AIDS), traumatic loss (drive-by shootings), or sudden onset of psychiatric illness in a family member. The leader must be able to stay close to the group process, but also be resilient enough to give the group hope and direction.

## Suggestion for the Therapist

If the therapist has not conducted a bereavement group, or has not had the opportunity to have co-therapy with another experienced professional, it is helpful to find a text that is reliable. *Bereavement and Support: Healing in a Group Environment* by Marylou Hughes provides structure, activities, and theoretical and pragmatic suggestions that are clear and comprehensive in a brief format.

## ☐ Summary

Looking back over this chapter, the reader may be struck by the major issue of timing and pacing. Always an important issue in the evolution of any group, it is of central importance in this type of support group. The first interview and the first three groups should be very closely considered: The group growth is protected and the therapist takes responsibility for the structure to be flexible but also a container that provides safety.

Careful selection of members to fit the proposed group will better ensure success. Women who have recently undergone the trauma of loss do not have to be retraumatized with a failed group experience. Losing a partner's support, and then losing a support group is a serious situation that must be guarded against. The interview may find another group of candidates that are compatible in another group, therefore, the interview is not discriminatory, it is protective.

Pacing is also vital. Structured suggestions in the first third of the group provide protection and security, as mentioned above. The goal is to move the group toward trust at the exact pace that reflects the group's temperament. This movement varies with every group, which demonstrates how attentive to this dynamic the therapist must be. Group dynamics are closely monitored (silently) and art expressions are tailored to harmonize with the group's stage of development. When the time comes, the therapist can withdraw from the more active role, and let the group become the facilitator. Even at this phase of comparative openness, the leader must be mindful of the dynamics and to be ready to guide. She must also have art projects planned and prepared that will integrate with the verbal flow. The proper use of the art facilitates and activates the interactive exchange that is essential to group cohesion.

In addition, the way women work together should be well understood by the therapist. Some background on gender differences and the feminist viewpoint will help the therapist to open up to modifications in theoretical thinking. Parallel to this education, the therapist should be educated about the type of trauma that is the theme of the group. Loss, illness, divorce, and other external traumas require attention in individual areas. To be uninformed about the central theme of a group is irresponsible.

The last consideration that is of major importance is that the therapist must be clear with herself that this is a *support* group. The group will no doubt engender therapeutic changes, but the changes are made within the structure of support not therapy. The difference is delicate, as the line between intrapsychic and interpsychic approaches is always somewhat blurred. However, this is no time to uncover unresolved issues of the past. This time of bereavement is a time of healing and gathering resources. All of the client's psychic energy should be mustered to have them resume the most effective life that they desire.

# ☐ References

Allen, P. B. (1995). *Art is a way of knowing: A guide to self-knowledge and spiritual fulfillment through creativity.* Boston: Shambala.

Engel, G. I. (1980). A group dynamic approach to teaching and learning about grief. *Omega, 11,* 45–59.

Gilligan, C. (1993). *In a different voice: Psychological theory and woman's development.* Cambridge, MA: Harvard University Press.

Hughes, M. (1995). *Bereavement and support: Healing in a group environment.* Washington, DC: Taylor & Francis.

Riley, S. (1997). Conflicts in treatment, issues of liberation, connection, and culture: Art therapy for women and their families. *Art Therapy, 14,* 102–108.

Roberts, J. (1991). *Taking care of caregivers.* Palo Alto, CA: Bull.

Seigel, D. J. (1999). *The developing mind.* New York: Guilford Press.

Vernon, A. (1992). Group counseling: Loss. In D. Cappucci and D. R. Gross (Ed.), *Introduction to group counseling.* Denver, CO: Love.

Walsh, F., & McGoldrick, M. (1991). *Living beyond loss: Death in the family.* New York: Taylor & Francis.

White, M. (2000). *The ritual of telling, retelling, and re-retelling.* Presented at the Evolution of Psychotherapy Conference, The Milton Erickson Foundation. Anaheim, CA, May 25–28, 2000.

# ☐ Suggested Readings

Achterberg, J., Dossey, B., & Kolkmeir, L. (1994). *Rituals of health and healing: Using imagery for health and wellness.* New York: Bantam.

Bertman, S. L. (1991). *Facing death: Images, insight, and interventions. A handbook for educators, health care professionals, and counselors.* Washington, DC: Hemisphere.

Capacchione, L. (1979). *The creative journal: The art of finding yourself.* Chicago: Swallow Press.

Cappachione, L. (1989). *The well being journal: Drawing upon your inner power to heal yourself.* North Hollywood, CA: Newcastle.

Childs Gowell, E. (1992). *Good grief, rituals.* Barrytown, NY: Station Hill Press.

Cohen, B. M., Barnes, M. M., & Rankin, A. B. (1995). *Managing traumatic stress through art: Drawing from the center.* Lutherville, MD: Sidran Press.

Lazarus-Leff, B. (1998). Art therapy and the aesthetic environment as agents for change: A phenomenological investigation. *Art Therapy, 15,* 120–126.

Malchiodi, C. A. (1999). *Medical art therapy with adults.* London: Jessica Kingsley.

Manheim, A. R. (1998). The relationship between the artistic process and self-actualization. *Art Therapy, 15,* 99–106.

Pennebaker, J. (1997). *Opening up: The healing power of confiding in others.* New York: Guilford Press.

Rogers, N. (1993). *The creative connection: Expressive arts as healing.* Palo Alto, CA: Science and Behavior Books.

Sanders, C. M. (1989). *Grief: The mourning after.* New York: Wiley.

Sanders, C. M. (1992). *Surviving grief. . . and learning to live again.* New York: Wiley.

Volkan, V. D., & Zimtl, E. (1993). *Life after loss.* New York: Macmillan.

# A Group for Therapists Dealing with Secondary Post-Traumatic Stress Syndrome Induced by Their Abused Clients' Art Products

This chapter will explore how group therapy provides a successful and therapeutic stress reduction experience for therapists who are working with the severely abused patient. Even the most experienced clinicians become emotionally fatigued processing the life-traumas of their clients, a process which is an inescapable part of the therapeutic procedure. As a result, many therapists experience excessive distress, secondary post-traumatic stress syndrome. Attending to this condition is of primary importance if the therapist is to continue to provide optimum care for the client (Guy, 1987). Williams (1996) observes: "Working with traumatized individuals can challenge the therapist's belief system of safety, trust, power, esteem, and intimacy. Therefore, it is important to have a support network available to use to talk over cases and process secondary trauma in the therapist" (p. 159).

## ☐ Introduction

The therapist who works with clients who have been subjected to extreme abuse often find that visual products are their clients first relief from past trauma when the painful memories are externalized

236

through art products. The visible product is the first mode of accessing the repressed memories. For the traumatized client, this imagery becomes doubly valuable when it is shared with the therapist, who becomes the holding agent for some of the distress. The therapist affirms the client's imagery through empathy and confirmation of the recalled memory. However, in the process of this experience, the therapist will often find that the empathic encounter leaves an emotional and visual residue that impinges on their lives. An uninvited shadow of their client's ordeal remains with them, which may interfere with their own reality. To deal with the second-hand imagery that is often horrific, it is valuable and sometimes necessary, to externalize and transform this toxic imagery. This is addressed by the therapist making his or her own visual products, created in a stress reduction group, with other therapists who also have become holding agents for their clients' distress. The art product takes on a double life—imagery of the abused client interacting with imagery of the artmaker. To untangle the two superimposed images is the challenge (Speigel et al., 1993).

How a group of professionals has dealt with this dilemma, through the use of art, group process, and relevant dialogue follows.

## ☐ Visual Knowing

Therapists have traditionally recognized the importance of examining their countertransference reactions and they utilize this awareness to ensure that they are able to serve their clients without being over-influenced by their own personal processes. However, in working with severely abused clients, there is an area of psychic exchange that makes such a traumatic impact on the emotional-cognitive centers of the brain that it is often disregarded or rarely brought to consciousness. The reaction is so powerful that most therapists instinctively repress their emotions to preserve the therapeutic neutrality that makes continuing the relationship possible.

To better understand this problem, which is the cause of burnout and fatigue with many therapists, one must explore a domain of knowing that few people take into consideration. This form of intelligence lies in the silent, visual knowing that greatly influences cognitive awareness.

Neuropsychologists recognize that the mind has the capacity to know the world through images alone. This understanding is silent, without words, and profoundly influential upon one's opinions and choices in many areas (Tinnin, 1991). "Nonverbal memory is already well established at birth. It functions parallel to verbal memory but its retention is effortless, image based, and timeless. It continues to function despite conditions such as anesthesia, sedation, and altered states of consciousness" (Tinnin, 1994, p. 1).

The visual images recorded, or the visualizations created in the mind by associations and stimuli, involve our emotional reactions. These reactions are commonly acknowledged by accepting that one "falls in love at first sight," are often "attracted or repelled" by strangers, "recognize criminals by their look," and countless other unexplainable and irrational opinions and interactions in daily life. Yet, in spite of strong responses to visual stimuli, people lack logical evidence to confirm these impressions and are hard pressed to put these behaviors into words. One may know the world through several channels, verbal and nonverbal, but the visual knowing remains silent until the cognitive, verbal capacities of the thinking processes brings the impressionistic meanings to awareness through language. This process of the interface between nonverbal visual understanding and verbal cognizance is another interpretation for countertransference reactions. It provides a different way of understanding some of the roots of one's projections. Since these responses are based to a large extent on a wordless, image-knowing system, it takes stimulus to start the translation into the cognitive capacities of the brain. In other words, choices are made when words are brought to image.

The above speculation on the workings of the mind lead to the hypothesis that a stress reduction group requires the use of visual expression combined with the verbal narration to facilitate effective relief.

## ☐ The Nexus of the Challenge

The clinicians discussed in this chapter were not seeking a therapy group. They were interested in using art expressions to deal with their own fatigue with their practice, which dealt with severely abused adults and with some clients who claimed to have multiple personalities. The group would focus on the secondary trauma that were caused by visual images made by their clients. However, the stress reduction group proved to be therapeutic in a variety of ways.

One of the primary burdens that therapists working with an abused population carry, are the appalling and frightful images conveyed to them through their clients' descriptions of their mistreatment. There is no way that the practitioner can avoid taking in these client-generated descriptions and storing them in their own image bank. This is even more powerfully reinforced when abuse is seen in the client's artwork, since the image (amplified by the client's narration) is incorporated into the visual intelligence of the therapist. Therefore, the therapist acquires the client's abuse by absorbing (on a sensory level) the stories and pictures of the horrors recounted in the session. The therapist often introjects the visions, which had triggered the client into a state of anxiety, the therapist is then triggered when these visualizations are recalled. The trauma of the client becomes the acquired trauma of the therapist (Tinnin, 1994).

## Traumatic Imagery

To quote Tinnin (1991),

> After the trauma a vivid fixed image often haunts the patient, intruding into consciousness as a post-traumatic symptom. Typically, the image coincides with the fixed idea and represents the person's experience of the trauma at the moment of being overwhelmed, just before entering into that altered state that interrupted the stream of consciousness. If a person can draw this image and "unfreeze" it by integrating it into a graphic narrative of the event then the dissociative experience can be transformed into a conscious historical memory (p. 347).

Understanding some of these functions of the mind, helps one appreciate how central the image is to the treatment of severely abused persons, and how easily the image can influence the therapeutic relationship. When visual memories are shared it is done so at some cost. The client recalls graphically the moment, and the therapist "lives" the moment with the client through exposure to their imagery.

## Approaches that Fit the Problem

In the group the power of the image is acknowledged and combated with the same tools that lie at the formation of the stress. Art psychotherapy has traditionally recognized the advantage of personifying personal difficulties in a visual form, which leads to a better comprehension of how the problem impacts the individual. Through scrutinizing the concrete expression the client–creator allows themselves to observe from a safe distance the undesirable situations or problematic behaviors. This same process is at the heart of the stress reduction group. The therapist group members externalize material that originated through another person's experience and was expressed visually. They, in turn, rendered their version of the client's imagery as it filtered through their brain centers. The client's image and the therapist's image are certain to be different, since it is not possible to exactly reproduce an emotionally projected experience. By creating their own art expressions and sharing observations, they find the relief needed to continue to be effective in their clients' lives.

## *Process*

When the group convenes, the members discuss a variety of distressful situations they have found particularly burdensome during the period between meetings. Often the artwork of the client is brought in, and they share the overwhelming tragic, visual images which they are unable to put aside. On another occasion, the issue may be their frustrations around a clinical issue that refuses to respond to treatment, or it may be the inability to defend against hearing one more tale of horror. There is tension to be dealt with that is created by unrealistic expectations that a "good" therapist can always find a therapeutic channel for the client's relief. When the therapist fails to meet this goal of perfection, there is fatigue and sadness, even rage. Most persons in the field have experienced these emotions, some even fear being criticized by their colleagues for incompetence. This harsh allegation is instigated solely by their own internalized judge. They also imagine criticism from their clients. It is hard to face their humanness, the inability to quickly take away the pain they see, and admit that they are not omnipotent. This admission is often accompanied by apprehension and stressful feelings of tension.

A therapist who is familiar with the art process can facilitate the group interactions by making educated suggestions. They are comfortable with providing ways to project on paper the above mentioned concerns that are toxic to the group members' well being. The therapist clearly establishes that there are no standards of aesthetics that might stand in the way of free expression. Through scribbles, marks, and magazine collage pictures, the group projects their anguish, which is often related to the cruel experiences their clients have represented in their artwork. The other members can see and hear what the difficulty appears to be, since verbal and nonverbal systems are used simultaneously in the process. The group becomes both an ancillary container of the stressful images and a vehicle to assist eradication of the internalized representations. It is the group support and understanding that complements the relief experienced when the group member materializes the unwanted traumatic memory (in the art). Both verbal and nonverbal processes are needed to instigate the reduction of stress. Sharing their visual impressions that have been internalized, not the actual circumstantial description offered by the client, preserves patient confidentiality without reducing the efficacy of the group process (Yalom, 1995; Corey et al., 1988).

## The Group Leader

It is important to have a professional trained in the use of art as leader of the group. Their training can be used to offer helpful media that facilitates expression and to suggest various art tasks that have proven productive in past group experiences. It helps to have been trained to synthesize theory and practice and transform them into action, and in addition, an experienced therapist is aware of the responsibility to protect group members from experiencing additional trauma through an encounter with some material of a personal nature that may be evoked through the art idiom. Visual externalization can easily circumvent the defensive barrier, and repressed material will surface without invitation. It is by providing this feeling of safety, within the freedom of creative expression, that all of the members have the opportunity to have a positive experience.

One member of the group remarked, "There is no other place where we can talk so openly about feelings that are elicited by our clients. If we did so in case conference we would be open to criticism. However, it is this permission to talk about the forbidden reactions to our clients that is the essence of facing vulnerabilities and gathering renewed strength from others to continue the battle against harm perpetrated upon our clients."

## Caveats

The art therapy product illustrates the narrative of the clients story told (Riley & Malchiodi, 1994). Therefore, the visual expression does not exist in a vacuum, but rather, is firmly integrated with the legend that is being discussed. This runs counter to the notion that an art therapist has a set of directives that fit many psychotherapeutic situations, or the power to interpret another person's images. Each decision about the subject matter of an artform will rise from the client–therapist dialogue and be unique to that circumstance and no other. The major danger with post-traumatic stressed individuals, first or secondarily impacted, is the fear of retriggering the psychologically damaging reaction to the memory. Even memory traces can stimulate this reaction, so the greatest caution must be used when the imagery begins to emerge. Never push the activity, make interpretations too early, or feel you have a better understanding of the events than the client. The therapist's job is to wait and support and be ready to encourage the next step—not to make the step first.

As a rule, this attitude and limitation regarding interpretation of client work is discussed at length when meeting a new stress reduction therapist group member. It is a principle impressed on the professionals who use image-making with their clients.

## Examples of the Group Process

In this world of brief therapies, often motivated by managed care structures rather than by client need, the treatment of the severely abused and dissociative client continues to be recognized as long-term therapy. The very fact that the therapeutic alliance often continues for years exacerbates the impact of the client's process upon the therapist. The stress factor and the toxic visual overload becomes cumulative over time. In response to this need, the following group exercises were created cooperatively by the group members input and therapist's involvement. At the beginning, group members had some concerns that they would not meet the artistic level that they imagined would be prerequisite for success with this modality. This was quickly set aside when all members became aware that important personal significance may reside in scribbles and primitive drawings, and that there is no need for aesthetics. The simplicity of the art had no bearing on the meaning embedded in the product or the power to externalize feelings. It soon became evident that there was a direct connection between the partiscipants' imagery and the creative process which brought the graphic narrative onto the page. Art in therapy has very little to do with fine art, indeed, artists may have a difficult time staying close to their feelings while they are art making and struggle not to use their art training as a defense against self-knowledge.

## *Example*

One group member therapist was reflecting on the first meeting of the group, comparing an educational discussion group that had been meeting regularly with these same therapists, to her personal experience with the expressive art. She explained the difference: "Now, we were more vulnerable, more exposed to each other than we had ever been. Sharing a big piece of paper, drawing in each other's space, not talking, putting feelings out there, risking with each other, being clients together. This was new for us. It was fun! It was a childlike feeling. Here was new freedom!"

The only male member of the group, and perhaps, the most hesitant member to start the creative process, had this to say about his experience: "I have learned not to compare my work with other person's visual productions; to draw abstractly, not realistically; that I do not have to have to explain the meaning of my art, that is, place a value on my feelings. I could allow anger and depression; it was possible to release negative feelings in a safe environment. I lost my fear of expressing myself in a room full of women; no woman would make fun of me; I could let my fingers do my thinking expressively; exhibit feelings nonverbally; watch myself as I developed a freer rendering of line and color. As the weeks passed, I had warmer feelings and they were reflected in my using warmer colors, my pictures moved from restricted straight lines to shapeless masses with heavy borders for containment, to my most recent product, a flowering sturdy tree with deep roots and branches that could shade others."

This insightful explanation of the group experience is inspiring and is a reminder of how the power of the visual, verbal opportunity can expedite self-learning.

## Fusing Art Tasks with Group Goals

The group members created many murals focused on the subject of stress. The murals were composed by all the members drawing on the same large sheet of paper. This format is useful for several reasons. At the formation of a group, creating an image cooperatively and discussing this shared experience enhances cohesion and establishes the mutual concerns and goals of the members (Yalom, 1995). The group art task can be completed in several ways. Everyone can draw on the large paper, any issue on which they choose to focus—the traumatic images generated by the client's art expressions, their feelings about their practice, their distress around feeling fatigued, or a subject that emerged in the group discussion. In fact, the drawing may contain all of the above concerns simultaneously. Each projection of stress will be rendered by the creator in response to their inner vision. The abstract images are fully understandable only upon interpretation by the one who produced the product, and yet, very soon stylist mannerisms become recognizable and add intimacy to the process. The participants find comfort in identifying that many of the problems and challenges are not unique to them, and solutions are not easy to discover.

Another approach to a large, shared group drawing is created in the following manner. The participants individually draw a current dilemma, in any manner they choose, on a smaller piece of paper; they follow this activity by a discussion, exchanging opinions and support. A question is then posed, "What part of this drawing are you willing to part with and contribute it to a composite image created by all in the group?" The members, if they wish, then cut up whatever part, or all, of their original drawing and assemble the pieces (with the other member's contributions) with glue onto the large paper. The result is a group collage. The symbolic actions of destroying toxic images and restoring them in another context is parallel to the process and purpose of the group.

## A Variety of Stressors

Other art tasks addressed a variety of issues—the distress of financial concerns rising from the therapist's desire to be therapeutic and disregard money, the burden of balancing personal demands and client's demands during the holidays, how pressures are exacerbated by the client's unhappiness at holiday time. Questions arise, such as how the troubles of clients interfere with the therapists own problem solving skills; are therapists dependent on their clients; is there a door of escape to flee from client's stories; when do the client's images trigger in the therapist a similar manner that they trigger themselves; how dependent is self-esteem, on the progress of the client? Many pragmatic and emotional stress producing situations that have immediate bearing on the group participants have been the subject matter of the drawings.

A three-dimensional art task offers a problem-solving approach that differs from two-dimensional drawings. It is the creation of the "self-box." The group member brings in a box about the size of a shoe-box. The challenge is to represent on the outside the part of self that is generally known to clients or acquaintances, the inside of the box represents the private, personal portions of one's self, known to only a select number of persons. The interior may contain many surpressed emotions around being a therapist, the ambivilant felings about the stories of abuse, the imposition of the horrific images on memory, as well as other intimate concerns. The suggested media is collage from a collection of magazine pictures. This media provides rich, metaphorical images and reduces the threat of having to artistically render the symbols needed to complete the task.

This piece of therapeutic art has been a very moving experience for many people. It provides the container for "who we are," invites the group members to be their own self-observer, and protects them from the threat of having to share more than they wish. The creator can always keep the lid on the box!

## Illustrations

The following illustrations will demonstrate how apparently simple the drawing can be, yet filled with meaning and how complex the thought process are behind it. In addition, it should be noted that the media used in this group is extremely limited, partly because a permanent meeting place has not been established, and in part because familiarity with felt pens and oil pastels give another level of comfort. Space here does not allow for a full display of all the art in each group.

Figure 11.1 is an example of a drawing created early in group by a group member responding to her need to externalize her client's depression and regain her therapeutic equilibrium.

Two examples of the holiday stress-time are depicted in Figures 11.2 and 11.3. In Figure 11.2 one member shows her feelings of a 100,000 pound load bearing down on her, comprised of her own commitment to gifts and food for the family, financial problems, and clients' holiday-related distress. In the drawing, she indicated that her support flowed upward and stemmed from her spiritual beliefs. Figure 11.3 shows another member's feelings about how she was a large black bowl, from which radiated all the complex feelings that personal and professional concerns stirred up at this holiday time. She was relieved by externalizing the excess load.

Figure 11.4 shows a therapist lost in the troubles, pressures, and

**FIGURE 11.1.** A therapist's artwork, externalizing depression and regaining therapeutic equilibrium.

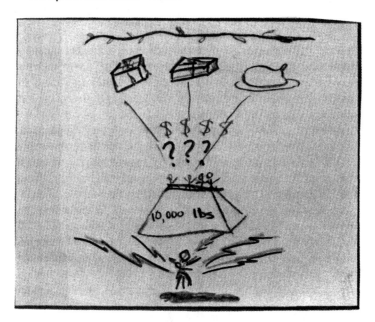

**FIGURE 11.2.** Holiday stress: 10,000 pounds of worries.

images of client pain. Figure 11.5 and Figure 11.6 are examples of the self-box, looking at both the interior and exterior representations of self.

Two drawings of how the therapist can become over-involved or dependent on the client relationship are shown in Figure 11.7 and Figure 11.8. Figure 11.7 depicts a tree buffeted by negative images but still struggling to stand strong against the onslaught. Figure 11.8 is an abstract rendering of the intrusion of toxic visual material into the center of the therapist's person.

Figure 11.9 is an example of how much thought process existed behind what appears to the outside observer as a formless and nonsubjective abstract scribble. The creator describes the drawing:

> This is a depiction of a mirror process between my client and myself when we are in harmony. The inner circles represent the client and myself. The arrows in opposing directions are the give and take in our dialogue. The wavy lines towards the bottom, with no beginning or ending, are the internal exchange. This exchange is not intellectual, not cognition, it is inconsistent. The shaded area at the bottom grounds us; it keeps me aware of my therapeutic skills and responsibilities. The arches at the top of the drawing hold the mirroring process and deepens the reflections. There is a oneness that unites, yet remains above, neither spoken or ignored. (Hume, 1995)

**FIGURE 11.3.** "I feel like a big black bowl. All the mixed feelings radiate out at the holidays."

**FIGURE 11.4.** A therapist "Lost in the troubles, pressures, and client's pain."

FIGURE 11.5. Exterior of a self-box—a projection of "self-in-the-world."

In Figure 11.10 a large group drawing was created by three members of the group in response to (1) supporting one person who was "overwhelmed," (2) one who was highly defended, and recuperating from an unexpected reversal in fortunes, and (3) another member who was recalling an exposure to a new therapeutic approach that she wanted to re-experience in the drawing. At the completion of the group drawing, each therapist discussed the imagery and then offered symbolic support by drawing connective lines that represented their feelings toward each other. It was a concrete expression of the powerful relationships that had developed during the life of this group.

FIGURE 11.6. Interior of a self-box, representing the internal world of the creator.

**FIGURE 11.7.** "Buffeted by negative images."

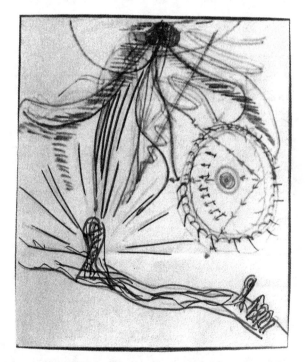

**FIGURE 11.8.** A depiction of some of the toxic visual (client) images intruding into the therapist's memory.

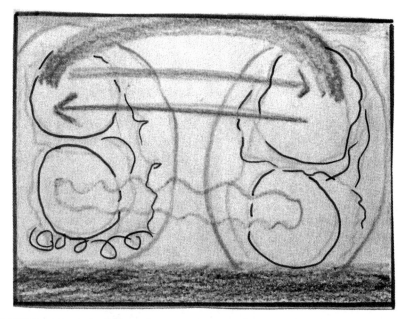

**FIGURE 11.9.** A depiction of a mirror process between the client and therapist when they are in harmony.

**FIGURE 11.10.** "My client's images are always swirling in my mind."

These illustrations are examples of how the products in an art therapy stress reduction group may be far from artistic. However, the process is highly aesthetic, in the sense of the beauty of the therapeutic support that can be derived from this mode of combining imagery with verbal expression.

# ☐ Conclusion

A stress reduction group, with experienced therapists as group members, employed art as the primary language of expression. This proved to be a positive experience. It provided an additional avenue for communication and an opportunity to externalize traumatic visions held in the therapists' personal memory banks. The art product became an entrée into the silent capacity of the mind to know the world through images, reflective emotions, and memories. It became apparent that stressful knowing cannot be discharged unless a methodology is employed that is in harmony with the problem. Just as the traumatized client used the capacity to let images lead the way to resolution, the stress-burdened therapists need to follow the same path.

The group discussed in this chapter represents a homogenous group of clinicians, social workers, counselors, and psychologists, who work with a similar population. They were all experienced and capable of treating victims of severe abuse and were well-educated in the field. This commonality enhanced the group cohesion and the trust was more easily established. However, this format could be used for any group of clinicians or interns in the world of psychological services. The uncertainties and systemic pressures take their toll in all mental health environments. Stress is a common phenomena and burn out is a result of neglecting to provide a forum for relief and support. The addition of the creative qualities that are inherent in an art therapy group can make the goal of stress reduction a more accessible reality.

Sharon Loeschen, LCSW, an experienced and competent therapist, published author, and member of the group has written:

> My experience in the art therapy support group for therapists treating dissociate disorders and other life threatening trauma, has been very positive. The severe difficulties that my clients share with me, affect me deeply and yet I find very little release for these feelings. The traditional case consultation has its place, but it does not provide the much needed avenue for externalizing the absorbed pain, terror, rage and grief. Through the media of pastels, I find a kinesthetic release. This is only possible, however, under the direction of the art therapist who guides us before we begin the process, observes us during our process, and helps us

discuss our process afterwards. I highly recommend such a group to others.

# References

Corey, G., Corey, M., & Callanan, P. (1988). *Issues and ethics in the helping professions.* Pacific Grove, CA: Brooks/Cole.

Guy, J. (1987). *The personal lives of psychotherapists.* New York: Wiley.

Riley, S., & Malchiodi, C. (1994). *Integrated approaches to family art therapy.* Chicago: Magnolia Street.

Spiegel, D., Kluft, R. P., Lowensein, R. J., Putnam, F. W., & Steinberg, M. (1993). *Dissociative disorders: A clinical review.* Lutherville, MD: Sidran Press.

Tinnin, L. (1991). Creativity and mental unity. *Perspectives in Biology and Medicine, 34,* 347–354.

Tinnin, L. (1994). Prevebal Memory (pp. 1–5). Presented at conference, Explorations in Unity and Multiplicity. Pittsburgh, Pennsylvania.

Tinnin, L. (1994). *Art Therapy-Amanuensis: Resolving dissociation by drawing* (pp. 1–3). Paper presented at Conference on Trauma, Dissociation, and Multiple Personality, Akron, Ohio.

Williams, M. B. (1996). Trauma and the family. In M. Harley (Ed.), *Treating the changing family* (pp. 163–190). New York: Wiley.

Yalom, I. D. (1995). *The theory and practice of group psychotherapy* (4th ed.). New York: Basic Books.

# Suggested Readings

Cohen, B., Mills, A., & Kwapien Kijak, A. (1994). An introduction to the Diagnostic Drawing Series: A standardized tool for diagnostic and clinical use. *Art Therapy, 11,* 105–110.

Cohen-Lieberman, M. S. (1994). The art therapist as expert witness in child sexual abuse. *Art Therapy, 11,* 260–265.

Hagood, M. M. (1994). Diagnosis or dilemma: Drawings of sexually abused children. *Art Therapy, 11,*

Jacobson, M. (1994). Abreacting and assimilating traumatic, dissociated memories of MPD through art therapy. *Art Therapy, 11,* 48–52.

Mills, A. (1995). Outpatient art therapy with multiple personality disorder: A survey of current practice. *Art Therapy, 12,* 253–256.

Morris, M. B. (1995). The diagnostic drawing series and the tree rating scale: An isomorphic representation of multiple personality disorder, major depression, and schizophrenic populations. *Art Therapy. 12,*

Murphy, P. S. (1994). The contribution of art therapy to the dissociative disorders. *Art Therapy, 11,* 43–47.

Rankin, A. (1994). Tree drawings and trauma indicators: A comparison of past research with current findings from the diagnostic drawing series. *Art Therapy, 11,* 127–130.

# Some Final Thoughts

Looking through this book as though I was a reader not an author, which is almost impossible to do since self-observation is always biased, I was struck by one motif than seemed to be present in every chapter. The theme I observed was, that when I told the story of the various groups it became obvious that most groups had developed very individual meanings and procedures. Traditionally, when writers discuss the theory behind group process they note how it conformed to Yalom (1995) and Corey's (1990) basic principles. It was striking how the impact of mental health providers and the severity of the client's problems had forced drastic modifications of these principles. Both the above experts laid out the normal evolution of group process, and their guidelines still are important, however, the external pressures and cultural shifts have had high impact on the classic interpretation of group. It is still true that we strive for a cohesive group involvement—but think of the composition of so many groups today. It is not reasonable to expect attention deficit boys to move in the direction of trust in the same manner or at the same pace that an eating disorders women's group advances. Every group is created in the frame of its context and content. I have tried to show how the language of art informs the therapist about the internal and external factors at work in the process. Examples of these deviations from the classic mold make up the body of this text.

For example, it was proposed that the present day adolescent client is usually mandated to group therapy in specialized settings. They are often potentially violent and frequently disillusioned with the therapeutic system. They may have had numerous social workers or case managers, and been disappointed with them all. The caseworker, on the other hand, may have 40 or 50 cases to manage, and have fled the position to regain their own mental stability—but the child does not see it that way, only as one more abandonment. Similarly, the hospitalized and residential patient is herded into large groups that defeat the notion of group process. It takes an inventive therapist to create interventions that will in some manner balance these inequities. For these two extremes it still seems plausible that the stressful group is better than isolation. If nothing else, the group members can feel they are part of a larger assembly of peers who feel as they do. There is comfort in banding against the enemy and the societal or therapeutic system is often the culprit. When we learn how to manage the groups in a way that is congruent with their needs we can stop being adversaries.

## ☐ Fresh Look at the Interpretation of Group Structure

Many chapters in this book have addressed the unique challenge that the system and the clients present at this time. It may be a new millennium but the situational problems are not new, for example, the difficult world of the autistic child. When the autistic youth is, at last, able to make some social contact with one other youth, can we name it a group? In this case the size has nothing to do with the challenge of becoming more socialized. One other person looms like a group to the autistic person. I believe we can look at the service that a group provides without counting heads. In contrast, it would be of little use to put two elderly dementia clients together, and call it group. It would be a limited learning experience for the participants, to say the least.

The positive recognition that group therapy has earned is not diminished because the structural change of the mental health providers has made a dramatic impact. The most basic fact still remains that we often learn best from our peers, and for that reason group therapy will survive. It is not the small focused group that is in question, it is the wholesale marketing of huge groups that is destructive. Defining the terminology or the description of group therapy is needed, and as therapists we can increase the scope of the definition.

For example, large groups of 12 or more disturbed adults or children make a farce of group practice. The art expression is lost in the shuffle and the only hope is that the immediate art experience had some inner regulatory gain for the client. To counteract the unrealistic expectations of some agencies we have suggested means to breakdown the groups into small units and let art tasks give a focus to the reduced number of participants.

## ☐ How Therapists Think

These mechanical challenges are not the major changes with which I am concerned. I question the resistance of therapists to enter into a comprehensive attitude of co-construction in all forms of therapeutic relationships with their clients. It seems to me to be anti-therapeutic to second guess the client. Particularly in a group format, it is not helpful to do individual therapy with the group as audience. Group is a viable here-and-now experience, and it is only in the present that change can come about.

There have been examples in all the chapters where the group task was made visible through the art in the session. It is striking the imprint the art has on the group process. The artwork anchors each member's contribution in an impactful manner. The empty page says something about the group member, as well as the creative picture. It is not enough to elicit drawings from the group; it is what the members and the leader *do* with the product. Walking into the drawing and bringing the images alive, encouraging the images to find their own voice, is ideal. The leader is lead by the image, and interpretation is left to the creator of the art piece. The philosophy of "trust in the client" permeates throughout the chapters. Structure and careful design does not conflict with this belief. Just because imagery has been introduced into the group process does not mean that it has been of therapeutic service. The therapist must have a notion of how the art can move the therapy and provide opportunities for self-awareness. Mindless art projects are as useless as unfocused verbal digressions. Art used in group should be a part of the process on every level, and the understanding of the psychobiological rationale for the use of visualization gives form to therapeutic reasoning.

## ☐ The Value of Group Treatment

Group therapy is the most demanding therapeutic setting for "controlled non-control." This means that the leader is responsible for opportunities, not for knowledge that supersedes the clients present understanding. There is an amazing synergistic interaction between group members if the group is embraced by the facilitator and becomes a haven for the members.

There are so many stories that could be interjected with every art illustration throughout the text: the bravery of the young burn-injured boys and girls, the tears of gratitude in the eyes of the parents when these recovered children visited the newly burned hospitalized child. These moving moments could not have been created unless there was the safe support of the group. The art they made was a gift for the child suffering the first trauma of burns. The group gave a tangible therapeutic gift at the crisis time. Can we question how a chain loop of construction paper, with good wishes written on the paper, can become magic at a time of distress? The art stays, it doesn't slip away when medication dulls the mind.

Throughout these chapters, perhaps the reader has become aware that each group forms its own personality and dynamic function. It poses a problem to me to find an overall description of group process. It seems to reduce to more than one person forming a relationship, with the support of a leader that is dedicated to the benefit of each individual in connection with other. As an individual makes progress, the other members find connective themes in their lives, and move in consort with each other. I am convinced that group therapy will soon be offered again as a preventative tool, as it has been in the past. The newspapers feature articles daily that describe facilities that open their door to persons who are in distress. The human need to "group" and to be in contact assures us that group will remain. It is the professional community that must relinquish the static formulation of group and rethink the vehicle that will benefit the client need.

## ☐ Suggestions

I have emphasized how important I find the initial pre-group interview. The assessment is not created to eliminate certain types of personalities, however, it is helpful not to have too many persons of the same difficult behavior, which predicts trouble. Most of us have had the "I won't talk," hostile client. Imagine an entire group of withdrawn persons. On the other hand, two reclusive personalities in a group of six or eight would be acceptable. The opposite is true as well. The "constant talker" can be helped to gain control by group pressure, but not if the entire group had the same trait.

Exploring these ordinary human habits in the initial interview is not the same as searching for pathology. If pathology is a dominant consideration of the therapist the group will reflect that bias. Even in a group of patients in the hospital, the pathology should not be the binding force of the group. The quests for abilities, survival strengths, coping skills, and the capacity to love or nurture, are the traits to uncover. Group members can find these skills in each other, and they become more valuable when discovered by a peer. Often the person has overlooked these capacities and is astonished when the group reinforces these positive virtues.

An early evaluation of the group "mix" will provide a high percentage of positive group outcomes. It is almost unethical to casually accept anyone into a group and then expect the group to struggle with solving the problems that could have been averted early on. This is particularly true considering the fact that many groups are provided in a brief therapy format. It is the responsibility of the therapist to clarify all the issues of structure and group composition.

The assessment can be helped if the therapist asks the group applicant to draw a picture as part of the intake. The directive should be created to have meaning to the person, particularly in groups built around a theme. For example, an adolescent might be willing to draw "What issues bug a teenager?," or the geriatric client might be able to pick a collage picture and tell what it represented. The first request would give the therapist a notion of the adolescent's worldview, the second, a mini-look at the cognitive abilities of the prospective program applicant. Again, why not use all the capacities of our mind and brain? Why is it better to eliminate all forms of communication except verbal?

## ☐ Final Thought

This last paragraph is a message to the creative person that dwells in us all and is particularly viable in the trained therapist. I hope the information in this book is practical and flexible, and reassures the creative person hiding inside, that they can find a creative outlet in group therapy—and enjoy!

## ☐ References

Corey, G. (1990). *Theory and practice of group counseling.* Pacific Grove, CA: Brooks/Cole.
Yalom, I. D. (1995). *The theory and practice of group psychotherapy.* New York: Basic Books.

# APPENDIX: TEACHING GROUP DYNAMICS

For many years I have been privileged to teach a class in group dynamics to Master's level students in two educational settings. I put together a series of art tasks that reflected the goals of, first, providing a safe environment, and later, promoting group cohesion. I do not claim these tasks were original. I probably took the ideas long ago from many sources. However, if the reader would like a short cut to creating a learning group for group dynamics, I share the following condensed protocol, with nine meetings offered in a two-hour framework. I want to emphasize that I am offering only the "bones" of this course, the process and therapeutic skills are appropriate for another entire text.

**First class:** Usual introductions, then I pass around the "hand" tracing ritual paper (described in chapter 1). We establish the "rules" of the group with an emphasis on confidentiality. Although every effort is made to teach group dynamics, and not group therapy, material is bound to surface, often through the art product. Therefore, the leader must remind the participants on a regular basis to self-regulate their disclosures, and be prepared to steer the person away from material that should be handled in personal therapy.

Following this opening move, which introduces the topic of trust, I ask the group to make a symbol for themselves, using any media they prefer. I allow time, and try to make the environment casual and comforting. The question of whether to talk about the drawings or not is a decision individual to each group. Adequate time is the first consideration, whether or not the group members seem eager to verbalize. If it seems to be appropriate to let the drawing do the talking, they can be put in the center of the room and observed silently. At this time an educational rumination about the ability of art expressions to speak to the creator may be appropriate. Self-therapy can arise from the image if it is seriously contemplated and self-interpreted.

**Second class:** In a first move to find some commonality between the members, the class is asked to pick a partner and choose a single color in marking pen or pastel. They are directed to have a conversation on paper, each taking turns and responding to the other in any manner they choose. The conversation should not use pictorial symbols (i.e., smiley faces or stick figures). This exercise is nonverbal. After completion, which is self-dictated, they can take time to review how they felt when their marks were responded to or ignored, what they were trying to convey, and other dynamics of the experience.

Secondly, the same dyad is asked to create a picture together; verbalization is now allowed. They can choose the subject matter and plot the drawing together. They discuss this experience with each other.

When these two drawings are completed, the class is requested to share their observations and feelings, and consider where an exercise such as these could be used with a clinical population. An educational dialogue is encouraged.

**Third class:** A similar directive, as given in the second class, is repeated. This time with four participants drawing together. After discussion of the process the class is asked to be aware of their feelings of trusting two more people and giving up the intimacy of the previous dyadic experience. Before further discussion, the group members are asked to make a drawing which reflects this dynamic.

The class dialogues about this experience, draws clinical parallels, such as resistance to change, suspicion of strangers, and many others, which can surface from this simple task.

**Fourth class:** Class is asked to breakup into two sections. A drawing is made by each member of the mini-group, then passed sequentially around the group. Each member draws with a singular color. At each move, the receiver adds a complimentary shape to the ones that have been added before. After the drawings have made the rounds of the circle, the small groups talk about their feelings upon receiving their drawing, and ask questions of the other members if they choose.

This task rarely has profound meaning, it is, as the reader is no doubt aware, another step toward consolidating the group. As the art task gradually includes more participants, the relationships are tested, supported, challenged, and entire complexes of situational opportunities are offered. Each member will react to these tasks in a manner that reflects their personality and comfort level.

From this point on, the class will begin to explore media as well as dynamics. The readers should remind themselves that this formula is a teaching format and does *not* reflect a model that is recommended for all groups. It is basically a grab bag of techniques for the beginner. I tell the students that they should be sensitive to what the group needs, but if they are, as beginners, stuck, here are some ideas to pull out of their pocket.

**Fifth class:** Creating a mural, with all member participating. This can be done in several ways. The members can step to the wall (large mural paper) and draw as they wish. They can trace around their hand, decorate it, cut it out, and tape it to the mural wall. In every case, the purpose is to give the visual impact of the entire group, working as a group. Changes are recommended and relationships discussed (i.e., "How did you feel being surrounded by three images?" "Did you have any thoughts when someone marked over your image?").

This exercise is often the beginning of the group personality and mode of relating. Some of these observations can be discussed with the participants, others are reserved by the leader to enable her to make adjustments to this group and lead them into a positive experience. This is a class, not therapy.

**Sixth class:** Creating the "Island of Your Choice. A Place Where You Can Have Anything You Wish to Have."

Again this is a tried and true stand-by art task, but it works. I often ask the group members to assume the role of an adolescent. This serves two purposes: It teaches a task that is often useful in adolescent group, and simultaneously, it allows the member to distance themselves as a group member and pretend. Of course, the adolescent within usually comes forth, and the group is often very lively and revealing.

The members can decide if they wish to keep one color for each person, which makes the individual more apparent, or use any color at will. The island is discussed developmentally, territorially, emotionally (past memories of adolescence), and symbolically. Did the group provide food and shelter for themselves? Were friends invited? Was there a feeling of cooperation or defensiveness? It is always interesting to see how many issues will rise from this exercise. Sometimes, I think I will never do it again, and then the occasion arises and I am pleased with the results. The group members are usually extremely insightful about the second-level messages sent through the art and by the activity of the members. There is no need to strain to interpret a volcano, a massive fence, sharks in the water, and on the positive side, markets, food stores, homes, recreation areas, churches, and occasionally schools.

**Seventh class:** An alternative to the island directive is to create a collage that reflects the emotional ambiance of their family of origin. This task invites the students to appreciate the power that the family environment has on all of us. Terms such as "hot," "cold," "stuffy," "poisonous," and more can be represented more easily with a collage picture from a magazine than by a drawing. This exercise is a lead in for the family sculpture, which is the task for class eight. The collage should be created on sturdy paper and act as a backdrop for the family created in three dimensions.

The discussion of environments can be revealing to the members of the group, who are encouraged to see the symbolic meaning in the magazine pictures and the metaphors that arise from this project.

**Eighth class:** Create a family sculpture of Plasticine; demonstrate relationships by size, shape, and color. Do not be bound by literal physical appearance—for example, if baby brother ruled the family, he should be the biggest figure. Try using abstract shapes to represent family members—a red block of clay with toothpicks and nails embedded in the clay that could represent the rageful member. Relationships can be demonstrated by applying mom's color on daughter and dad's color made into a rope that binds them to him (see chapter 1 for illustrations of Plasticine families).

This is the group that is most likely to create powerful emotions in the group members. I make every effort to regulate the presentations by safety rules, and I call upon the class to be attentive to one another and help me keep the group a safe place. This discussion often takes two groups to complete. The Plasticine family may be created at home if the course period is running short.

The sculpture is an excellent introduction to systems thinking and the principles of family therapy. As a group task it is the final step toward group cohesion. Everything that follows will reflect the courage that it takes to bring our family alive and share them with others. There are group members in an educational class that are not willing to talk about their family of origin. That is always an option that is clearly stated by the leader. If the member has had a traumatic childhood they are invited to invent a family and do the sculpture. In that manner they will have the experience but not the trauma.

**Ninth Class:** Because the sculptures take time to create and explore, the classic termination art expression I have used is the "self-box." The member is asked to bring in a box that they will decorate as a projection of themselves. I first did this task as a student with Helen Landgarten, and I could recreate it to the last detail these many years later.

The outside of the box is the persona that is shared with the world. The inside is the receptacle of personal, private feelings and desires (both positive and negative). Many people place precious mementos inside the box, such as pictures of departed parents or lovers and tokens of success and failures. The self-box can be an ongoing project that becomes richer as associations are stimulated by memories and connections. For the class to process these boxes, I suggest that at least two meetings be reserved for discussion.

# ☐ Conclusion

The above process of teaching group dynamics is just a suggestion that uses the old tried and true exercises that are perhaps not as interesting as they were years ago. However, the principle of moving from individual, to dyads, to a gradually larger task that requires cooperation and interactions is a way to achieve a cohesive group. Through these exercises, the leader has the advantage of observing on several levels the dynamics of the group. The art is the companion language, and the art products speak for themselves even if the artmaker is silent.

I am concerned that these exercises may seem superficial and repetative. I must remind myself that these tasks are only the scaffolding on which the group is built. The sensitivity and ability of the therapist to allow process to make unique meanings from these basic materials is why I trust that the reader will make these suggestions their own by modifying them to suit their purpose.

# INDEX

abstract scribbles, 63, 246, (illus.)247
  art inhibition and, 7
  two-way, 21–22, 38
abuse, suffered by clients:
  burn injuries, 52–53, 58
  stress of therapists and, 236–237
action-oriented therapeutic tasks, 54
adolescents, xxii
  autistic clients, 109–112
  burn-injured, 52–53
aesthetic developmental process, 211–
  212
affect, emotional state *vs.*, 173–174,
  178
aging, fear of, 180
Alzheimer's disease, 157–161, 186
America On-Line (AOL), 161
American Art Therapy Association, 8
anger, in bereavement therapy, 228–
  229
animal kingdom project, 137
anti-group phenomenon, 213
anxiety:
  appraisal-arousal process, of brain,
    176
  helped by rituals, 173
architect project, 136
art projects, 135–137, 260
  (*See also individual project names*)
Art Therapy Association, American, 8
*Art Therapy for Groups: A Handbook of
  Themes, Games, and Exercises*
  (Liebmann), 25
Asperger's syndrome, 83, 89
assessment:
  for 72-hour model, 194–195
  art used for, 93–96, 120
  for burn-injured children, 58
  for elderly groups, 169

parent interview for, 125–126
for social skills interventions, 88–91
attachment, in parenting process, xxii,
  35–47, 203
attendance, of group members, 98, 126
attention deficit/hyperactivity disorder
  (*see* behavior disorders)
attention span, 93
  of adolescents, 150
  of elderly, 166
autistic children, xxii, 82–113, 254
avoidance, 37, 88, 89–90
awkwardness, social, 89–90

background issues, 15
banner project, 136
baseball hat project, 79–80
Beckett, Samuel, xii
beginning-stage group, 213
  (*See also* initial group session)
behavior disorders, xxii, 115–137
behavioral difficulties, 101, 103
belief system, of leader, 7–8
Benderly, B.L., 34
*Bereavement and Support: Healing in a
  Group Environment* (Hughes), 233
bereavement groups, 221–234
bias, of therapist, 7–9
body drawing, for burn victims, 64–66
body knowledge, 211, 214, 218
"body trust," 216
bonding (*see* attachment)
boundaries, of clients, 94
Bowlby, J., 34
boys:
  in adolescent groups, 144
  art themes of, 123–124
  latency age, xxii

**263**